Sutton-cum-Duckmanton Parish Register 1662–1837

Edited by
Pamela Kettle and Philip Riden

Derbyshire Record Society
Volume XVIII, 1992

Published by the Derbyshire Record Society
9 Caernarvon Close, Chesterfield S40 3DY

First published 1992

ISBN 0 946324 15 8

Sutton-cum-Duckmanton Parish Register published by courtesy of the Rector, Churchwardens and Parochial Church Council of St Mary the Virgin, Sutton Scarsdale

Typeset at Oxford University Computing Service
Printed by Technical Print Services Ltd
Brentcliffe Avenue, Carlton Road
Nottingham NG3 7AG

CONTENTS

ACKNOWLEDGEMENTS

Our sincere thanks are due to the Rector of Sutton-cum-Duckmanton, the Revd Nigel Johnson, for confirming the permission originally given by his predecessor, the late Revd Peter Hicks, for the register to be published; to Mrs Margaret Roberts of Sutton for undertaking much of the typing involved; to Howard Llewellyn of Cardiff for his hard work with both typing and indexing; to Keith Williams and Liz Atkinson of the University Computing Service in Cardiff for help with preparing the text for typesetting; and to Stephen Miller at Oxford University Computing Service for similar help there.

INTRODUCTION

The parish of Sutton-cum-Duckmanton occupies some 4,300 acres a few miles to the south-east of Chesterfield. As its name implies, the modern parish was created by the amalgamation of two older units. In 1558 Sir Francis Leeke of Sutton (1509–81) secured permission to combine that parish, where he was patron and sole owner, with Duckmanton, immediately to the north, where he had succeeded Welbeck Abbey, again as both patron and owner.[1] Leeke was thus able to create a single estate which included all the land of both parishes, together with two livings. Presumably because it lay immediately adjacent to his mansion, Leeke chose to retain the church at Sutton and to demolish that at Duckmanton.

The Leeke family remained at Sutton until shortly after the death of Nicholas, the fourth and last Earl of Scarsdale, in 1736, when the estate was sold to pay his debts.[2] The earldom, created in 1645, took its name from the hundred of Scarsdale, in which Sutton lies, which in turn led to the use of the name Sutton Scarsdale for the hall and adjoining hamlet; previously it had been known as Sutton-en-le-Dale, to distinguish it from Sutton-on-the-Hill in south Derbyshire. The mansion at Sutton Scarsdale was rebuilt to the design of Francis Smith of Warwick in 1724–9, who thus created one of the most splendid houses of the period anywhere in Derbyshire.[3]

The Sutton estate was purchased, after Nicholas Leeke's death, by Godfrey Clarke of Chilcote in the south of the county. After the death of Gilbert Clarke, a lunatic, in 1786, the estate remained in the hands of trustees, who included a cousin, Clement Kynnersley of Loxley, Staffs., who occupied Sutton occasionally in the early nineteenth century. Following his death in 1816, the estate reverted to the Clarke family, one of whom, Anna Maria

---

[1] D. & S. Lysons, *Magna Britannia. V. Derbyshire* (1817), pp. 135, 270–72; P. Kettle, *Sutton Scarsdale's story. Part 1: The Leekes of Sutton* (Ilkeston, 1988), pp. 21–7.

[2] Lysons, *Magna Britannia*, pp. 270–72; Kettle, *Sutton Scarsdale*, pp. 54–8.

[3] Kettle, *Sutton Scarsdale*, pp. 61–4; M. Craven and M. Stanley, *The Derbyshire country house* (Derby, 2nd. ed., 1991), pp. 204–206.

Katherine, married an Irish peer and thus became the Marchioness of Ormonde. After the death of the marquess in 1820, Sutton was bought by Richard Arkwright, the son of Sir Richard Arkwright, the builder of the cotton mills at Cromford, for his own son Robert, and the estate remained in the hands of this family until the whole property was sold in 1919.[1] Since then the former Sutton Scarsdale estate has become divided between numerous small owners, while the mansion itself, stripped of its interior decoration and damaged by partial demolition, survives as an impressive but gaunt ruin.

Since 1558, Sutton and Duckmanton have formed a single parish for both civil and ecclesiastical purposes, although in the nineteenth century the boundary between the two could still be identified and separate acreages were calculated for each half of the parish.[2] In 1854 Robert Arkwright built a 'large and commodious room for the use of the parish' on the site of the medieval church at Duckmanton: sixteen skeletons were found during the construction of this but nothing appears to have been recorded, either then or earlier, concerning the appearance of the church, which was dedicated to St Peter and St Paul.[3] The new building was probably used as a chapel-of-ease from the start (with the medieval dedication retained) but separate marriage registers have only been kept for the church since 1951.[4] Throughout the period covered by this volume, however, the parish was served only by St Mary's church at Sutton.

The baptism, marriage and burial entries printed here, together with other notes, are taken from five separate books, the earliest of which is a general register, beginning in 1662.[5] This was the oldest volume in the custody of the parish at the time of Archdeacon Butler's visitation in 1823:[6] presumably at some date before then one earlier book, perhaps starting in 1558, had disappeared. Because of the loss of the first part of the register, it is impossible to be certain that the church at Duckmanton was abandoned

---

[1] Lysons, *Magna Britannia*, pp. 270–2; a fuller account of the later history of the estate will be given in the forthcoming second part of Mrs Kettle's history of Sutton Scarsdale.

[2] *White's Derbyshire Directory* (1857), pp. 779–80.

[3] *White's Derbyshire Directory*, p. 780, gives the date of building as 1856, but according to the MS diary of Daniel Gladwin, the clerk at Duckmanton Ironworks (in Chesterfield Local Studies Library), it was completed between August and November 1854.

[4] See a short history of SS Peter & Paul, Duckmanton, by Harold Taylor, in Derbyshire Record Office, D2223A PI 36–37; the marriage registers are now PI 4/1–3.

[5] All the older registers for both St Mary's and SS Peter & Paul were deposited in the Derby Diocesan Record Office in 1980 and now form part of DRO, D2223A. The general register of 1662–1812 is D2223A PI 1/1.

[6] M.R. Austin (ed.), *The church in Derbyshire in 1823–4* (Derbyshire Archaeological Society Record Series, 5, 1969–70), p. 164.

as soon as the two parishes were combined, although according to local tradition, recorded in the early nineteenth century, it was taken down around 1558.[1] The register of 1662 is a tall, narrow ledger, consisting of paper sheets bound in vellum-covered boards. Only one page appears to have suffered significant damage, resulting in the loss of some burial entries for 1671.

The entries for baptisms and burials extend from 1662 until the introduction of new registers under the Act of 1812; those for marriages end in 1754, with the adoption of the separate marriage register under Hardwicke's Act of that year. Entries for all three events form a single chronological sequence, although separated into two parallel series, with baptisms on the right and burials and marriages on the left of each opening. Because of this division, the entries have been printed here in three separate sections; the opportunity has also been taken to convert all dates to New Style.

Although the book appears to be virtually intact, there is a hiatus in the registration of all three events between about 1716 and 1732, when some eight pages have been left blank, as though entries were intended to be copied in but have not been.[2] This gap can only be partially remedied by the use of the bishop's transcripts, which are themselves incomplete for this period. Throughout much of this first volume, especially after the gap of 1716–32, the entries have the appearance of being copied up some time after the event.

For the seventeenth century and most of the eighteenth, there is little or no detail in each entry, beyond the bare minimum, except for those involving members of the Leeke family or perhaps the incumbent. For a few years prior to 1812, however, baptism entries generally give dates of birth, while burial entries record age and the cause of death. The production of transcripts at visitations by both the archdeacon and the bishop, normally held at Chesterfield, is noted on various occasions, as is the collection of the stamp duty imposed on entries in parish registers for ten years following an Act of 1783.[3] The register was inspected by the local collector of stamps, John Bower, and a note inserted as to the amount paid.[4] Between 1678 and

[1] Lysons, *Magna Britannia*, p. 135.

[2] See pp. 19, 73–4; the gap in burial entries is as stated in the text; baptisms are only lost for 1718–29.

[3] W.E. Tate, *The parish chest. A study of the records of parochial administration in England* (Cambridge, 3rd ed., 1969), p. 50.

[4] The signatory 'J. Bower' can be identified (e.g. from *Bailey's Northern Directory*, 1781) reasonably confidently as John Bower, the Chesterfield attorney, who was evidently the local collector of stamps.

1689 burials in woollen are recorded in some detail, including the name of the justice of the peace certifying that the event might proceed.[1] At the end of the register there are various miscellaneous memoranda, including a list of briefs under which collections were made, a note about the poor harvest of 1796 and a short list of pauper apprentices. At the front is an eighteenth-century reference to the amalgamation of Sutton and Duckmanton in 1558.

The other volumes from which entries have been printed call for little comment. The two marriage registers covering the years 1754–1812 and 1813–37 are of the form prescribed in the Acts of 1753 and 1812; the former continued to be used for banns until 1823, when the modern series of banns registers begins.[2] Finally, entries have been extracted from the baptism and burial registers kept under the Act of 1812 down to the end of June 1837, the eve of the introduction of birth and death registration.[3] Although it is possible that there are baptisms and burials recorded in the same volumes after 1 July that year for which there is no corresponding birth or death entry in the civil registers at Chesterfield (or elsewhere), it would be difficult to justify deviating from the long-established convention in parish register publishing that entries after this date are not worth extracting.

Since the bishop's transcripts at Lichfield do not in general survive prior to 1662, it is impossible to augment from that source the information presented here from the original register, except for the hiatus of 1716–32. For a few eighteenth-century burials some additional details can be gleaned from monumental inscriptions at St Mary's and anything of this sort has been incorporated into the transcript printed here, enclosed in square brackets. The resulting volume thus forms the fullest possible record that can obtained of baptisms, burials and marriages at St Mary's, Sutton, from the commencement of the surviving register down to the beginning of civil registration. Sutton-cum-Duckmanton is in fact the first parish in the diocese of Derby for which the register has been published in full in this way.

As one might expect in a parish with only one owner, the population of both Sutton and Duckmanton remained small for much of the period covered by the register.[4] Until the end of the eighteenth century, most of the families in both townships would have relied on the land for their livelihood, whether as farmers or labourers, with the rest engaged in blacksmithing and other village crafts, or else employed at the hall. As in other parishes

[1] Tate, *Parish chest*, pp. 67–8.
[2] DRO, D2223A PI3/1–2, PI 5/1–6.
[3] DRO, D2223A PI 2/1, 7/1.
[4] See Kettle, *Sutton Scarsdale*, for a general account of the parish.

around Chesterfield, there may have been some framework-knitting, but as bye-employment, rather than a main occupation. Similarly, since Sutton and Duckmanton lie on the North Derbyshire coalfield, there would have been some small-scale mining from an early date.

This picture changed somewhat after the establishment of an ironworks at Duckmanton Moor in about 1799 by a family named Smith, who already had a similar enterprise in Chesterfield.[1] The Adelphi Ironworks, as it became known, represented the first attempt to exploit the ironstone of the parish and appears to have prospered modestly during the Napoleonic Wars, with two blast furnaces, a foundry, brickworks and the usual collieries and pits. The mines were linked by tramroad to the works, which also had a tub-boat canal running to the main road from Duckmanton to Staveley, where finished goods could be transferred to the Chesterfield Canal. The opening of the ironworks makes an immediate impact on the parish register. A wider of range of occupations is recorded; newcomers from distant parishes are noted; and both the ironworks and a new colliery are given as places of residence. Those employed by the Smiths would have lived at Duckmanton, rather than Sutton, which remained a much smaller, entirely rural, hamlet and this too is evident from the more frequent appearance of the former name in the register in the early nineteenth century.

It might have been supposed that the arrival of industry in Duckmanton would have led to the establishment of a dissenting congregation there, although in a closed parish the owner would probably have been able to prevent the building of a meeting-house. The rector of Sutton, in returning answers to Archdeacon Butler's visitation in 1823, mentions the existence of 'Calvinists',[2] presumably at Duckmanton, but there was no nonconformist place of worship in the parish in 1851.[3] It is quite possible that some children of miners and ironworkers went unbaptised during this period but there is no way of measuring the incidence of under-registration. On the other hand, it is clear that many of those employed by the Smiths did choose to have their children baptised at Sutton, even though the church lay a couple of miles from where they lived.

[1] P.M. Robinson, *The Smiths of Chesterfield. A history of the Griffin Foundry, Brampton, 1775–1833* (Chesterfield, 1957), pp. 37–40.

[2] Austin, *Church in Derbyshire*, p. 165.

[3] We are indebted to Mrs Margery Tranter of Leicester University for confirming that only the parish church appears in the 1851 census of worship (PRO, HO 129/448/75), the Derbyshire returns from which she is preparing for publication by the Record Society. *White's Directory* (1857), pp. 779–81 makes no mention of nonconformity in the parish, although there was an Independent meeting-house at nearby Calow, erected in 1837 (Ibid., p. 715), which residents of Duckmanton would have attended.

The development of the ironworks was probably mainly, if not wholly, responsible for the fairly substantial rise in the population of the parish recorded in the early censuses. From 515 in 1801, the population rose to 700 in 1831, after which the works began to decline. Only 628 people were living in the parish in 1841, a figure which had fallen to 587 ten years later, at a time when most parishes around Chesterfield were experiencing a modest but clear growth in population.[1] The ironworks closed down about 1850 (although some of the buildings remained in use as estate offices)[2] and Duckmanton reverted to being a largely agricultural community until almost the end of the nineteenth century. Only in the 1880s were the Arkwrights tempted to lease their coal to the major local colliery concern, the Staveley Coal & Iron Co.,[3] who proceeded to build a new village at Duckmanton Moor at the turn of the century, named Arkwright Town. This marked the beginning of Duckmanton's modern history, now drawing to a close, as a mining community, whereas Sutton has remained rural, with only limited residential development near the church and hall.

All this, however, lies beyond the period covered by the register printed here. Although some will see page after page of the names of those baptised, married and buried in one, fairly thinly populated, parish as a publication of strictly limited interest, we nonetheless feel the effort involved in transcription and indexing has been worthwhile. Not only is the resulting volume easier to read than the original register (and much easier to read than a microfilm copy), the indexes make it possible to locate individual families quickly and also to trace references to particular places. More generally, no source can compare with a parish register as a chronicle of everyday life in a community, and as more examples are published, thus facilitating easy study and comparison, so more will be learned of this most familiar and fascinating source for the local historian and genealogist.

[1] *White's Derbyshire Directory* (1857), pp. 658–9, provides a convenient conspectus of the Scarsdale figures for 1801–51.

[2] Robinson, *Smiths of Chesterfield*, p. 40; *White's Directory*, p. 780, says in 1857 that 'Many of the inhabitants [of Duckmanton] are employed at the collieries and iron-works in the immediate neighbourhood'. Either this is intended to refer to Staveley Works, about three miles away, or it has been copied un-checked from an earlier directory.

[3] J.E. Williams, *The Derbyshire miners. A study in industrial and social history* (1962), pp. 200–201.

REGISTER OF BAPTISMS, MARRIAGES AND BURIALS 1662–1812

[Note in Latin on front paste-down that in 1558 the parish church of Sutton-in-le-Dale was united with the vicarage of Duckmanton alias Dogmanton and that the instrument of union may be found in the Lichfield diocesan archives. Attested by – Buckeridge, 1775.]

August 30th 1662: Memorandum that the day and year above written Nicholas Richardson was put in to be clerk of the parish church of Sutton.

BAPTISMS

1662

Richard son of Robert and Elizabeth Withers bapt. 21st Sept.
Sarah dau. of John and Sarah Ashberie born 27th Sept. and bapt. 8th Oct.
Georg son of William and Anne Douman born 20th Oct. and bapt. 5th Nov.
Sarah dau. of Richard and Sarah White born 2nd and bapt. 9th Nov.

1663

Thomas son of Robert and Ann Allwood born the 8th and bapt. 20th Jan.
James son of Robert and Katherin Battman was bapt. 1st March.
Katherin dau. of Henry and Elizabeth Chantery born 27th April and bapt. 3rd May.
Barbara dau. of Rodger and Elizabeth Richardson born 23rd [May] and bapt. 15th June.
Edward son of Edward and Elizabeth Arddin born 31st [June] and bapt. 7th July.
Sarah dau. of William and Margot Roberts born 19th and bapt. 23rd Aug.
Marie dau. of Thomas and Elizabeth Freeman born 11th and bapt. 17th Sept.

William son of Thomas and Ann Hille born 29th Sept. and bapt. Oct. [*Part of page torn away*].
Ann dau. of William and Alise Tabernor born 19th and bapt. 26th Oct.
Sarah dau. of Richard and Ann Turner born 15th Oct. and bapt. 2nd Nov.
Francis son of Thomas and Marie Flint born 31st Oct. and bapt. 4th Nov.
Katheren dau. of Nicholas and Marie Marsh born 2nd and bapt. 8th Nov.
Simon son of John Robinson being a poor traveller bapt. 19th Dec.

[*Inserted in a hand of c. 1750 (possibly that of Francis Tallents, parish clerk) opposite the baptism entry of 17 Sept. 1663*:] Surgunt indocti et caelum sapient et nos cum doctrinis nostris sine corde (ecce) voluntamur in carne et sanguine. [They grow up untaught and discern the Heavens and we with our soulless doctrines – lo – we are occupied with flesh and blood.]

1664

Jane dau. of Jerom Shaw bapt. 14th Feb.
Francis son of Francis and Mary Turner born 1st April and bapt. 1st May.
Thomas son of William and Ann Collgrieve born 28th and bapt. 30th June.
Ann dau. of Godfrey and Dorothy Flint born 15th July and bapt. 1st Aug.
Job son of William and Mary Scales born 28th Sept. and bapt. 11th Oct.
Richard son of Nicholas and Mary Redfern born and bapt. 17th Oct.
Ann dau. of Henry and Elizabeth Fern born 26th Oct. Mary dau. of Godfrey and Mary Tallents bapt. 11th Dec.

1665

Gerard son of Thomas and Elizabeth Freeman born Saturday 14th Jan. and bapt. Tuesday 31st Jan.
Mary dau. of Robert and Catherine Bateman bapt. 19th Feb.
John son of Christopher Upton bapt. 24th and bur. 27th Feb.
Mary dau. of Edward and Elizabeth Arden bapt. 10th April.
Lydia dau. of John and Sarah Ashbury bapt. 11th April.
Nicholas son of Richard and Ann Richardson bapt. 24th April.
George son of Jeroam Shaw bapt. 30th July and bur. 4th Aug.
Robert son of Henry and Catherine Carter bapt. 11th Aug.
Mary dau. of Henry and Elizabeth Chantry bapt. 20th Aug.

1666

Ales dau. of William and Margaret Roberts born 20th Dec. 1665 and bapt. 18th
    Feb.
Ann dau. of Edward and Elizabeth Arden born 23rd March and bapt. 17th April.
Elizabeth dau. of William and Mary Moar born 15th and bapt. 19th Aug.
Christopher son of Christopher and Ales Upton born 23rd and bapt. 26th Aug.
Charles son of Thomas and Elizabeth Freeman born 7th and bapt. 25th Oct.
John son of Henery and Ales Whitworth born 10th and bapt. 23rd Oct.
Ann dau. of Jerom and Mary Shaw born 1st and bapt. 9th Dec.

1667

Mary dau. of Henery and Catherin Carter born 7th and bapt. 14th Jan.
Richard son of Richard and Ann Turner born 10th and bapt. 17th Feb.
Mighel son of Edward and Joane Haslam born 14th and bapt. 26th Feb.
Marie dau. of Thomas and Sara Allwood born 18th Feb. and bapt. 28th March.
Godfrey son of Godfrey and Dorothy Flint born 21st June.
Elizabeth dau. of William and Ann Douman bapt. 3rd Aug.
John son of John and Mary Bland bapt. 25th and bur. 28th Aug.
Elizabeth dau. of William and Elizabeth Walker born 12th and bapt. 21st Nov.

1668

An dau. of Robert and Elen Hardy born 24th and bapt. 29th March.
Godfrey son of Godfrey and Elizabeth Richardson bapt. 3rd May.
John son of Henry Onion bapt. 4th May.
Godfrey son of Godfrey and Mary Tallents born 29th May and bapt. 28th June.
Sara dau. of Henery and Elizbeth Chantry born and bapt. 23rd Sept.
John son of Peter and Isabell Vickerstaff bapt. 27th Sept.
Robert son of Robert and Catherin Batman bapt. 4th Oct.
Henery son of Henery and Catherin Carter born 17th and bapt. 22nd Nov.
Sara dau. of Edward and Elizabeth Arden born 24th and bapt. 29th Nov.

1669

Ann and Dorothie daus. of John and Sara Ashbury born and bapt. 2nd March.
Elizabeth dau. of Thomas and Elizabeth Freeman born 13th March and bapt. 1st
    April.

Elizabeth dau. of Godfrey and Dorothy Flint bapt. 7th April.
Nickolas son of Nickolas and Mary Marsh born 26th April and bapt. 2nd May.
Alese dau. of John and Ann Benet bapt. 20th May.
An dau. of Francis and An Turner bapt. 31st May.
Elizabeth dau. of William and Elizabeth Outram born 30th Oct. and bapt. 10th
    Nov.
Edward son of Edward and Jone Haslam born 18th Oct.

1670

John son of John and Helen Clark bapt. 24th April.
Georg son of Henery and Elizabeth Onion bapt. 19th May.
Robert son of Henery and Elizabeth Furne bapt. 26th June.
Josef son of John and Sara Ashbury bapt. 7th Aug.
Francis son of John and Isabell Glosop bapt. 11 Sept.

1671

John son of Robert and Elen Hardy born, bapt. and died 28th Jan.
Ralph son of Thomas and Elizabeth Freeman born 12th and bapt. 31st Jan.
William son of William and Margrett Roberts born 25th Jan. and bapt. 3rd Feb.
Thomas son of Godfrey and Mary Tallents born 10th March and bapt. 3rd April.
Nickolas son of Thomas and Mary Thornally bapt. 7th May.

1672

Ann dau. of Reginald and Mary Woodhead born 27th Jan. and bapt. 13th Feb.
Alice dau. of Robert and Catherine Bateman bapt. 10th March.
William son of William and Elizabeth Outram bapt. 10th March.
John son of John and Catherine Brett born 14th and bapt. 24th March.
Thomas son of Thomas and Sara Allwood born 14th and bapt. 29th March.
Ann dau. of John and Ann Bennet bapt. 9th April.
Robert son of John and Elizabeth Rogers bapt. 5th May.
Ales dau. of William and Ann Douman bapt. 26th June.
William son of William and Sara Rodgers bapt. 28th July.
Mary dau. of Jerom and Mary Shaw bapt. 28th July.
Samuel son of Thomas and Elizabeth Freeman born 24th and bapt. 28th Aug.
Robert son of Robert and Elin Hardy born and bapt. 27th Aug.

1673

John son of John and Sara Ashbury born 24th Dec. 1672 and bapt. 6th Jan.
William son of William and Ann Watkinson bapt. 16th March.
Mary dau. of Nicholas and Mary Marsh bapt. 4th May.
Elizabeth dau. of Henery and Alls Whitworth bapt. 1st June.
Mihell son of John and Katherin Brett bapt. 3rd Aug.
William son of William and Elizabeth Marsh bapt. 21st. Oct.
Mary dau. of Thomas and Mary Thornally bapt. 17th Nov.
Francis son of Godfrey and Mary Tallents born 22nd Oct. and bapt. 18th Nov.
Mary dau. of Georg and Mary Widesonn bapt. 18th Nov.

1674

Francis son of William and Elizabeth Outram bapt. 13th Sept.
Robert son of Thomas and Elizabeth Freeman born 8th and bapt. 11th Oct.

1675

John son of Robert and Ellen Hardy born 26th April and bapt. 3rd May.
William son of William and Ann Douman born 29th May and bapt. 14th June.
Ann dau. of Edward and Joane Haslam born 10th and bapt. 20th June.
John son of John and Ann Hallom born 22nd and bapt. 29th Aug.
Ann dau. of John and Catherin Brett bapt. 28th Nov.
John son of William and Elizabeth Marsh born 14th and bapt. 30th Dec.

1676

Roger son of William and Ann Watkinson bapt. 12th March.
Francis son of Nicholas and Mary Marsh born 11th March and bapt. 10th April.
William son of Godfrey and Mary Tallents born 30th March and bapt. 2nd April.
Robert son of John and Isabel Glossop bapt. 30th April.
Richard son of Richard and Sara White bapt. 7th May.
Joshua son of Thomas and Marie Thornally bapt. 27th Aug.

1677

John son of Samuell and Susanna Stevenson bapt. 15th July.
Marie dua. of William and Elizabeth Outram bapt. 15th July.

Sara dau. of John and Rebecka Allwood bapt. 14th Oct.
Marie dau. of Charles and Elinor Waine bapt. 24th Nov.

1678

Frances dau. of William and Ann Coulgreave bapt. 20th May.
Ann dau. of John and Ann Hallom born 29th May and bapt. 25th June.
Febe dau. of John and Catherine Brett bapt. 14th July.
Margaret dau. of Richard and Mary Benit bapt. 21st July.
Elizabeth dau. of William and Elizabeth Marsh bapt. 5th Aug.
George son of William and Ann Watkinson bapt. 7th Oct.
George son of Nicholas and Mary Marsh bapt. 4th Nov.
Samuel son of Godfrey and Mary Tallents bapt. 24th Nov.

1679

Daniel son of William and Mary Bradley of Ryley bapt. at Sutton 1st Jan.
Elizabeth dau. of Henry and Catherine Carter bapt. 9th Feb.
Dorothy dau. of Johna and Rebecca Allwood bapt. 27th Feb.
Sarah dau. of Samuel and Susanna Stimpson bapt. 23rd March.
Francis son of James and Elizabeth Taylor bapt. 6th April.
Edward son of John and Anne Bennet bapt. 15th April.
Mary dau. of Richard and Ann Shaw bapt. 19th May.
Elizabeth dau. of Thomas and Mary Thornally bapt. 20th Oct.
Samuel son of Henry and Barbara Unwin bapt. 26th Oct.
[Blank] dau. of John and [Blank] Rogers bapt. 22nd Dec.

1680

Frances dau. of Charles and Elianor Wayne bapt. 6th Jan.
Elizabeth dau. of Thomas and Elizabeth Naylor bapt. 17th Feb.
Francis son of John and Catherine Brett bapt. 11th April.
Robert son of John and Ann Hallam bapt. 27th April.
Ellen dau. of John and Ellen Clarke of Normanton bapt. 30th April.
Robert son of John Elizabeth Shaw bapt. 13th June.
Ralph and Francis sons of Robert and Hellen Hardy bapt. 15th July.
Ann dau. of Thomas Chapman and his wife bapt. 1st Aug.
Elizabeth dau. of James and Elizabeth Taylor bapt. 15th Aug.
Abigail dau. of William and Ann Doeman bapt. 22nd Aug.

Rebechah dau. of John and Rebecka Allwood bapt. 12th Nov.

1681

Elizabeth dau. of Henry Unwin junior and Barbara his wife bapt. 2nd Jan.
Thomas son of Richard and Ann Shaw bapt. 13th Jan.
Martha dau. of Edward and Joane Haslam bapt. 25th Jan.
Mary dau. of Samuel and Susanna Stevenson bapt. 9th Feb.
Dinah dau. of Godfrey and Mary Tallents bapt. 13th Feb.
John son of Daniel and Ellen Bateman bapt. at Sutton 9th March.
Mary dau. of William and Mary Scales bapt. 20th April.
Thomas son of William and Elizabeth Marsh bapt. 29th April.
Thomas son of Howsley and Judith Freeman born 16th and bapt. 23rd Oct.
Thomas son of Thomas and Ann Lawrence bapt. 27th Oct.

1682

John son of William and Alice Wingfield bapt. 4th April.
Thomas son of Thomas and Elizabeth Naylor bapt. 24th May.
Alice dau. of Samuel and Jane Unwin bapt. 25th June.
Henry son of Henry and Barbara Unwin bapt. 13th July.
John son of Edward and Joane Haslam bapt. 18th July.
Francis son of Revel and Margaret Shaw bapt. 23rd July.
John son of Thomas and Mary Bennet bapt. 3rd Sept.
William son of John and Elizabeth Rogers bapt. 10th Sept.
Robert son of Charles and Elianor Wayne born 3rd and bapt. 26th Sept.
Jane dau. of Robert and Ellen Hardie bapt. 17th Oct.
Mary dau. of Arthur and Sarah Nelson bapt. 4th Dec.

1683

Elizabeth dau. of Howsley and Judith Freeman born 18th and bapt. 25th March.
Jonathan son of John and Elizabeth Shaw bapt. 1st April.
Elenor dau. of Godfrey and Mary Tallents bapt. 4th June.
Joseph son of James and Alice Taylor bapt. 26th Dec.

1684

John son of Henry and Barbara Unwin bapt. 14th Jan.
Katherine dau. of John and Katherine Brett bapt. 15th Jan.
William son of Daniel and Elen Bateman bapt. 26th Jan.
[*Blank*] son of Thomas and Ann Lawrence bapt. 26th May.
Samuel son of Samuel Stimpson and his wife bapt. 19th Aug.
Samuel son of Samuel and Jane Unwin bapt. 2nd Sept.

1685

John son of Revel and Margaret Shaw bapt. 2nd Jan.
Samuel son of Michael and Elizabeth Brett bapt. 14th Jan.
Richard son of John and Elizabeth Shaw bapt. 20th Jan.
William son of William and Alice Wingfield bapt. 20th Jan.
John son of James and Alice Taylor bapt. 27th Feb. and bur. 1st March.
Elizabeth dau. of Robert and Anne Stanley born 21st and bapt. 31st March.
Ann dau. of Francis and Hannah Holsworth bapt. 6th March.
Elizabeth dau. of Francis and Sarah Tallents bapt. 3rd May.
John son of Robert and Catherine Finnie bapt. 10th May.
Francis son of Robert and Elin Hardie bapt. 8th June.
William son of Thomas and Isabel Chapman bapt. 13th July.
Sara dau. of Thomas and Margaret Parks bapt. 3rd Aug.
Mary dau. of William and Elizabeth Marsh bapt. 9th Dec.

1686

Alice dau. of Robert and Isabel Butcher bapt. 10th Jan.
Robert son of Robert and Ann Stanley bapt. 8th April.
Jonathan son of Michael and Elizabeth Brett bapt. 10th May.
Alice dau. of Alice Swindale bapt. 16th May.
Mary dau. of Henry and Barbara Unnian bapt. 21st May.
William son of Thomas and Ann Colliar bapt. 24th May.
Robert son of Thomas and Ann Lorance bapt. 22nd June.
Charles son of Mr Charles Waine and Elnor his wife born 26th July and bapt.
    6th Aug.
Francis son of Arthur and Sarah Nolson bapt. 10th Oct.
Alice dau. of John Rogers bapt. 21st Nov.
Thomas son of Thomas and Mary Bennitt bapt. 2nd Dec.
Mary dau. of Samuel and Jane Unnian bapt. 26th Dec.

1687

Elizabeth dau. of John and Elizabeth Shaw bapt. 2nd Feb.
Robert son of Francis and Sara Tallents bapt. 20th March.
Lettice dau. of John and Lettice Heath bapt. 1st May.
Joshua son of Jonathan and Mary Swallow bapt. 20th June.
Ann dau. of William and Ann Watkinson bapt. 11th July.
Ann dau. of William and Mary Richardson bapt. 1st Aug.
Elizabeth dau. of Robert and Isabel Butcher bapt. 21st Aug.
Elizabeth dau. of William and Jone Baumfort bapt. 11th Sept.
Sara dau. of Godfrey and Mary Tallents bapt. 11th Sept.
Thomas son of William and Ann Winfield bapt. 12th Sept.
Ann dau. of Revill and Margaret Shaw bapt. 20th Sept.
Jeremiah son of William and Mary Shaw bapt. 16th Oct.
John son of Thomas and Sara Colgreave bapt. 8th Nov.
Isabel dau. of Francis and Sara Tallents bapt. 28th Dec.

1688

Thomas son of Robert and Ann Standley bapt. 18th Jan.
Elizabeth dau. of Robert and Catherine Finney bapt. 25th Jan.
Ann dau. of Samuel and Susannah Steemson bapt. 19th Feb.
Margaret dau. of Henry and Dorothy Johnson bapt. 11th March.
Elizabeth dau. of Edward and Elizabeth Gill bapt. 26th March.
Mary dau. of Godfrey and Mary Shipston bapt. 26th March.
Hennerry son of Hennerry and Barbara Unnian bapt. 28th March.
Alice dau. of Thomas and Ann Colliar bapt. 18th Sept.
Wiliam son of Leonard and Jane Woodhead bapt. 3rd Oct.
Francis son of Thomas and Ann Lorans bapt. 24th Oct.

1689

Thomas son of Thomas and Sarah Colgreave bapt. 8th Jan.
John son of Robert and Frances Steemson bapt. 4th Feb.
Elizabeth dau. of William and Ann Unnian bapt. 5th Feb.
Paule son of Samuel and Jane Unnian bapt. 11th Feb.
John son of John and Elizabeth Shaw bapt. 18th March.
John son of John and Ann Holmes bapt. 30th April.
Ann dau. of Thomas and Mary Bennett bapt. 30th April.
Mary dau. of William and Mary Richardson bapt. 23rd May.

Hellen dau. of John and Hellen Frith of the parish of Bolsover, bapt. 29th May.
Francis son of Thomas and Ann Vessey bapt. 15th July.

1690

Mary dau. of Robert and Catherine Finney bapt. 4th Jan.
Thomas son of Robert and Isabel Butcher bapt. 22nd Jan.
William son of Francis and Sara Tallents bapt. 5th Feb.
Elizabeth dau. of William and Mary Shaw bapt. 10th Feb.
Jonathan son of Jonathan and Mary Swallow bapt. 10th March.
Alice dau. of Henry and Barbara Unnian bapt. 30th March.
Ann dau. of William and Ann Bennit bapt. 13th May.
Robert son of Robert and Frances Steemson bapt. 7th Sept.
Samuel son of William and Alice Winfield bapt. 7th Oct.
Isabel dau. of William and Joan Baumfort bapt. 18th Nov.

1691

Ann dau. of William and Ann Unnian bapt. 7th Jan.
Sara dau. of William and Sara Citching bapt. 25th March.
Joseph son of John and Helen Heath bapt. 11th May.
Mary dau. of Thomas and Mary Bennet bapt. 16th June.
Thomas son of Thomas and Elizabeth Thornaly bapt. 20th July.
Thomas son of Thomas and Ann Colliar bapt. 3rd Nov.
William son of William and Ann Bennit bapt. 30th Nov.
Elizabeth dau. of William and Mary Richardson bapt. 15th Dec.

1692

John son of Leonard and Jane Woodhead bapt. 4th Feb.
Susannah dau. of Thomas and Ann Vessey bapt. 24th Feb.
Barbara dau. of Robert and Isabel Butcher bapt. 7th March.
Francis son of Francis and Ann Richardson *alias* Gregory bapt. 10th March.
Catherine dau. of Robert and Caterine Finnie bapt. 17th April.
Catherine dau. of Henry and Sara Carter bapt. 19th June.
Mary dau. of John and Elizabeth Shaw bapt. 10th July.
William son of William and Elizabeth Shaw bapt. 22nd Aug.
Epiphanius son of Jobe and Elizabeth Scales bapt. 23rd Oct.
Hannah dau. of Henry and Barbara Unnian bapt. 21st Nov.

William son of William and Ann Unwin bapt. 5th Dec.
Francis son of Richard and Isabel Bennet bapt. 26th Dec.

1693

James son of William and Alice Winfield bapt. 14th Feb.
Edmund son of Thomas and Mary Bennit bapt. 19th Feb.
John son of Robert and Ann Standley bapt. 20th Feb.
Joseph son of Joseph and Ann Allwood bapt. 21st March.
Thomas son of Francis and Elizabeth Butcher bapt. 6th July.
Francis son of Thomas and Elizabeth Thornally bapt. 5th Nov.

1694

Mary dau. of Samuel and Mary Tallents bapt. 3rd July.
Mary dau. of William and Ann Bennet bapt. 5th Sept.
Jane dau. of Thomas and Mary Bennet bapt. 20th Nov.
Mary dau. of Thomas and Ann Colier bapt. 26th Nov.

1695

Francis son of Francis and Elizabeth Butcher bapt. 4th March.
Jane dau. of Robert and Ann Standley bapt. 23rd May.
Sara dau. of Thomas and Elizabeth White bapt. 28th May.
Joseph son of Edward and Elizabeth Hodgkinson bapt. 26th June.
Mary dau. of William and Ann Onian bapt. 1st Sept.
Robert son of Robert and Catherine Finney bapt. 16th Sept.
Mary dau. of Thomas and Mary Colgrave bapt. 15th Oct.
Elizabeth dau. of George and Jane Dowman bapt. 16th Oct.
Sara dau. of James and Sara Brailsford bapt. 22nd Oct.
George son of Henry and Barbara Unnian bapt. 17th Nov.
Mary dau. of Thomas and Lydia Marsh bapt. 17th Nov.
Sara dau. of Thomas and Ann Rogers bapt. 22nd Dec.
Elizabeth dau. of Robert and Frances Steemson bapt. 29th Dec.

1696

Elizabeth dau. of Francis and Ann Richardson *alias* Gregory bapt. 7th Jan.

Samuel son of Samuel and Mary Tallents bapt. 1st March.
Ann dau. of [*Blank*] bapt. 12th April.
Francis son of William and Alice Winfield bapt. 7th May.
Samuel son of Thomas and Elizabeth Thornally bapt. 12th July.
Grace dau. of Mr Ralph Heathcoate and Elizabeth his wife bapt. 3rd Sept.
Henry son of Robert and Mary Ferne bapt. 5th Nov.
Elizabeth dau. of William and Ann Bennit bapt. 29th Nov.
Sara dau. of Thomas and Mary Bennit bapt. 21st Dec.

1697

Robert son of William and Elizabeth Shaw bapt. 1st Feb.
John son of John and Mary Scales bapt. 18th Feb.
Francis son of Philip and Catherine Tallents bapt. 21st Feb.
Elizabeth dau. of Francis and Elizabeth Butcher bapt. 9th March.
John son of Robert and Elizabeth Hardy bapt. 10th March.
Elizabeth dau. of Thomas and Hannah Rolin bapt. 5th April.
Rebecah dau. of Samuel and Mary Tallents bapt. 23rd April.
James son of James and Sarah Brailsford bapt. 3rd June.
Francis son of Godfrey and Mary Shipston bapt. 7th June.
Ann dau. of Arthur and Sarah Noleson bapt. 11th Oct.
Georg son of William and Ann Onnion bapt. 12th Oct.
Ralph son of Ralph Heathcoate, rector of this church, and Elizabeth his wife
    bapt. 4th Nov.
Anne dau. of Robert and Anne Stanley bapt. 4th Nov.
Anne dau. of John and Margaret Thomlinson bapt. 14th Nov.
Anne dau. of George and Jane Dowman bapt. 29th Dec.

1698

Samuel son of Robert and Frances Stevenson bapt. 13th Feb.
George son of Thomas and Anne Lawrence bapt. 5th April.
William son of Godfrey Tallents junior and Mary his wife bapt. 15th May.
Edward son of Edward and Elizabeth Hodgkinson bapt. 13th June.
Elizabeth dau. of Thomas and Elizabeth White bapt. 5th July.
Thomas son of Thomas and Anne Rodger bapt. 12th July.
Francis son of Francis and Anne Richardson bapt. 9th Aug.
Samuel son of Christopher and Elizabeth Upton bapt. 21st Aug.
Elizabeth dau. of William and Mary Hill bapt. 15th Sept.
Emme dau. of Robert and Mary Ferne bapt. 21st Sept.

John son of James and Sarah Brailsford bapt. 6th Oct.

1699

Elizabeth dau. of Ralph Heathcoate, rector of this church, and Elizabeth his wife
    bapt. 16th Feb.
Anne dau. of John and Elizabeth Shaw bapt. 19th Feb.
Mary dau. of John and Anne Wood bapt. 5th March.
Sarah dau. of William and Anne Bennet bapt. 14th March.
William son of Francis and Elizabeth Butcher bapt. 16th April.
John son of Michael and Elizabeth Brett bapt. 23rd April.
William son of John and Isabell Barker bapt. 1st June.
Godfrey son of Robert and Anne Stanley bapt. 24th Aug.
Elizabeth dau. of Thomas and Mary Bennet bapt. 17th Sept.
Ellen dau. of Robert and Elizabeth Hardy bapt. 26th Sept.

1700

Mary dau. of Jonathan and Mary Swallow bapt. 1st Jan.
John son of William and Elizabeth Shaw bapt. 28th Jan.
Joseph son of William and Ann Unwin bapt. 25th Feb.
Alice dau. of George and Jane Dowman bapt. 1st April.
Mary dau. of Thomas and Anne Lawrence bapt. 1st April.
Richard son of Thomas and Elizabeth White bapt. 9th April.
Robert son of Samuel and Mary Tallents bapt. 16th April.
Mary dau. of Thomas and Hannah Rawlins bapt. 2nd June.
Elizabeth dau. of John and Mary Castle bapt. 28th July.
Elizabeth dau. of John and Isabel Barker bapt. 1st Sept.
John son of John and Margaret Thomlinson bapt. 9th Sept.
Elizabeth dau. of William and Alice Wingfield bapt. 24th Sept.
Mary dau. of Robert and Frances Stevenson bapt. 20th Oct.
Elizabeth dau. of Ralph Heathcoate, rector of this church, and Elizabeth his wife
    bapt. 29th Oct.
John son of Thomas Thornally, a poor man, and Elizabeth his wife bapt. 15th
    Dec.
Elizabeth dau. of Godfrey Tallents junior and Mary his wife bapt. 26th Dec.

1701

Sarah dau. of John and Mary Scales bapt. 6th Feb.

John son of Edward and Elizabeth Hodgkinson bapt. 12th May.

Jacob son of Michael Brett, a poor man, and Elizabeth his wife bapt. 10th June.

William son of John Shaw, a poor man, and Elizabeth his wife bapt. 13th July.

John son of John and Sarah Unwin bapt. 10th Aug.

Joseph son of William and Anne Bennet bapt. 12th Aug.

Mary dau. of Robert and Mary Ferne bapt. 18th Aug.

John son of John and Elizabeth Eyre bapt. 8th Sept.

Robert son of Francis and Elizabeth Butcher bapt. 21st Sept.

Robert son of Robert and Elizabeth Hardy bapt. 29th Sept.

Elizabeth dau. of Thomas and Anne Rodger bapt. 30th Sept.

Godfrey son of Ralph Heathcoate, rector of this church, and Elizabeth his wife bapt. 11th Nov.

Abigail dau. of Ralph Heathcoate, rector of this church, and Elizabeth his wife bapt. 11th Nov.

Joseph son of Robert and Anne Stanley bapt. 29th Dec.

1702

Roger son of William and Alice Winfield bapt. 3rd Feb.

Robert son of James and Sarah Brailsford bapt. 10th Feb.

Thomas son of William Shaw, a poor man, and Elizabeth his wife bapt. 6th April.

Joseph son of Thomas and Anne Lawrence bapt. 28th April.

John son of John Wood, a poor man, and Anne his wife bapt. 17th May.

Esther dau. of John Thomlinson, a poor man, and Margaret his wife bapt. 24th May.

Thomas son of Thomas and Elizabeth White bapt. 28th July.

Thomas son of Samuel and Mary Tallents bapt. 11th Aug.

James son of James and Elizabeth Darcy bapt. 23rd Aug.

Peter son of Joseph and Mary Ashbury bapt. 28th Sept.

George son of Ralph and Elizabeth Heathcoate bapt. 6th Nov.

1703

Robert son of William and Elizabeth Peace bapt. 13th Jan.

Sarah dau. of William and Ann Unwin bapt. 14th March.

Anne dau. of John and Isabel Barker bapt. 11th April.

William son of John and Mary Scales bapt. 6th May.
Robert son of William and Mary Wing bapt. 12th May.
Thomas son of James and Sarah Brailsford bapt. 16th Aug.
John son of John and Mary Lievesly bapt. 26th Sept.
Jane dau. of George and Jane Dowman bapt. 7th Oct.
Alice dau. of William Bennet, a poor man, and Anne his wife bapt. 27th Oct.
Ralph son of William Roberts junior and Sarah his wife bapt. 17th Dec.

1704

John son of Robert Butcher, a poor man, and Ann his wife bapt. 2nd Jan.
Henry son of Thomas and Hannah Rawlins bapt. 26th March.
Benjamin son of Thomas and Anne Lawrence bapt. 4th April.
William son of Robert and Anne Stanley bapt. 8th May.
Francis son of Samuel and Mary Tallents bapt. 12th May.
Lydia dau. of Thomas and Elizabeth White bapt. 16th May.
Benidicta dau. of Thomas and Anne Rodger bapt. 11th June.
Elizabeth dau. of Robert and Mary Ferne bapt. 12th June.
John son of James and Sarah Brailsford bapt. 30th Aug.
Elizabeth dau. of William and Margery Outram bapt. 2nd Oct.
Phebe dau. of Godfrey and Mary Tallents bapt. 31st Oct.
Ellen dau. of George and Anne Clark bapt. 1st Nov.
Elizabeth dau. of Sampson and Alice Johnson bapt. 7th Dec.
Jane dau. of William and Dorothy Peace bapt. 12th Dec.

1705

Sarah dau. of Joseph and Mary Ashbury bapt. 28th Jan.
John son of John Pogmore, [a] poor [man], and Sarah his wife bapt. 11th March.
John son of John and Frances Christian bapt. 16th March.
Elizabeth dau. of Robert and Elizabeth Hardy bapt. 27th March.
Edward son of Ralph Heathcote, rector of this church, and Elizabeth his wife
    bapt. 12th April.
Willoughby son of William and Sarah Roberts bapt. 15th May.
Godfrey son of Samuel and Mary Tallents bapt. 31st May.
Nicholas son of Nicholas and Mary Marsh bapt. 15th July.
Sarah dau. of Robert Butcher, a poor man, and Anne his wife bapt. 5th Aug.
Samuel son of John and Sarah Unwin bapt. 7th Oct.

1706

Isabel dau. of John and Isabel Barker bapt. 1st Jan.
Joseph son of John and Mary Lievesly bapt. 13th Jan.
John son of William and Anne Bennet bapt. 11th Feb.
Samuel son of Thomas and Elizabeth White bapt. 26th March.
Robert son of William and Anne Unwin bapt. 14th April.
Samuel son of Henry and Joane Unwin bapt. 14th May.
Joseph son of John and Mary Scales bapt. 20th May.
Ralph son of Thomas Bennet, a poor man, and Mary his wife bapt. 20th May.
Thomas son of John and Mary Stevenson bapt. 11th June.
Anne dau. of John Pogmore, a poor man, and Sarah his wife bapt. 11th June.
Elizabeth dau. of John and Frances Christian bapt. 7th July.
Sarah dau. of John and Mary Bennet bapt. 25th Aug.
Sarah dau. of Thomas and Anne Lawrence bapt. 1st Sept.

1707

Mary dau. of Joseph and Mary Ashbury bapt. 2nd Jan.
Sarah dau. of William and Sarah Roberts bapt. 8th Jan.
Robert son of Robert and Anne Butcher bapt. 9th Feb.
William son of William and Dorothy Peace bapt. 20th May.
Elizabeth dau. of Henry and Joane Unwin bapt. 22nd May.
Dinah dau. of Godfrey and Mary Tallents bapt. 22nd May.
William son of John and Margaret Thomlinson bapt. 29th Oct.
John son of John and Mary Stevenson bapt. 5th Dec.

1708

Isabella dau. of Thomas and Ann Rodger bapt. 20th Jan.
John son of Samuel and Mary Tallents bapt. 13th May.
Elizabeth dau. of Nicholas and Mary Marsh bapt. 27th June.
Ann dau. of Edward and Jane Haslam bapt. 5th July.

1709

Margaret dau. of William and Sarah Roberts bapt. 16th Jan.
John son of Thomas and Elizabeth White bapt. 18th Jan.
Elizabeth dau. of Joseph and Mary Ashbury bapt. 25th Jan.

John son of Francis and Elizabeth Butcher bapt. 13th March.
Thomas son of John and Elizabeth Eyre bapt. 10th April.
Edward son of John and Mary Scales bapt. 15th May.
Joseph son of Francis Tallents junior and Catherine his wife bapt. 29th May.
Sampson son of Sampson and Alice Johnson bapt. 26th June.
Mary dau. of John and Frances Christian bapt. 3rd July.
Edward son of Edward and Jane Haslam bapt. 5th July.
Edward son of Robert and Anne Stanley bapt. 30th Aug.
William son of John and Sarah Pogmore bapt. 16th Sept.
Robert son of Robert and Mary Ferne bapt. 20th Sept.
Anne dau. of John and Anne Wood bapt. 20th Oct.
Stephen son of Henry and Joane Unwin bapt. 25th Oct.
George son of John and Anne Madin bapt. 25th Oct.
John son of Nicholas and Mary Marsh bapt. 30th Oct.
Joseph son of Robert and Ann Butcher bapt. 6th Nov.
Elizabeth dau. of John and Margaret Thomlinson bapt. 11th Dec.
Godfrey son of Godfrey and Mary Tallents bapt. 27th Dec.

1710

Phillip son of Samuel and Mary Tallents bapt. 2nd Feb.
Francis son of Francis Tallents junior and Catherine his wife bapt. 2nd July.
Margaret dau. of Edward and Jane Haslam bapt. 28th July.
Anne dau. of John and Mary Stevenson bapt. 6th Aug.
Barbara dau. of William and Anne Bennet bapt. 10th Sept.
Mary dau. of John and Patience Siddon, strangers, bapt. 10th Sept.
Mary dau. of William and Sarah Roberts bapt. 24th Sept.
Anne dau. of William and Abigail Marsden bapt. 29th Oct.
John son of John and Ann Maden bapt. 27th Dec.

1711

Mary dau. of John and Mary Bennet bapt. 30th Jan.
Mary dau. of John and Sarah Pogmore bapt. 4th Feb.
Mary dau. of Thomas and Mary Cousen bapt. 31st July.
Anne dau. of Joseph and Mary Ashbury bapt. 19th Aug.
David son of Francis and Catherine Tallents bapt. 21st Oct.
Francis son of John and Ann Glossop bapt. 28th Oct.
Thomas son of Thomas and Elizabeth Vessey bapt. 4th Nov.

1712

Mary dau. of John and Margaret Thomlinson bapt. 15th March.
William son of Edward and Jane Haslam bapt. 1st April.
Eleanor dau. of Godfrey and Mary Tallents bapt. 15th May.
Mary dau. of William and Abigail Marsden bapt. 26th May.
Richard son of Robert and Elizabeth Hardy bapt. 6th May.
Gilbert son of Thomas and Elizabeth White bapt. 30th June.
William son of Robert and Ann Butcher bapt. 13th July.
Richard son of Nicholas and Mary Marsh bapt. 24th Aug.
Mary dau. of Sampson and Ales Jonson bapt. 19th Oct.
Ann dau. of Richard Stimson bapt. 9th Nov.
William son of William and Sarah Robards bapt. 5th Dec.
Henry son of Henry and Joan Unwin bapt. 26th Dec.

1713

Elizabeth dau. of Francis and Catherine Tallents bapt. 6th March.
John son of John and Isabel Barker bapt. 29th March.
Thomas son of Thomas and Mary Cousen bapt. 12th April.
Elizabeth dau. of Edward and Jane Haslam bapt. 29th Oct.
Joseph son of Joseph and Mary Ashbury bapt. 13th Nov.

1714

Mary dau. of John and Mary Stephenson bapt. 24th Feb.
John son of Francis and Anne Nelson bapt. 7th March.
Margaret dau. of John and Margaret Tomlinson bapt. 7th March.
William son of William and Abigail Marsden bapt. 21st March.
Katherine dau. of Francis and Katherine Tallents bapt. 7th April.
Elizabeth dau. of Francis and Elizabeth Britt bapt. 24th April.

1715

Ruth dau. of Thomas and Elizabeth White bapt. 2nd March.
Elizabeth dau. of Francis and Elizabeth Brett bapt. 24th April.
Ann dau. of Godfrey and Anne Flint bapt. 18th May.
Anne dau. of William and Margarory Outram bapt. 10th July.
Peter son of Robert and Ann Butcher bapt. 18th Sept.

Sarah dau. of Francis and Anne Nelson bapt. 14th Nov.
Jane dau. of Paul and Jane Unwin bapt. 2nd Dec.

1716

Thomas son of Thomas and Margaret May bapt. 1st May.
Elizabeth dau. of Francis and Catherine Tallents bapt. 30th Sept.
Anne dau. of Stephen Ward, rector of Sutton, and Anne his wife bapt. 15th Dec.

1717

Mary dau. of Francis and Elizabeth Brett bapt. 27th March.
Anne dau. of John and Elizabeth Bennet bapt. 10th June.
Sarah dau. of Thomas and Margaret May bapt. 18th June.
John son of Nathaniel and Anne Bradshaw bapt. 29th Aug.
Thomas son of Thomas and Elizabeth Shaw bapt. 17th Sept.

1718–19

Joseph son of Godfrey and Mary Tallents bapt. 3rd April.
John son of John and Elizabeth Palmer bapt. 16th June.
Ellen dau. of John and Margaret Tomlinson bapt. 3rd Sept.
Elizabeth dau. of William and Jane Richardson bapt. 2nd April 1719.
[*No further baptism entries until 1729; eight pages left blank into which the
missing entries should evidently have been copied.*]

1729

John son of Joshua and Anne Deabanks bapt. 10th Nov.
Francis and William sons of John and Mary Frith bapt. 10th Nov.

1730

Elizabeth dau. of Francis and Anne Nelson bapt. 5th April.
Thomas son of Thomas and Mary Low bapt. 25th June.
Francis son of Francis and Sarah Wingfield bapt. 7th Aug.
Joseph son of John and Elizabeth Scales bapt. 26th Dec.

1731

Samuel son of John and Elizabeth Turner bapt. 31st March.
Robert son of John and Jane Hewitt bapt. [*Date missing*].
James son of James and Anne Hewitt bapt. [*Date missing*].
Joshua son of Joshua and Anne Deabanks bapt. 1st Nov.
William son of William and Anne Plant bapt. 18th Nov.

1732

[*Blank*] dau. of John and Hannah Mettam bapt. 31st Jan.
Ellen dau. of Joseph and Ellen Hodgkinson bapt. 11th May.
Thomas son of Francis and Sarah Wingfield bapt. 25th June.
Elizabeth dau. of Elizabeth Palmer bapt. 25th June.
Hannah dau. of Jonathan and Sarah Swallow bapt 27th June.
Hannah dau. of Henry and Elizabeth Rawlins bapt. 31st July.
Elizabeth dau. of John and Mary Turner bapt. 30th July.
Doeman son of John and Elizabeth Scales bapt. 27th Dec.

1733

Anne dau. of John and Elizabeth Turner bapt. 1st Jan.
Grace dau. of Catherine Holmes bapt. 6th Feb.
Elizabeth dau. of Frances Twells bapt. 18th Feb.
Samuel son of Thomas and Mary Cantrell bapt. 18th Feb.
[*Blank*] of Samuel and Mary Tallents bapt. 3rd June.
Jane dau. of Mary Dowley bapt. 24th Aug.
Thomas son of Joseph and Elizabeth Bennet bapt. 30th Aug.
Robert son of Robert and Elizabeth Finney bapt. 1st Oct.
William son of John and Hannah Mettam bapt. 24th Oct.
Elizabeth dau. of Thomas and Dorothy Talyor bapt. 10th Dec.

1734

Anne dau. of Francis and Elizabeth Rodger bapt. 1st Jan.
John son of William and Anne Plant bapt. 1st Jan.
Anne dau. of Joshua and Anne Deabanks bapt. 7th Jan.
John son of Sampson and Frances Johnson bapt. 25th March.
William son of Thomas and Elizabeth Lowe bapt. 10th May.

Thomas son of Francis and Sarah Wingfield bapt. 12th May.

James son of John and Jane Hewitt bapt. 22nd July.

Elizabeth dau. of James and Elizabeth Wingfield bapt. 8th Dec.

1735

Mary dau. of John and Elizabeth Scales bapt. 1st March.

Samuel son of Richard and Ann Johnson bapt. 1st April.

John son of John and Mary Turner bapt. 6th May.

Elizabeth dau. of Joseph and Elizabeth Scales bapt. 23rd Sept.

Edward son of Ann Tallents bapt. 12th Oct.

Anne dau. of John and Ellen Revel bapt. 4th Nov.

Anne dau. of Joseph and Anne Lievesley bapt. 24th Nov.

1736

Thomas son of Thomas and Elizabeth Stanley bapt. 17th March.

Phebe dau. of John and Anne Nelson bapt. 17th March.

William son of Joseph and Dorothy Unwin bapt. 2nd April.

George son of John and Hannah Mettam bapt. 7th April.

Edward son of Francis and Sarah Wingfield bapt. 27th June.

William son of Thomas and Mary Cantrell bapt. 27th June.

Elizabeth dau. of Francis and Elizabeth Rodger bapt. 29th Aug.

Anne dau. of William and Anne Plant bapt. 12th Sept.

William son of Joshua and Anne Deabanks bapt. 29th Sept.

John son of John and Mary Pogmore bapt. 10th Oct.

Francis son of Francis and Anne Tallents bapt. 28th Dec.

1737

Robert son of John and Mary Dawson bapt. 27th Jan.

William son of William and Mary Peace bapt. 1st Sept.

Richard son of John and Susanna Motte bapt. 22nd Sept.

Richard son of Joseph and Anne Newton bapt. 23rd Oct.

[Blank] son of Anne Tallents spinster bapt. 23rd Oct.

John son of Sarah Stork spinster bapt. 26th Dec.

Sarah dau. of John and Anne Nelson bapt. 27th Dec.

1738

Henry son of Henry and Elizabeth Rawlins bapt. 5th Feb.
Joseph son of Jos. and Anne Lievesley bapt. 15th Feb.
Samuel son of John and Hannah Mettam bapt. 3rd May.
Thomas son of Richard and Benedicta White bapt. 26th June.
Joseph son of John and Sarah Bacon bapt. 27th June.
Sampson son of Sampson and Frances Johnson bapt. 27th June.
Sarah dau. of William and Anne Plant bapt. 7th Aug.
Anne dau. of Peter and Anne Tallents bapt. 17th Sept.
Joseph son of John and Mary Pogmore bapt. 19th Nov.
Margaret dau. of Joshua and Susanna Wetheral bapt. 28th Nov.
Ruth dau. of John and Mary Turner bapt. 27th Dec.

1739

Samuel son of Joseph and Elizabeth Bennet bapt. 12th Jan.
Samuel son of Godfrey and Martha Tallents bapt. 28th Jan.
Samuel son of Francis and Sarah Wingfield bapt. 30th Jan.
Mary dau. of Thomas and Mary Cantrill bapt. 11th Feb.
Anthony son of Joshua and Anne Debanke bapt. 13th Feb.
Sarah dau. of Francis and Anne Tallents bapt. 16th Feb.
James son of William and Mary Peace bapt. 23rd April.
Isabel dau. of Thomas and Sarah Bennett bapt. 8th July.
Mary dau. of John and Rebecca Lawrence bapt. 11th Dec.
Mary dau. of Sampson and Frances Johnson bapt. 31st Dec.

1740

Anne dau. of Richard and Benedicta White bapt. 3rd Feb.
John son of Joseph and Ann Lievesley bapt. 6th Feb.
Diana dau. of Peter and Anne Tallents bapt. 10th Feb.
James son of William and Anne Plant bapt. 29th June.
Anne dau. of John and Anne Nelson bapt. 29th June.

1741

Anne dau. of Paul and Anne Unwin bapt. 1st Jan.
Philip son of Godfrey and Martha Tallents bapt. 20th Feb.

Anne dau. of Thomas and Elizabeth Mellar bapt. 18th Feb.
Anne dau. of Thomas and Mary Sales bapt. 9th March.
Anne dau. of Joseph and Anne Newton bapt. 15th March.
John spurious son of Susanna Tomlinson bapt. 22nd March.
Mary dau. of William and Mary Peace bapt. 29th June.

1742

Peter son of Peter and Anne Tallents bapt. 6th March.
Anne dau. of Sampson and Frances Johnson bapt. 19th April.
Thomas son of Joseph and Anne Lievesley bapt. 27th June.
Benjamin son of William and Anne Plant bapt. 5th Oct.

1743

Edward son of Edward and Anne Stanley bapt. 8th March.
Ruth dau. of John and Anne Nelson bapt. 20th June.
Robert son of William and Mary Peace bapt. 28th Oct.
Mary dau. of Francis and Anne Tallents bapt. 13th Nov.
Anne dau. of John and Sarah Bacon bapt. 21st Dec.

1744

Thomas son of Henry and Elizabeth Rawling bapt. 22nd Feb. [*Unclear from register if this entry is for 1744 or 1745 new style*].
Sarah dau. of Peter and Sarah Glossop bapt. 5th April.
John son of Edward and Anne Stanley bapt. 30th April.
Godfrey son of Godfrey and Mary Flint bapt. 10th May.
Mary dau. of Thomas and Mary Sales bapt. 10th June.
Hannah dau. of John and Anne Nelson bapt. 3rd July.
Samuel son of Joseph and Anne Lievesley bapt. 6th Sept.
Anne dau. of Francis and Sarah Nelson bapt. [*No date*].
Elizabeth dau. of Sampson and Frances Johnson bapt. [*No date*].

1745

Sarah dau. of Michael and Mary Scales bapt. 13th March.
Robert son of Edward and Anne Stanley bapt. 23rd Aug.

Anne dau. of William and Mary Peace bapt. 16th Sept.

1746

Mary dau. of Francis and Anne Wingfield bapt. 9th Jan.
James son of John and Anne Wood bapt. 14th Jan.
Thomas son of William and Anne Plant bapt. 26th Dec.

1747

Mary dau. of Ralph and Mary Bennett bapt. 1st Jan.
Anne dau. of Edward and Anne Stanley bapt. 19th Jan.
John son of Michael and Mary Scales bapt. 22nd Feb.
Mary dau. of Peter and Sarah Glossop bapt. 25th March.
Elizabeth dau. of John and Anne Nelson bapt. 25th March.
John son of John and Mary Bennett bapt. 7th April.
Mary dau. of Francis and Sarah Nelson bapt. April.
Edward son of Sampson and Frances Johnson bapt. 20th April.
Ellen dau. of Edward and Susanna Woodhead bapt. 25th May.
Thomas son of Thomas and Mary Sales bapt. 8th June.
William son of Joseph and Anne Lievesley bapt. 23rd Aug.
John son of William and Anne Shaw bapt. 30th Aug.
William son of Francis and Ann Wingfield bapt. 31st Aug.
James son of Godfrey and Mary Flint bapt. 29th Oct.
Sarah dau. of Willam and Esther Frost bapt. 26th Dec.

1748

Benedicta dau. of Thomas and Elizabeth Rodgers bapt. 13th March.
Edmund son of Willam and Catherine Ferne bapt. 2nd May.
Samuel son of Thomas and Mary Pogmore bapt. 22nd May.
John son of John and Anne Wood bapt. 26th June.
Thomas son of Ralph and Mary Bennett bapt. 27th June.
Dorothy dau. of William and Mary Peace bapt. 28th June.
Elizabeth dau. of John and Anne Frith bapt. 12th Sept.
James son of James and Hannah Swallow bapt. 25th Oct.
Catherine dau. of Francis and Anne Tallents bapt. 20th Nov.

1749

Anne dau. of Michael and Mary Scales bapt. 16th April.
Susannah dau. of Edward and Susannah Woodhead bapt. 24th April.
George son of George and Elizabeth Brett bapt. 30th May.
John son of John and Anne Nelson bapt. 30th July.
Elizabeth dau. of William and Ann Shaw bapt. 14th Aug.
Elizabeth dau. of Francis and Sarah Nelson bapt. 17th Sept.
Stephen son of Sampson and Frances Johnson bapt. 2nd Oct.
Mary dau. of Thomas and Ellen Fern bapt. 24th Oct.
Robert son of Joseph and Anne Lievesley bapt. 26th Dec.
Mary dau. of John and Mary Bennett bapt. 26th Dec.

1750

Elizabeth dau. of Richard and Mary Marsh bapt. 2nd Feb.
Ellen dau. of Peter and Anne Tallents bapt. 25th Feb.
Thomas son of Thomas and Mary Pogmore bapt. 1st July.
Samuel son of Francis and Anne Wingfield bapt. 15th July.
Joseph son of Thomas and Mary Cantrell bapt. 29th July.
John son of William and Elizabeth Woodhead bapt. 5th Sept.
Elizabeth dau. of William and Ann Barlow bapt. 20th Nov.
Anne dau. of George and Elizabeth Brett bapt. 26th Dec.
Anne dau. of John and Anne Frith bapt. 26th Dec.
Mary dau. of William and Esther Frost bapt. 26th Dec.

1751

Elizabeth dau. of William and Catherine Ferne bapt. 1st Jan.
Sarah dau. of Thomas and Anne Reddish of Heath bapt. 1st. Jan.
Ralph son of Ralph and Mary Bennet bapt. 10th Jan.
John son of John and Elizabeth Lowe bapt. 5th Feb.
Elizabeth dau. of Michael and Mary Scales bapt. 19th Feb.
Anne dau. of Francis and Anne Tallents bapt. 24th March.
Joseph son of John and Anne Wood bapt. 24th March.
Mary dau. of John and Elizabeth Renshaw bapt. 23rd April.
Jane dau. of Edward and Susannah Woodhead bapt. 29th July.
Hannah dau. of Thomas and Mary Sales bapt. 1st Nov.
John son of Samuel and Margaret Swift bapt. 30th Nov.
William son of William and Anne Shaw bapt. 26th Dec.

1752

William son of William and Elizabeth Woodhead bapt. 10th Feb.
Mary dau. of Thomas and Anne Marsh bapt. 25th March.
Sarah dau. of Francis and Sarah Nelson bapt. 30th March.
William son of John and Mary Bennett bapt. 7th May.
Job son of Michael and Mary Scales bapt. 18th May.
Thomas son of William and Ann Barlow bapt. 24th May.
John son of James and Hannah Swallow bapt. 7th June.
Sarah dau. of George and Elizabeth Brett bapt. 28th June.
James son of Francis and Anne Wingfield bapt. 16th Aug.
Richard son of Richard and Mary Marsh bapt. 31st Oct.
Edward son of Edward and Susannah Woodhead bapt. 21st Nov.

1753

Mary dau. of William and Catherine Ferne bapt. 4th March.
Gervase son of Sampson and Francis Johnson bapt. 6th March.
Anne dau. of Ralph and Mary Bennet bapt. 16th March.
Elizabeth dau. of John and Elizabeth Renshaw bapt. 6th May.
John son of Thomas and Anne Pogmore bapt. 1st July.
Mary dau. of Joseph and Ann Lievesley bapt. 1st July.
Jane dau. of William and Elizabeth Woodhead bapt. 2nd July.
Mary dau. of John and Ann Frith bapt. 19th Aug.
Mark son of John and Ann Wood bapt. 9th Dec.

1754

William son of William and Anne Barlow bapt. 30th June.
Hannah dau. of Francis and Anne Tallents bapt. 14th July.
Joseph son of James and Elizabeth Wilson bapt. 21st July.
Thomas son of William and Anne Shaw bapt. 1st Sept.
Robert son of Francis and [Blank] Wingfield bapt. 15th Sept.
Hannah dau. of William and Esther Frost bapt. 1st Oct.
Abraham son of George and Elizabeth Brett bapt. 6th Oct.

1755

William son of Thomas and Mary Sales bapt. 1st Jan.

Joseph son of John and Mary Bennett bapt. 1st Jan.
Alice dau. of William and Elizabeth Woodhead bapt. 6th Jan.
Hannah dau. of Francis and Sarah Nelson bapt. 1st April.
Samuel son of Edward and Ann Stanley bapt. 29th June.
Thomas son of James and Hannah Swallow bapt. 30th June.
Joseph son of Edward and Susannah Woodhead bapt. 25th Aug.
John son of John and Ann Frith bapt. 19th Oct.
Thomas and Anne son and dau. of Thomas and Grace Rodgers bapt. 26th Dec.
Elizabeth dau. of John and Elizabeth Lowe bapt. 26th Dec.

1756

Elizabeth dau. of Sampson and Frances Johnson bapt. 24th Feb.
William son of William and Sarah Beane bapt. 21st March.
David son of George and Elizabeth Brett bapt. 9th May.
Anne dau. of John and Elizabeth Lowe bapt. 27th June.
Anne dau. of William and Anne Shaw bapt. 19th Sept.
Elizabeth dau. of William and Anne Barlow bapt. 26th Sept.
John son of John and Elizabeth Renshaw bapt. 18th Oct.
Elizabeth dau. of William and Elizabeth Wood bapt. 19th Oct.

1757

Absalom son of Michael and Mary Scales bapt. 23rd Jan.
William son of John and Anne Wood bapt. 30th Jan.
Mathew dau. [sic] of John and Mary Bennit bapt. 27th June.
Frances dau. of George and Elizabeth Brett bapt. 27th Dec.

1758

Abraham son of William and Esther Frost bapt. 25th Jan.
Lydia dau. of Francis and Sarah Nelson bapt. 8th March.
John son of John and Anne Bennett bapt. 17th March.
Thomas son of William and Elizabeth Woodhead bapt. 22nd May.
Mary dau. of William and Dorothy Watkinson bapt. 13th June.
Roger son of Francis and Ann Wingfield bapt. 2nd July.
William son of Thomas and Elizabeth Renshaw bapt. 25th Dec.

1759

Thomas son of Thomas and Betty Wingfield bapt. 4th Jan.
Frances dau. of William and Anne Barlow bapt. 29th May.
Sarah dau. of William and Ann Shaw bapt. 1st July.
Mary dau. of Michael Scales and his wife bapt. 3rd July.
Charles son of Henry Cantrill and his wife bapt. 5th Aug.
James son of George and Elizabeth Thornley bapt. 5th Aug.
Ann dau. of John and Elizabeth Mott bapt. 24th Sept.
Richard son of Edward and Susanna Woodhead bapt. 8th Oct.
William son of John and Elizabeth Renshaw bapt. 26th Dec.
William son of Sampson and Frances Johnson bapt. 27th Dec.
George son of George and Elizabeth Hewit bapt. 27th Dec.

1760

Charles son of John and Ann Wood bapt. 6th Jan.
John son of John and Elizabeth Lowe bapt. 20th Feb.
Martha dau. of John and Mary Bennett bapt. 8th April.
Sarah dau. of John and Ann Frith bapt. 27th April.
Lydia dau. of Edmund Reddish and his wife bapt. 8th June.
Hellen dau. of William and Elizabeth Woodhead bapt. 30th June.
Joseph son of Joseph and Ann Ashbury bapt. 3rd Aug.
Dolly dau. of William and Dolly Watkinson bapt. 17th Aug.
Sarah dau. of Thomas and Betty Wingfield of Duckmanton bapt. 28th Sept.
Joseph son of Francis and Sarah Nelson of Duckmanton bapt. 5th Oct.
Thomas son of George and Elizabeth Hewit of Sutton bapt. 22nd Oct.
Godfrey son of John and Sarah Glossop of Duckmanton bapt. 22nd Oct.
Alexander son of Thomas and Elizabeth Clark of Duckmanton bapt. 26th Dec.

1761

Joseph son of Thomas and Elizabeth Renshaw bapt. 9th June.
Ann dau. of Edward and Ann Hodgkinson of Duckmanton bapt. 28th June.
Betty dau. of John and Mary Lowe bapt. 28th June.
Ann dau. of William and Ann Barlow bapt. 5th July.
Samuel son of Mary Cantrel bapt. 12th July.

1762

Ann dau. of William and Catharine Parkins bapt. 1st. Jan.

Elizabeth dau. of Joseph Bennett junior and Elizabeth his wife bapt. 6th Jan.

William son of Richard and Mary Marsh of Sutton bapt. 15th Feb.

William son of George and Elizabeth Hewit of Sutton bapt. 23rd Feb.

William son of William Unwin and his wife bapt. 28th Feb.

Hellen dau. of John and Ann Frith of Duckmanton bapt. 4th April.

Mary dau. of Thomas and Elizabeth Clarke of Duckmanton bapt. 18th April.

Hannah dau. of James and Hannah Swallow of Duckmanton bapt. 9th May.

William son of John and Mary Lowe bapt. 11th July.

Ann dau. of John and Elizabeth Renshaw of Sutton bapt. 18th July.

Sarah dau. of James and Sarah Newton bapt. 1st Aug.

Peter son of Joseph Ashbury deceased and Ann his wife of Duckmanton bapt.
    8th Aug.

Francis Septimus son of John and Ann Wood bapt. 5th Sept.

Leonard son of Edward and Susanna Woodhead bapt. 12th Oct.

Elizabeth dau. of John and Ann Pogmore bapt. 18th Oct.

Rebecca dau. of William and Dorothy Watkinson of Sutton bapt. 7th Nov.

Mary dau. of Edmund and Mary Reddish of Sutton bapt. 28th Nov.

1763

Esau and Jacob sons of Thomas and Hannah Butcher bapt. 9th Jan.

Sarah dau. of William and Catharine Parkins bapt. 30th Jan.

George son of William and Ann Shaw bapt. 6th Feb.

Elizabeth dau. of Thomas and Ann Bennett bapt. 13th Feb.

Francis son of Richard and Ann Rogers bapt. 6th April.

Alice dau. of George and Elizabeth Brett bapt. 24th April.

Francis son of Francis and Sarah Nelson bapt. 8th May.

Benedicta dau. of Thomas and Mary White bapt. 26th June.

John son of Edward and Ann Hodgkinson bapt. 27th June.

Ann dau. of John and Mary Bennett bapt. 27th June.

Ann dau. of George and Elizabeth Thornely bapt. 27th June.

Mary dau. of Samuel and Mary Johnson bapt. 21st Aug.

Susy dau. of John and Mary Law bapt. 4th Sept.

Benjamin son of Thomas and Elizabeth Renshaw bapt. 13th Nov.

1764

Margaret dau. of Joseph and Elizabeth Bennett bapt. 5th Jan.
Thomas son of Joseph and Elizabeth Mellars bapt. 3rd Feb.
Hannah dau. of Godfrey Lindley and his wife bapt. 20th April.
Thomas son of Thomas and Elizabeth Clarke bapt. 24th April.
Elizabeth dau. of George and Elizabeth Hewit bapt. 14th June.
Joseph son of Richard and Mary Marsh bapt. 2nd July.
Hannah dau. of Hannah Froggatt spinster bapt. 12th Aug.
Ann dau. of William and Elizabeth Woodhead bapt. 20th Aug.
John son of John and Mary Revill bapt. 2nd Sept.
James son of William and Dorothy Watkinson bapt. 2nd Dec.

1765

Joseph son of James and Sarah Newton bapt. 6th Jan.
Moses son of George and Elizabeth Brett bapt. 17th Feb.
Hellen dau. of Edward and Ann Hodgkinson bapt. 7th April.
Mary dau. of Thomas and Ann Bennett bapt. 7th April.
Elizabeth dau. of Robert and Ann Hewitt bapt. 8th April.
Joseph son of William and Ann Booker bapt. 27th May.
Joseph son of Richard and Ann Rogers bapt. 30th July.
John son of John and Ann Pogmore bapt. 18th Aug.
Sarah dau. of Thomas and Mary White bapt. 25th Aug.
Hellen dau. of John and Sarah Glossop bapt. 29th Sept.
Ann dau. of Samuel and Mary Johnson bapt. 29th Sept.
Mary dau. of John and Dorothy Lievesly bapt. 12th Nov.
George son of John and Ann Frith bapt. 24th Nov.
Samuel son of William Unwin and his wife bapt. 25th Dec.

1766

James son of William and Ann Shaw bapt. 1st Jan.
Ann dau. of Thomas and Elizabeth Clarke bapt. 9th Feb.
William son of Thomas and Hannah Butcher bapt. 9th Feb.
Moses son of Thomas and Elizabeth Renshaw bapt. 3rd March.
Samuel son of Edmund and Mary Reddish bapt. 23rd March.
Ann dau. of Robert and Ann Hewitt bapt. 30th March.
Sarah dau. of Francis and Sarah Nelson bapt. 29th June.
Anne dau. of Joseph and Martha Mellars bapt. 3rd Aug.

Thomas son of Thomas and Ann Law bapt. 17th Aug.
Mary dau. of Edward and Susanna Woodhead bapt. 28th Oct.
William son of Henry and Elizabeth Cantrel bapt. 2nd Nov.
Anne dau. of George and Elizabeth Hewit bapt. 20th Nov.

1767

Robert son of John and Mary Revel bapt. 4th Jan.
Ann dau. of John and Ann Pogmore bapt. 8th Feb.
Sarah dau. of Thomas and Ann Bennett bapt. 5th March.
Joseph son of Edward and Ann Hodgkinson bapt. 29th March.
Ann dau. of William and Ann Booker bapt. 20th April.
Lydy dau. of William and Dolly Watkinson bapt. 23rd May.
Sarah dau. of John and Betty Lowe bapt. 14th June.
Richard son of Samuel and Mary Johnson bapt. 28th June.
Elizabeth dau. of Thomas and Mary White bapt. 29th June.
John son of Richard and Isabel Sharman bapt. 20th Sept.
Mary dau. of John and Mary Parkin bapt. 20th Dec.

1768

Aaron son of George and Elizabeth Brett bapt. 1st Jan.
[Blank] of William Unwin [Blank].
Hannah dau. of John Renshaw and his wife bapt. 6th March.
Sarah dau. of Thomas and Elizabeth Clarke bapt. 1st April.
Millicent dau. of [Blank] bapt. 17th April.
Samuel son of Godfrey and Sarah Lindley bapt. 24th April.
Robert son of John and Ann Frith bapt. 8th May.
John son of John and Mary Cox bapt. 29th May.
Robert son of James and Sarah Newton bapt. 12th June.
Sarah dau. of Henry and Elizabeth Cantril bapt. 12th June.
Anne dau. of Thomas and Mary Lievesley bapt. 7th Sept.
Richard son of Richard and Anne Rogers bapt. 2nd Oct.
Sarah dau. of Joseph and Susanna Smith bapt. 27th Nov.
[Blank] Raddish [Blank] bapt. 27th Nov.
Stephen son of Christopher and Martha Wilson bapt. 26th Dec.
John son of Joseph and Benedicta Parker bapt. 27th Dec.
Hannah dau. of William and Ann Shaw bapt. 27th Dec.

1769

Francis son of John and Mary Revel bapt. 5th Feb.
Hannah dau. of Thomas and Hannah Butcher bapt. 19th Feb.
Anne dau. of Thomas and Mary White bapt. 12th March.
Joseph son of Thomas and Ann Bennit bapt. 19th March.
Robert son of Robert and Anne Hewit bapt. 27th March.
Anne dau. of Joseph and Martha Mellars bapt. 2nd April.
Mary dau. of Edward and Anne Hodgkinson bapt. 18th April.
Samuel son of Thomas and Mary Elizabeth Renshaw bapt. 23rd July.
Peter son of James and Mary Fidler bapt. 17th Sept.
William son of William and Dolly Watkinson bapt. 19th Nov.
Elizabeth dau. of Obadiah and Anne Bunting bapt. 19th Nov.
Samuel son of Samuel and Mary Johnson bapt. 24th Nov.

1770

Mary dau. of William and Hannah Bennit bapt. 2nd Feb.
Lydia dau. of John and Ann Pogmore bapt. 4th March.
Anne dau. of Richard and Isabel Sharman bapt. 11th March.
Stephen son of John and Sarah Glossop bapt. 8th April.
William son of John and Mary Parkins bapt. 29th April.
Ellen dau. of John and Mary Revel bapt. 6th May.
Sarah dau. of Thomas and Mary Lievesley bapt. 6th May.
Elizabeth dau. of John and Hannah Bennet bapt. 2nd July.
Betty dau. of William and Ann Booker bapt. 3rd July.
Thomas son of Samuel and Mary Unwin bapt. 26th Aug.
Joseph son of John and Dolly Lievesley bapt. 2nd Sept.
Elizabeth dau. of Thomas and Elizabeth Clarke bapt. 16th Sept.
James son of Robert and Anne Hewit bapt. 21st Oct.
Ann dau. of James and Ellen Plant bapt. 24th Oct.
William son of Richard and Anne Rodgers bapt. 5th Nov.
Anne dau. of Edmund Reddish and his wife bapt. 18th Nov.
Mary dau. of Peter and Hannah Broadhead bapt. 5th Dec.
John son of Thomas and Anne Bennit bapt. 26th Dec.
Joseph son of Joseph and Benedicta Parker bapt. 26th Dec.
John son of Godfrey and Sarah Lindley bapt. 27th Dec.

1771

Ann dau. of David and Ann Handley bapt. 3rd March.
Mary dau. of Luke and Ellen Frith bapt. 10th March.
William son of William and Elizabeth Milward of Sutton bapt. 23rd May.
John son of Elizabeth Lowe bapt. 23rd June.
Aaron son of George and Elizabeth Brett bapt. 30th June.
Sarah dau. of Thomas and Elizabeth Green bapt. 30th June.
Susanna dau. of Joseph and Susanna Smith bapt. 15th July.
Richard son of Richard and Isabel Sharman bapt. 28th July.
Mathew and Elizabeth twins of Hannah Fox widow bapt. 11th Aug.
Elizabeth dau. of William and Hannah Bennet bapt. 18th Aug.
Sophia dau. of Henry and Elizabeth Cantrel bapt. 15th Sept.
Jane dau. of John and Mary Wood bapt. 6th Oct.
Jane dau. of Robert and Ann Hewit bapt. 27th Oct.
John son of Francis and Elizabeth Hudson bapt. 2nd Dec.
Thomas son of Thomas and Mary White bapt. 26th Dec.

1772

Anne dau. of John and Hannah Bennet bapt. 1st Jan.
Richard son of William and Ann Shaw bapt. 5th Jan.
Mary dau. of John and Sarah Glossop bapt. 2nd Feb.
Martha dau. of John and Ann Frith bapt. 8th March.
Joseph son of John and Ann Pogmore bapt. 8th March.
John son of Obadiah and Ann Bunting bapt. 19th April.
Daniel son of William and Dorothy Watkinson bapt. 26th April.
James son of James and Hellen Plant bapt. 12th July.
Sarah dau. of James and Mary Fidler bapt. 2nd Aug.
Elizabeth dau. of William and Elizabeth Milward bapt. 18th Aug.
Elizabeth dau. of James and Elizabeth Swallow bapt. 18th Oct.
John son of Thomas and Mary Bennet bapt. 22nd Nov.
Anthony son of Thomas and Elizabeth Radish bapt. 20th Dec.
Francis son of John and Mary Revel bapt. 28th Dec.

1773

Deborah dau. of John and Mary Revel bapt. 1st Jan.
Richard son of Samuel and Mary Johnson bapt. 24th Jan.
James son of Hannah Taylor of Calow bapt. 7th Feb.

Paul son of Samuel and Mary Unwin bapt. 14th Feb.

Anne dau. of Benjamin Lawrence lately deceased and Mary his wife bapt. 21st March.

Betty dau. of Thomas and Mary Lievesley bapt. 4th April.

William son of Joseph and Benedicta Parker bapt. 12th April.

William son of William and Anne Booker bapt. 12th April.

John son of John and Mary Parkin bapt. 18th April.

Joseph son of Edward and Ann Woodhead bapt. 2nd May.

Ellen dau. of William and Hannah Bennet bapt. 30th May.

Paul son of Paul and Mary Unwin bapt. 6th June.

Mary dau. of Richard and Isabel Sharman bapt. 6th June.

John son of David and Ann Handley bapt. 8th Aug.

John son of John and Mary Johnson bapt. 29th Aug.

Edward son of Edward and Ann Hodgkinson bapt. 5th Sept.

Patty dau. of Charles and Hannah Hudson bapt. 17th Oct.

1774

Hannah dau. of John and Hannah Bennit bapt. 1st Jan.

Thomas son of Thomas and Ann Allein bapt. 1st Jan.

Joseph son of Francis and Sarah Lowe bapt. 4th April.

Elizabeth dau. of Joseph and Frances Giles bapt. 4th April.

James son of James and Mary Fidler bapt. 11th April.

Abraham son of Robert and Elizabeth Renshaw bapt. 24th April.

Hannah dau. of Thomas and Ann Bennit bapt. 1st May.

Sarah dau. of John and Sarah Glosop bapt. 25th May.

Francis son of Obadiah and Ann Bunting bapt. 12th June.

Mary dau. of Joseph and Susanna Smith bapt. 12th June.

Richard son of Thomas and Mary White bapt. 26th June.

Hellen dau. of James and Hellen Plant bapt. 26th June.

Nanny dau. of John and Mary Revil bapt. 26th June.

Ann dau. of William and Elizabeth Milward bapt. 12th Aug.

Hellen dau. of Richard and Mary Raddish bapt. 9th Oct.

Solomon son of Solomon and Ephsheba Wood bapt. 16th Oct.

Molly dau. of William and Elizabeth Peace bapt. 5th Nov.

Susannah dau. of Francis and Elizabeth Hudson bapt. 26th Dec.

Thomas son of John and Mary Wood bapt. 26th Dec.

John son of William and Hannah Bennit bapt. 27th Dec.

1775

Mary dau. of Godfrey and Mary Lindley bapt. 1st Jan.
William son of George and Dolly Clarkson bapt. 2nd Feb.
Richard son of Samuel and Margaret Lievesley bapt. 24th Feb.
Mathew spurious son of Sarah Brett bapt. 14th April.
Elizabeth dau. of Joseph and Benedicta Parker bapt. 17th April.
Dorothy dau. of Henry and Elizabeth Cantrel bapt. 26th June.
James son of Robert and Ann Hewit bapt. 16th July.
Betty dau. of Samuel and Mary Johnson bapt. 27th Aug.
Hannah dau. of Paul and Mary Unwin bapt. 15th Oct.
Elizabeth Nancy dau. of James and Ann Tallents bapt. 14th Nov.
George son of John and Ann Pogmore bapt. 26th Dec.

1776

Gilbert son of Thomas and Mary White bapt. 30th June.
Charles son of Charles and Hannah Hudson bapt. 30th June.
John son of James and Elizabeth Swallow bapt. 30th June.
Nevil son of Thomas and Elizabeth Reddish bapt. 23rd July.
Samuel son of Thomas and Ann Bennit bapt. 1st Sept.
William son of Jarvis and Elizabeth Johnson bapt. 1st Nov.
Hannah dau. of William and Elizabeth Milward bapt. 18th Nov.
Samuel son of Richard and Mary Reddish bapt. 18th Nov.
Peter son of Joseph and Susannah Smith bapt. 1st Dec.
William son of James and Ellen Plant bapt. 19th Dec.

1777

Alice dau. of William and Hannah Bennet bapt. 18th Jan.
Sarah dau. of Robert and Ann Hewitt bapt. 19th Jan.
William son of William and Elizabeth Peace bapt. 19th Jan.
Robert son of Thomas and Mary Lievesley bapt. 2nd Feb.
John son of William and Anne Booker bapt. 27th April.
William son of John and Mary Revill bapt. 30th May.
Alice dau. of John and Mary Wood bapt. 26th June.
Charles son of Thomas and Mary Pogmore bapt. 26th June.
Elizabeth dau. of Richard and Isabella Sharman bapt. 1st July.
Sarah dau. of John and Anne Pogmore bapt. 7th Sept.
Mary dau. of Benjamin and Mary Rodgers bapt. 14th Sept.

Elizabeth dau. of Edward and Ann Woodhead bapt. 21st Sept.
Elizabeth dau. of Samuel and Mary Unwin bapt. 12th Oct.
Elizabeth dau. of George and Dolly Clarkson bapt. 19th Oct.
Anne dau. of Joseph and Benedicta Parker bapt. 30th Oct.

1778

Thomas son of Joseph and Elizabeth Cantrel bapt. 18th Jan.
Thomas son of Jos. and Hannah Cantrel bapt. 18th Jan. [*Not clear if this entry
is for 1778 or 1779; possibly duplicates preceding.*]
Anne dau. of Solomon and Ephsheba Wood bapt. 15th Feb.
Hannah dau. of Thomas and Sarah Sales bapt. 18th March.
Mary dau. of James and Ellen Plant bapt. 8th April.
James son of William and Elizabeth Peace privately bapt. 27th April.
James son of James and Elizabeth Swallow bapt. 29th June.
Ann dau. of John and Elizabeth Renshaw bapt. 29th June.
Ellen dau. of Thomas and Ann Bennet bapt. 30th Aug.
William son of John and Hannah and Reddish bapt. 20th Sept.
John son of Paul and Mary Unwin bapt. 18th Oct.
Thomas son of John and Elizabeth Hopkinson bapt. 28th Dec.

1779

Mary dau. of Thomas and Mary White bapt. 11th Feb.
John son of Robert and Ann Hewitt bapt. 7th March.
Francis son of Jarvis and Elizabeth Johnson bapt. 5th April.
Thomas son of John and Ann Pogmore bapt. 27th June.
Hannah and Anne twin daus. of Richard and Mary Reddish bapt. 27th June.
Martha dau. of George and Dorothy Clarkson bapt. 27th June.
John son of William and Elizabeth Peace bapt. 30th June.
Benjamin son of Benjamin and Mary Rogers bapt. privately 9th July.
James illegitimate son of Mary Davenport privately bapt. 1st Oct.
Joseph son of Samuel and Margaret Lievesley bapt. 17th Oct.
James Tomlinson son of Sarah Elliott bapt. 10th Nov.

1780

Sarah dau. of Hugh and Hannah Heath bapt. 5th Jan.
Richard son of Joseph and Benedicta Parker bapt. 21st Jan.

Thomas son of Thomas and Ann Bennett bapt. 8th Feb.
Sarah dau. of Thomas and Ellen Reddish bapt. 19th March.
Ann dau. of James and Elizabeth Swallow bapt. 26th March.
John son of John and Elizabeth Renshaw bapt. 26th March.
Margaret dau. of Joseph and Elizabeth Woodhead bapt. 2nd May.
William son of Benjamin and Mary Rodgers privately bapt. 14th May.
William son of Robert and Ann Hewitt bapt. 16th May.
Joseph son of Joseph and Sarah Higginbotham bapt. 20th June.
William son of Thomas and Sarah Sales bapt. 26th June.
Susanna dau. of James and Ellen Plant bapt. 13th Aug.
Sarah illegitimate dau. of Janet Marrit bapt. 20th Aug.
Hannah spurious dau. of Elizabeth Lowe bapt. 1st Oct.
Joseph Ashbury son of Joseph and Susannah Smith bapt. 24th Oct.

1781

Eph[sheba] dau. of Solomon and Ephsheba Wood bapt. 1st Jan.
Ann dau. of Jarvis and Elizabeth Johnson bapt. 27th Feb.
Sarah dau. of Edward and Ann Woodhead bapt. 18th March.
Mary dau. of Joseph and Benedicta Parker bapt. 25th March.
Francis son of James and Ann Wingfield bapt. 15th April.
Thomas son of John and Mary Sculthorpe bapt. 16th April.
Ann dau. of William and Elizabeth Peace bapt. 6th May.
James son of William and Ann Booker bapt. 29th May.
Elizabeth dau. of Paul and Mary Unwin bapt. 3rd June.
Barbara dau. of John and Mary Revell bapt. 11th June.
James son of John and Ann Pogmore bapt. 1st July.
Ann dau. of Benjamin and Mary Rodgers bapt. 1st July.
Ann dau. of Thomas and Sarah Sales bapt. 2nd July.
Elizabeth dau. of John and Jane Marsh bapt. 8th July.
Richard son of Charles and Hannah Hudson bapt. 9th Sept.
William son of Thomas and Ann Bennett bapt. 18th Sept.
Thomas son of Thomas and Mary Bennett bapt. 4th Nov.
Lydia dau. of Henry and Elizabeth Hodgkinson bapt. 27th Dec.
Mary dau. of Samuel and Peggy Lievesley bapt. 30th Dec.

1782

John son of Joseph and Hannah Bennett bapt. 1st Jan.
William son of John and Elizabeth Renshaw bapt. 1st Jan.

Mary dau. of Joseph and Hannah Cantrel bapt. 1st Jan.
George spurious son of Hannah Middleton bapt. 27th Jan.
Sarah dau. of James and Ellen Plant bapt. 12th Feb.
George son of George and Dolly Clarkson bapt. 15th Feb.
Joseph son of Hugh and Hannah Heath bapt. 1st April.
Richard son of William and Martha Barlow bapt. 7th April.
John son of William and Lydia Renshaw bapt. 20th April.
Joseph son of Robert and Ann Hewitt bapt. 30th June.
Thomas son of Richard and Mary Reddish bapt. 30th June.
Mary dau. of William and Sarah Sales bapt. 30th June.
Elizabeth dau. of Joseph and Elizabeth Woodhead bapt. 1st July.
Richard son of John and Jane Marsh bapt. 18th Aug.
Thomas son of Joseph and Benedicta Parker bapt. 20th Oct.
Mary illegitimate dau. of Jane Marril bapt. 15th Dec.
Thomas son of George and Mary Dicken bapt. 22nd Dec.
Thomas son of James and Elizabeth Swallow bapt. 25th Dec.
Mary dau. of John and Mary Wood bapt. 25th Dec.

1783

Elizabeth dau. of Joseph and Susanna Smith bapt. 1st Jan.
William son of James and Ann Hardwick bapt. 16th Feb.
Mary dau. of Charles and Hannah Hudson bapt. 11th May.
Joseph son of Thomas and Sarah Sales bapt. 1st June.
John son of Henry and Elizabeth Hodgkinson bapt. 15th June.
Mary Ann dau. of John and Mary Sculthorpe bapt. 24th Aug.
Paul son of Paul and Mary Unwin bapt. 14th Sept.

Act for every christening and burial 3d.

Elizabeth dau. of Jervase and Elizabeth Johnson bapt. 26th Oct.
John son of John and Elizabeth Hopkinson bapt. 2nd Nov.
William son of Thomas and Mary Bennet bapt. 25th Dec.

1784

William son of John and Ann Pogmore bapt. 5th Jan.
Lydia dau. of William and Ann Booker bapt. 28th March.
John son of James and Ann Wingfield bapt. 11th April.
Thomas son of John and Elizabeth Renshaw bapt. 11th April.

38

Jane dau. of Robert and Ann Hewitt bapt. 18th April.
Hannah dau. of Samuel and Margaret Lievesley bapt. 2nd May.
George son of George and Mary Dicken bapt. 2nd May.
John son of Richard and Hannah Marsh bapt. 9th May.
Elizabeth dau. of William and Lydia Renshaw bapt. 30th May.
Ann dau. of William and Martha Barlow bapt. 27th June.
Mary dau. of Joseph and Hannah Bennet bapt. 27th June.
William son of Joseph and Hannah Cantril bapt. 27th June.
John son of Humphrey and Mary Belfit bapt. 27th June.
Hannah dau. of James and Ellen Plant bapt. 28th June.
Mary dau. of William and Ann Rodgers bapt. 28th June.
Ann dau. of Joseph and Elizabeth Woodhead bapt. 5th Nov.

1785

Richard son of Joseph and Benedicta Parker bapt. 1st Jan.

Inspected 8th Jan. 1785 for the year ending 1st Oct. 1784, christenings 18, duty 4s. 6d. By J. Bower, Collector of Duties, Chesterfield.

Susy dau. of Benjamin and Mary Rodgers bapt. 30th Jan.
John son of Charles and Hannah Hudson bapt. 12th June.
Sarah dau. of Richard Reddish, pauper and Mary his wife bapt. 26th June.
John son of John and Ann Bennett bapt. 26th June.
Thomas son of Thomas and Sarah Sales bapt. 27th June.
George son of Henry and Elizabeth Hodgkinson bapt. 10th July.
Eleanor dau. of John and Jane Marsh bapt. 28th Aug.
William son of William and Martha Barlow bapt. 9th Oct.
Keturah dau. of William and Elizabeth Peace bapt. 27th Dec.

1786

George son of John and Mary Sculthorpe bapt. 5th Jan.

Paid the above to 13th Feb. 1786.

Robert son of George and Mary Dicken bapt. 26th March.
Mary dau. of David and Mary Britt bapt. 16th April.
Sampson son of Jervase and Elizabeth Johnson bapt. 30th April.

Thomas and Samuel twin sons of Thomas and Mary Lievesley bapt. 29th April and christened 25th June.

William son of Robert and Sarah Dicken bapt. 6th Aug.

Sarah dau. of Abraham and Sarah Frost bapt. 6th Aug.

Hugh son of Hugh and Hannah Heath bapt. 10th Sept.

John son of Joseph and Susannah Smith bapt. 19th Nov.

1787

George illegitmate son of Elizabeth Law bapt. 1st Jan.

Thomas son of William and Ann Booker bapt. 2nd Jan.

Anna Maria dau. of Henry and Elizabeth Hodgkinson bapt. 4th Jan.

George son of John and Ann Bennett bapt. 11th Jan.

Ellen dau. of Robert and Ann Hewitt bapt. 18th Feb.

William son of Samuel and Peggy Lievesley bapt. 4th March.

William son of William and Elizabeth Renshaw bapt. 11th March.

Joseph son of Joseph and Benedicta Parker bapt. 6th April.

Mary dau. of John and Ann Hodgkinson bapt. 8th April.

Joseph son of James and Ellen Plant bapt. 9th April.

Martha dau. of William and Martha Barlow bapt. 15th April.

Joseph son of Joseph and Elizabeth Woodhead bapt. 16th April.

Elizabeth dau. of Charles and Hannah Hudson bapt. 28th May.

George son of Richard Reddish pauper and Mary his wife bapt. 1st July.

Mary dau. of Richard and Judith Marsh bapt. 1st July.

Joseph son of Joseph and Hannah Bennett bapt. 1st July.

Elizabeth dau. of David and Mary Britt bapt. 26th Aug.

John son of John and Jane Marsh bapt. 2nd Sept.

James son of William and Elizabeth Peace bapt. 14th Oct.

The above paid to Mr Bower.

1788

Mary Ann dau. of Robert and Sarah Dicken bapt. 1st Jan.

Benjamin son of John and Elizabeth Renshaw bapt. 1st Jan.

Godfrey son of John and Hannah Pogmore bapt. 15th Jan.

John illegitimate son of Mary Turton Wakefield bapt. 24th Feb.

William son of John and Mary Sculthorpe bapt. 24th March.

Ellen dau. of Joseph and Elizabeth Nelson bapt. 29th June.

Elizabeth dau. of Benjamin and Ann Goodwin bapt. 29th June.

Mary dau. of James and Mary Cree bapt. 29th June.
Abraham son of Abraham and Sarah Frost bapt. 29th June.
John son of Joseph and Ann Rodgers bapt. 29th June.
Mary dau. of William Barlow and his wife bapt. 6th July.
Stephen son of Jervase Johnson and his wife bapt. 6th July.
Sarah dau. of Richard and Hannah Marsh bapt. 3rd Aug.
William son of Hugh and Hannah Heath bapt. 17th Aug.
Mary dau. of John and Ann Pogmore bapt. 21st Sept.

1789

The above settled with Mr Bower Jan. 17th 1789.

Robert son of John and Mary Pineder bapt. 1st Feb.
Sarah dau. of John and Ann Bennett bapt. 15th Feb.
Joseph son of John and Ann Hodgkinson bapt. 1st March.
Betty dau. of Joseph and Hannah Cantril bapt. 22nd March.
Benedicta dau. of Joseph and Benedicta Parker bapt. 14th June.
Thomas son of William and Elizabeth Cooper bapt. 28th June.
Thomas son of Thomas and Elizabeth Ragg bapt. 28th June.
Samuel son of Samuel and Peggy Lievesley bapt. 28th June.
Henry son of Joseph Deakin and his wife bapt. 12th July.
Betty dau. of William and Hannah Meakin bapt. 23rd Aug.
Elizabeth dau. of Robert and Sarah Dicken bapt. 23rd Aug.
Samuel son of John and Hannah Pogmore bapt. 23rd Aug.
David Caleb son of David Brett and his wife bapt. 30th Aug.
James son of John Revill and his wife bapt. 11th Oct.
Richard and George twin sons of Richard Marsh and his wife bapt. 18th Oct.
John son of Richard Marshall and his wife bapt. 22nd Oct.

1790

The above paid to Mr Bower 2nd Jan.

Benjamin son of James and Ellen Plant bapt. 1st Jan.
John son of John and Ann Pogmore bapt. 3rd Jan.
Anna Maria Katharine dau. of Job Hart Price Clarke Esq. and Sarah his wife
    bapt. 5th Feb 1790 and christened 10th Oct. 1791.
Nancy dau. of Thomas and Elizabeth Ragg bapt. 18th May.
Ann dau. of Thomas and Elizabeth Steemson bapt. 7th June.

Edward son of Jervase and Elizabeth Johnson bapt. 27th June.
Thomas son of William Barlow and his wife bapt. 27th June.
William son of Joseph Bennett and his wife bapt. 27th June.
Esther dau. of John Sculthorpe and his wife bapt. 12th Sept.

14th Oct. paid the above to Mr Bower.

1791

Mary dau. of William and Hannah Makin bapt. 2nd Feb.
Robert son of Samuel and Margaret Lievesley bapt. 6th Feb.
Thomas son of John and Ann Bennett bapt. 20th Feb.
George son of Moses and Hannah Britt bapt. 27th Feb.
Richard illegitimate son of Ann Wright bapt. 6th March.
Samuel son of John and Ann Pogmore bapt. 26th June.
John son of John and Ann Hodgkinson bapt. 26th June.

A copy of this register delivered at the Visitation at Chesterfield 5th July 1791.

Hannah dau. of John Pogmore junior of Sutton and Hannah his wife bapt. 24th
    July.
Henry son of John and Jane Marsh born 7th Feb. bapt. 24th July.
Elizabeth dau. of Thomas and Elizabeth Stevenson bapt. 18th Sept.
Margaret dau. of Robert and Sarah Dicken bapt. 18th Sept.
Helen dau. of Joseph and Susannah Smith bapt. 25th Sept.
Joseph son of Joseph and Margaret Dakin bapt. 25th Sept.

Paid Mr Bower duty on christenings for year ending Oct. 1st 1791.

Thomas son of John Lowe junior and Sarah his wife bapt. 20th Nov.
Robert son of James and Mary Cree bapt. 25th Dec.

1792

Thomas son of Charles and Hannah Hudson bapt. 11th March.
Edward son of William and Ann Cutt of Duckmanton bapt. 8th April.
Francis Rogers posthumous son of the late Joseph Parker by Benedicta his wife
    bapt. 13th May.
Alice dau. of Gervase and Elizabeth Johnson bapt. 1st July.
Joseph son of Richard and Judith Marshall born 17th Nov. 1791 bapt. 1st July.

James son of Joseph Nixon *alias* Shendall by Mary his wife bapt. 2nd July.
James son of William and Hannah Dixon bapt. 2nd July.

Paid Mr Bower duty up to 1st Oct. 1792.

George son of Thomas and Elizabeth Stevenson bapt. 21st Oct.
William son of Richard Reddage pauper and Mary his wife bapt. 30th Dec.

1793

Joseph son of Joseph and Elizabeth Nelson bapt. 3rd Feb.
Ann and Sarah twin daus. of Samuel and Margaret Lievesley of Duckmanton
    bapt. 12th Feb.
Samuel son of William and Martha Barlow of Middle Duckmanton bapt. 7th
    April.
John son of John Pogmore junior and Hannah his wife of Sutton bapt. 20th May.
Matthew son of Moses and Hannah Britt of Duckmanton bapt. 30th June.
Edward son of John and Ann Hodgkinson of Duckmanton bapt. 30th June.
Martha dau. of Joseph and Hannah Bennett of Duckmanton bapt. 30th June.
Sarah dau. of William and Hannah Meakin of Duckmanton bapt. 30th June.
Vernon illegitimate son of Martha Fisher spinster bapt. 30th June.
Helen dau. of Joseph and Elizabeth Woodhead of Duckmanton bapt. 1st July.
Hannah dau. of Robert and Sarah Dicken bapt. 14th July.
Ann dau. of John and Mary Sculthorpe now of Duckmanton bapt. 14th July.
Thomas son of William and Ann Dalton of Totley bapt. 21st July.
William son of Richard and Hannah Marsh of Sutton bapt. 29th Dec.

1794

John son of John Lowe junior and Sarah his wife of Duckmanton bapt. 1st Jan.
John son of William and Ann Cutt of Duckmanton bapt. 12th Jan.
Ann dau. of John and Ann Pogmore of Middle Duckmanton bapt. 16th March.
Henry illegitimate son of Ann Revill spinster bapt. 23rd March.
Anne dau. of Joseph and Margaret Dakin of Sutton bapt. 23rd March.
George illegitimate son of Alice White spinster by George Richardson bapt. 13th
    April.
James son of Richard and Judith Marshall of Duckmanton bapt. 29th June.
John son of Gervase and Elizabeth Johnson bapt. 30th June.
George son of George and Elizabeth Beresford of Duckmanton bapt. 3rd Aug.

Paid Mr Bower the duty up to 1st Oct. 1794. Duty ceased.

Mary dau. of James and Frances Watkinson bapt. 28th Dec.

1795

Elizabeth dau. of William and Martha Barlow of Duckmanton bapt. 1st Jan.
John son of Joseph and Mary Nixon of Duckmanton bapt. 25th Jan.
Hannah dau. of Moses and Hannah Britt of Duckmanton bapt. 8th Feb.
Martha dau. of Robert and Sarah Frith of Duckmanton bapt. 22nd March.
Esther dau. of David and Ellen Gladwin bapt. 24th May.
George son of John Pogmore junior and Hannah his wife bapt. 24th May.
Joseph son of James and Mary Cree of Duckmanton bapt. 28th June.
Thomas son of Joseph and Elizabeth Richardson of Clown bapt. 28th June.

A copy of this register was delivered at the Visitation up to 1st July.

Elizabeth dau. of John and Mary Sharman born 9th April and bapt. 5th July.
Jane dau. of Thomas and Elizabeth Stevenson now of Long Course bapt. 1st
    Nov.
Francis son of Richard and Mary Reddage of Duckmanton bapt. 8th Nov.
Elizabeth dau. of Joseph and Hannah Bennett of Duckmanton bapt. 27th Dec.
Lydia dau. of Joseph and Elizabeth Nelson of Duckmanton bapt. 27th Dec.
Susannah dau. of Joseph and Elizabeth Woodhead of Duckmanton bapt. 30th
    Dec.

1796

Sarah dau. of John Lowe junior of Duckmanton and Sarah his wife bapt. 24th
    Jan.
Thomas son of George and Elizabeth Beresford of Duckmanton bapt. 15th May.
William son of Thomas and Mary Wingfield bapt. 26th June.
John son of William and Hannah Meakin bapt. 26th June.
Anne dau. of John and Anne Bennett of Duckmanton bapt. 26th June.
Thomas son of Samuel and Margaret Lievesley bapt. 26th June.
Thomas son of David Hopkinson of Calow and Elizabeth his wife, late Elizabeth
    Renshaw, bapt. 9th Aug.
Mary dau. of John and Mary Sharman of Sutton bapt. 16th Oct.
Thomas son of Joseph and Margaret Dakin of Sutton bapt. 6th Nov.
James son of James Hardwick of Sutton bapt. 25th Dec.

1797

Joseph son of John Pogmore junior of Sutton and Hannah his wife bapt. 12th Feb.

William son of James and Frances Watkinson of Sutton bapt. 12th Feb.

Richard son of Richard and Hannah Marsh of Sutton bapt. 2nd April.

Nanny dau. of Thomas and Elizabeth Stevenson of Long Course bapt. 24th April.

John son of David and Helen Gladwin of Sutton bapt. 5th June.

Elizabeth dau. of Moses and Hannah Britt of Duckmanton bapt. 25th June.

Samuel son of Gervase and Elizabeth Johnson of Duckmanton bapt. 26th June.

William son of John and Ann Hodgkinson of Duckmanton bapt. 16th July.

Richard son of Richard and Judith Marshall of Duckmanton bapt. 13th Aug.

Elizabeth dau. of George and Elizabeth Beresford bapt. 13th Aug.

William son of Joseph and Mary Nixon of Duckmanton bapt. 15th Oct.

William son of John and Ann Pogmore of Middle Duckmanton bapt. 24th Dec.

Mary dau. of John and Sarah Lowe bapt. 26th Dec.

1798

Mary illegitimate dau. of Mary White spinster of Sutton, born 31st Dec. 1797 and privately bapt. 10th Jan. 1798.

Sarah dau. of William and Martha Barlow of Duckmanton bapt. 21st Jan.

Thomas Farnsworth Fern son of Elizabeth Fern spinster bapt. 27th May.

George son of Thomas and Elizabeth Wragg of Duckmanton born 11th April, privately bapt. 14th and publicly bapt. 27th May.

Ann dau. of John Pogmore junior late of Sutton but now of Brampton, and Hannah his wife bapt. 28th May.

Ann dau. of William and Ann Cutt of Duckmanton bapt. 1st July.

John son of Richard Lievesley of Bolsover, tailor, and Hannah his wife bapt. 1st July.

Rebecca dau. of Thomas and Elizabeth Stevenson of Long Course bapt. 2nd July.

Robert and John twin sons of Robert and Sarah Frith of Duckmanton bapt. 2nd July.

Richard illegitimate son of Ann Johnson spinster of Duckmanton bapt. 2nd July.

Isabella dau. of John Sharman of Sutton and Mary his wife born 7th Oct., privately bapt. 8th Oct. and publicly bapt. 27th Feb. 1799.

Elizabeth dau. of Thomas and Mary Wingfield of Duckmanton bapt. 4th Nov.

Rebecca dau. of James and Frances Watkinson of Sutton bapt. 6th Jan.

Elizabeth dau. of Daniel and Thamar Watkinson of Sutton bapt. 6th Jan.

Robert son of John Spence (gardener to J.H. Price Clark Esqr.) and his wife Sarah bapt. 16th Jan.

Elizabeth dau. of William and Mary Pearce of Duckmanton bapt. 24th Feb.

Matthew son of Joseph and Hannah Bennett of Far Duckmanton bapt. 31st March.

Sarah dau. of James and Sarah Hardwick of Sutton bapt. 12th May.

William son of David and Helen Gladwin of Sutton privately bapt. by the Rev. Sherard Becher 23rd June, and publicly bapt. 8th Sept.

Joseph son of William and Martha Barlow of Duckmanton bapt. 30th June.

George son of Robert and Sarah Frith of Duckmanton bapt. 30th June.

Mary dau. of George and Elizabeth Beresford of Duckmanton bapt. 30th June.

William son of William and Hannah Meakin of Duckmanton bapt. 30th June.

Richard son of Richard and Ann Chapman of Duckmanton bapt. 11th Aug.

Abraham son of Moses and Hannah Britt of Duckmanton privately bapt. 14th Sept.

William son of Samuel and Mary Chattaway, late of Cubbington, Warwickshire, but now of Sutton bapt. 29th Sept.

Elizabeth dau. of Samuel and Margaret Lievesley of Duckmanton bapt. 24th Nov.

1800

Thomas son of William and Margaret Turner of Sutton bapt. 1st Jan.

George son of John and Ann Hodgkinson of Duckmanton bapt. 12th Jan.

Dorothy dau. of Thomas and Elizabeth Wragg of Duckmanton bapt. 19th Jan.

Mary dau. of Joseph and Mary Nixon of Duckmanton bapt. 16th Feb.

Humphry son of Humphry and Mary Belfield of Sutton bapt. 23rd Feb.

Richard son of Samuel Johnson junior and Mary his wife of Duckmanton Moor Top bapt. 13th April.

Joseph son of William and Ann Cutt of Duckmanton privately bapt. 27th April.

Betty dau. of Thomas and Hannah Cantrell now of Calow bapt. 29th June.

Elizabeth dau. of John Lowe junior and Sarah his wife of Duckmanton bapt. 29th June.

A copy delivered at the Visitation up to 20th Aug. 1800.

Helen dau. of Robert and Sarah Frith of Duckmanton bapt. 19th Oct.

Mary dau. of Ann Cantrell spinster of Duckmanton Moor Top bapt. 26th Oct.

John son of John and Mary Sharman of Sutton born 3rd Aug., privately bapt. 19th Aug. and publicly bapt. 28th Dec.

1801

Elizabeth dau. of John and Mary Sculthorpe formerly of Sutton but now of Chesterfield born 12th April 1796 and publicly bapt. at Sutton 1st Jan. 1801.

Mary dau. of John and Mary Sculthorpe born 24th Feb. 1800 and publicly bapt. at Sutton 1st Jan. 1801.

Mary dau. of William and Mary Pearce of Duckmanton bapt. 1st Jan.

John son of John Spence (gardener to J.H. Price Clarke Esqr.) and his wife Sarah born 2nd and privately bapt. 3rd Dec. 1800; publicly bapt. 16th Jan. 1801.

Mary dau. of William Fern of Duckmanton by Ann his wife (late Ann Goodwin) privately bapt. 16th Jan. and publicly bapt. 22nd Feb.

John son of Thomas and Elizabeth Stevenson of Long Course bapt. 6th Feb.

William son of William and Mary Revill of Duckmanton bapt. 1st March.

James son of James and Elizabeth Cowley of Duckmanton bapt. 1st March.

Harriet Wright Lloyd dau. of William and Sarah Lloyd of Duckmanton and late of Nottingham bapt. 8th March.

Anne dau. of George and Mary Shaw of Duckmanton Moor Top born 15th Sept. 1798 and publicly bapt. 22nd March 1801.

Elizabeth dau. of the above George and Mary Shaw publicly bapt. 22nd March.

Anne dau. of William and Hannah Watkinson of Duckmanton born 2nd May and publicly bapt. 28th June.

Frances dau. of William and Martha Barlow of Duckmanton bapt. 29th June.

Hannah dau. of Frances Johnson spinster of Duckmanton bapt. 29th June.

John son of Richard and Ann Chapman of Duckmanton publicly bapt. 2nd Aug.

Thomas son of Samuel and Catherine Renshaw of Moor Top publicly bapt. 20th Sept.

Hannah dau. of David and Helen Gladwin of Sutton privately bapt. 11th Oct.

John son of James and Sarah Hardwick of Sutton bapt. 1st Nov.

William son of William and Margaret Turner of Hagg publicly bapt. 22nd Nov.

John son of Humphrey and Mary Belfield of Sutton publicly bapt. 27th Dec.

1802

John son of Thomas and Elizabeth Barber of Duckmanton bapt. 1st Jan.

James son of James and Jane Hewitt of Duckmanton bapt. 17th Jan.

Abraham son of Moses and Hannah Britt of Duckmanton bapt. 21st Feb.

Sarah dau. of George and Elizabeth Beresford of Duckmanton bapt. 9th May.

John son of Samuel and Mary Johnson of Moor Top bapt. 27th June.

Elizabeth dau. of Joseph and Mary Nixon of Duckmanton bapt. 27th June.

Nanny dau. of Robert and Sarah Frith of Duckmanton bapt. 27th June.

Ann dau. of William Booker junior late of Duckmanton but now of Stone Gravels and Elizabeth his wife bapt. 27th June.

Anne dau. of William and Mary Parker of Moor Top born 27th and bapt. 30th June.

Henry son of Ruth Baguley spinster bapt. 11th July.

Hannah dau. of John and Sarah Spence privately bapt. 26th Sept. Born same morning.

Jane dau. of Thomas and Hannah Cantrell born 18th Sept. and publicly bapt. 10th Oct.

Sarah dau. of John and Mary Sharman of Sutton born 29th Oct. last and bapt. 7th Nov.

Elizabeth dau. of Joseph and Elizabeth Nelson of Duckmanton bapt. 28th Nov.

Elizabeth dau. of David and Eleanor Gladwin of Sutton born 28th Nov., privately bapt. 30th Nov. and publicly bapt. 10th Jan. 1803.

Thomas son of James and Elizabeth Cowley of Duckmanton bapt. 26th Dec.

1803

Thomas Christopher son of Daniel and Thamar Watkinson of Sutton born and bapt. 26th Dec. 1802, publicly bapt. 13th Feb. 1803.

George son of William and Mary Revill of Duckmanton publicly bapt. 3rd April.

Alsopp son of Peter and Mary Smith born 28th Jan. and publicly bapt. 31st May.

William son of Samuel and Catharine Renshaw of Moor Top publicly bapt. 26th June.

Mary dau. of Thomas and Elizabeth Stevenson late of Long Course publicly bapt. 27th June.

William son of George and Mary Shaw of Duckmanton Moor Top publicly bapt. 4th Sept.

Martha dau. of Thomas and Ann Shaw of Duckmanton Moor Top publicly bapt. 25th Sept.

Samuel son of Humphrey and Mary Belfield publicly bapt. 23rd Oct.

Joseph son of Richard and Ann Chapman of Duckmanton publicly bapt. 13th Nov.

John son of Richard and Elizabeth Barlow of Duckmanton privately bapt. 19th Nov.

Joseph son of Joshua and Hannah Davidson bapt. 27th Nov.

Thomas son of Thomas and Elizabeth Barber of Duckmanton bapt. 27th Nov.

James son of James and Frances Watkinson of Sutton publicly bapt. 25th Dec.

1804

Joseph son of Thomas and Mary Mason of Duckmanton publicly bapt. 8th Jan.

Ann dau. of George and Elizabeth Beresford of Duckmanton publicly bapt. 19th Feb.

Ralph son of Robert and Helen Lievesley of Duckmanton publicly bapt. 29th April.

Mary dau. of James and Sarah Hardwick of Sutton publicly bapt. 20th May.

Joseph son of Joseph and Ann Horton of Duckmanton born 13th Jan. publicly bapt. 1st July.

Joseph son of William and Margaret Pearce of Duckmanton publicly bapt. 1st July.

Thomas son of William and Hannah Meakin of Duckmanton publicly bapt. 1st July.

William son of William and Sarah Miles Lloyd of Duckmanton publicly bapt. 30th Sept.

Mary dau. of Robert Frith of Duckmanton by Sarah his wife publicly bapt. 4th Nov.

Jane dau. of Francis Johnson spinster of Duckmanton publicly bapt. 4th Nov.

William son of Daniel and Martha Bacon of Duckmanton New Colliery, publicly bapt. 25th Nov.

John son of James and Jane Hewitt of Duckmanton publicly bapt. 25th Nov.

Mary dau. of Moses and Hannah Britt now of Temple Normanton publicly bapt. 25th Dec.

1805

Herrod son of William Parker of Duckmanton Moor Top by Mary his wife, late Mary Herrod, publicly bapt. 1st Jan.

William son of Thomas and Hannah Cantrell of Duckmanton Moor Top publicly bapt. 10th Feb.

Samuel son of Joseph and Mary Nixon of Duckmanton publicly bapt. 3rd March.

Francis son of James and Elizabeth Cowley of Duckmanton born 7th March and privately bapt. 11th March.

John son of George and Elizabeth Beresford of Duckmanton publicly bapt. 31st March.

George son of Robert and Susannah Woodruff of Duckmanton New Colliery publicly bapt. 14th April.

James son of Humphrey and Mary Belfield of Sutton publicly bapt. 21st April.

Sampson son of William and Mary Revill of Duckmanton publicly bapt. 21st April.

Hannah dau. of Robert and Helen Lievesley of Duckmanton publicly bapt. 21st April.

Sarah dau. of Peter and Mary Smith of Sutton born 11th March, publicly bapt. 18th June.

John son of Samuel and Catharine Renshaw of Moor Top Duckmanton publicly bapt. 30th June.

Sampson son of Samuel Clay of Duckmanton, plasterer, and Elizabeth his wife publicly bapt. 28th July.

George son of William and Sarah Turner of Duckmanton New Colliery publicly bapt. 4th Aug.

A copy of this Register down to 20th Aug. was delivered at Chesterfield 4th Sept.

Hannah dau. of John and Mary Sharman of Sutton born 1st Feb. 1804, publicly bapt. 8th Sept. 1805.

William son of John and Mary Sharman of Sutton born 23rd June 1805, publicly bapt. 8th Sept 1805.

Sarah dau. of Joseph and Amey Sales of Duckmanton publicly bapt. 22nd Sept.

James son of John and Grace Wingfield of Duckmanton publicly bapt. 6th Oct.

1806

Lydia dau. of David and Thamar Watkinson of Sutton publicly bapt. 19th Jan.

David son of David Gladwin of Sutton publicly bapt. 26th Jan.

Anne dau. of John and Clara Hewitt of Duckmanton publicly bapt. 2nd Feb.

Andrew son of William Gray (gardener to Clement Kynnersley Esqr.) by Esther his wife publicly bapt. 2nd March. It appeared from a memorandum on a blank leaf of a small bible belonging to the said William Gray, that the said Andrew was born July 2nd 1801.

James son of the above named William and Esther Gray was also publicly bapt. March 2nd 1806, and it appeared from a memorandum similar to the above that he was born July 26th 1805.

Sarah dau. of the above named William and Esther Gray was also publicly bapt. March 2nd 1806 and it appeared from a similar memorandum that she was born July 26th 1805.

Anne dau. of Robert Gee of Duckmanton and his wife Lydia, late Lydia Booker, publicly bapt. 20th April.

Anne dau. of William and Margaret Turner of Sutton publicly bapt. 25th May.

Sarah dau. of Joseph and Hannah Wragg late of Baslow but now of Sutton publicly bapt. 25th May.

Daniel son of James and Frances Watkinson publicly bapt. 25th May.

Sophia dau. of William and Sarah Lloyd of Duckmanton publicly bapt. 29th June.

Anne dau. of Robert and Helen Lievesley of Duckmanton publicly bapt. 29th June.

John son of William and Margaret Pearce of Duckmanton publicly bapt. 29th June.

Anne dau. of Thomas and Elizabeth Barber of Duckmanton publicly bapt. 29th June.

Anne dau. of William and Sarah Turner of Duckmanton New Colliery publicly bapt. 14th Sept.

Anne dau. of John and Sarah Lowe of Duckmanton publicly bapt. 28th Sept.

Mary dau. of William and Mary Parker of Duckmanton Moor Top privately bapt. 1st Dec. 1806 and received publicly into the congregation 15th April 1808.

Sarah dau. of James and Jane Hewitt of Duckmanton publicly bapt. 25th Dec.

1807

Samuel son of Daniel and Martha Bacon of Duckmanton Moor Top privately bapt. 1st Jan. 1807 and publicly received into the congregation 8th March 1807.

William son of Thomas and Elizabeth Jarvis of Duckmanton publicly bapt. 18th Jan.

Mary dau. of Peter and Mary Smith of Sutton privately bapt. 19th Jan. and publicly received into the congregation 21st June.

John son of Robert and Susannah Woodruff of Duckmanton New Colliery publicly bapt. 25th Jan.

William son of William Robinson of Duckmanton but late of Nottingham, a moulder at the Iron Furnace, by Jane his wife born 25th Jan. and privately bapt. 26th Jan. 1807 and publicly received into the congregation 9th July 1809.

Jane dau. of George and Elizabeth Beresford of Duckmanton publicly bapt. 8th Feb.

Thomas son of Joseph and Amy Sales of Duckmanton bapt. 15th March.

William son of William Baker, corporal in 2nd Battalion of 59th Regt, by Mary his wife dau. of John Hodgkinson of Duckmanton, publicly bapt. 25th April.

John son of Robert and Helen Lievesley of Duckmanton publicly bapt. 16th May.

Sarah dau. of John and Sarah Spence formerly of Sutton but now of Attercliffe publicly bapt. 17th May.

George son of Richard and Anne Chapman of Duckmanton privately bapt. 8th June and publicly bapt. and received into the congregation 28th June.

Anne dau. of Charles and Martha Watts of Duckmanton publicly bapt. 28th June.

Hannah dau. of Samuel and Catharine Renshaw of Moor Top privately bapt. 3rd June and publicly received into the congregation 28th June.

David Caleb son of Moses Britt of Normanton Lodge by Hannah his wife born 9th Jan. and publicly received into the congregation 19th July.

Anne dau. of John and Mary Hardy of Sutton born 18th July and privately bapt. 19th July.

Thomas son of Robert and Sarah Frith publicly bapt. 2nd Aug.

Richard son of Mr Richard Birkett of Long Course and Jane his wife, born 24th Aug. privately bapt. 27th Aug. 1807 and publicly received into the congregation 20th May 1811.

Ann dau. of John and Mary Cupit privately bapt. 15th Oct. 1807 and publicly received into the congregation 1st Jan. 1808.

Mary Anne dau. of John and Grace Wingfield privately bapt. 15th Oct. and publicly received into the congregation 28th Feb. 1808.

Hannah dau. of Daniel and Tamar Watkinson of Sutton publicly bapt. 8th Nov.

Thomas son of William and Mary Revill of Duckmanton publicly bapt. 15th Nov.

William son of Humphry and Elizabeth Brookes of Sutton privately bapt. 24th Nov. 1807 and publicly received into the congregation 5th June 1808.

William son of Samuel and Elizabeth Bacon of Duckmanton Moor Top privately bapt. 15th Oct. and publicly received into the congregation at Chesterfield 25th Dec. 1807.

1808

Thomas son of William Miles Lloyd and Sarah his wife of Duckmanton born 24th Dec. 1807. publicly bapt. 24th Jan. 1808.

Richard son of Richard and Mary Johnson of Duckmanton born 13th and publicly bapt. 24th Jan.

Henry son of Thomas and Hannah Cantrill of Duckmanton Moor Top publicly bapt. 31st Jan.

Ann dau. of Joseph and Mary Nixon of Duckmanton privately bapt. 16th Feb. and publicly received into the congregation 20th March.

John son of Robert and Lydia Gee of Duckmanton privately bapt. 16th Feb. and publicly received into the congregation 17th April.

George son of John Roberts of Duckmanton and his wife Sarah, late Sarah Reddish, privately bapt. 16th Feb. and publicly received into the congregation 25th Sept.

Joseph son of James and Jane Hewitt of Duckmanton publicly bapt. 10th April.

Joseph son of James Plant junior of Duckmanton and Mary his wife privately bapt. 12th April and publicly received into the congregation 29th June.

William son of William and Margaret Pearce of Duckmanton privately bapt. 12th April and publicly received into the congregation 15th May.

George son of George and Mary Shaw of Duckmanton Moor Top publicly bapt. 17th April.

William son of William and Sarah Turner of the New Colliery, Duckmanton, publicly bapt. 1st May.

Isaac son of Thomas and Elizabeth Barber of Duckmanton publicly bapt. 8th May.

Jane dau. of Thomas and Lydia Parker of Duckmanton publicly bapt. 22nd May.

Charles son of James and Jane Eastwood of Duckmanton publicly bapt. 22nd May.

Elizabeth dau. of William and Margaret Turner of Sutton publicly bapt. 5th June.

Amy dau. of John and Mary Sharman of Sutton privately bapt. 13th Dec. 1807 and publicly received into the congregation 5th June 1808.

Mary dau. of David and Helen Gladwin of Sutton publicly bapt. 19th June.

Thomas son of William and Ann Charlesworth of Duckmanton born 11th June and publicly bapt. 6th July.

Anne dau. of James and Elizabeth Cowley of Duckmanton publicly bapt. 18th Sept.

Elizabeth dau. of Robert and Helen Lievesley of Duckmanton publicly bapt. 25th Sept.

Anne dau. of Samuel and Elizabeth Bacon of Moor Top privately bapt. 6th Oct.

Martha dau. of Humphrey Belfield of Sutton and Mary his wife publicly bapt. 21st Dec.

1809

John son of Paul Unwin junior and Anne his wife of Duckmanton publicly bapt. 29th Jan.

Hannah dau. of William and Hannah Meakin publicly bapt. 26th Feb.

Hannah dau. of James and Frances Watkinson of Sutton publicly bapt. 19th March.

Thomas son of Ann Reddish spinster publicly bapt. 9th April.

Samuel son of John and Mary Sharman of Sutton born 27th April and publicly bapt. 21st May.

William son of John Spence formerly of Sutton now of Attercliffe publicly bapt. 4th June.

Peter son of William and Elizabeth Pogmore of Sutton born 18th May, privately bapt. 20th May and publicly received into the congregation [Blank] 1809.

George son of Joseph and Hannah Wragg of Sutton born June [Blank] and publicly bapt. 11th June.

Joseph son of Peter and Mary Smith of Sutton publicly bapt. 18th June.

Thomas son of Joseph and Elizabeth Heath of Sutton Hagg privately bapt. 18th June and publicly received into the congregation 16th July.

Rhoda dau. of Samuel and Mary Johnson of Moor Top privately bapt. 19th June and publicly received into the congregaton 8th Oct.

Ann dau. of Joseph and Amy Sales of Duckmanton publicly bapt. 25th June.

John son of George and Jane Holmes of Duckmanton publicly bapt. 25th June.

Richard son of Mary Barlow spinster of Duckmanton publicly bapt. 9th July.

Esther dau. of William Robinson, late of Nottingham but now a moulder at the New Furnace, by Jane his wife born 9th Aug. 1804 and publicly bapt. 9th July 1809.

John son of the above named William and Jane Robinson born 21st June 1809 and publicly bapt. 9th July 1809.

George son of Stephen and Sarah Thompson of Moor Top born 9th June and publicly bapt. 16th July.

William son of John and Mary Jepson of Sutton privately bapt. 13th Aug. and publicly received into the congregation 24th Dec.

Abigail dau. of Charles and Martha Watts of Duckmanton publicly bapt. 17th Sept.

Elizabeth dau. of Samuel and Catharine Renshaw privately bapt. 6th Oct. and publicly received into the congregation 12th Nov.

Joseph son of William and Mary Parker of Duckmanton Moor Top born 30th Sept., privately bapt. 15th Oct. 1809 and publicly received into the congregation 1st Jan. 1810.

Mary dau. of William and Mary Revill of Duckmanton publicly bapt. 19th Nov.

William son of George and Elizabeth Beresford of Duckmanton publicly bapt. 10th Dec.

1810

Joseph son of Humphrey and Elizabeth Brookes of Sutton privately bapt. 30th Jan.

John son of John and Grace Wingfield of Duckmanton publicly bapt. 25th March.

Susannah dau. of Richard and Mary Johnson of Duckmanton born 28th Feb. and publicly bapt. 1st April.

Helen dau. of William and Margaret Pearce of Duckmanton publicly bapt. 15th April.

Thomas son of Robert and Helen Lievesley of Duckmanton publicly bapt. 22nd April.

John son of Thomas and Mary Mason publicly bapt. 6th May.

Phillis dau. of William and Sarah Miles Lloyd of Duckmanton publicly bapt. 3rd June.

George son of Daniel and Thamar Watkinson of Sutton born 11th March and publicly bapt. 10th June.

James son of James and Hannah Fidler of Sutton Mill publicly bapt. 1st July.

Joseph son of Thomas and Hannah Cantrell of Moor Top publicly bapt. 5th Aug.

Henry son of Robert and Sarah Frith of Duckmanton publicly bapt. 19th Aug.

A copy of this Register from Lady Day 1805 to Lady Day 1810 was delivered at Chesterfield 20th Sept. 1810.

Joseph son of William and Sarah Turner of the New Colliery, Duckmanton, publicly bapt. 23rd Sept.

Mary dau. of Samuel and Mary Unwin of Duckmanton publicly bapt. 30th Sept.

Helen dau. of James Plant junior and Mary his wife of Duckmanton publicly bapt. 30th Sept.

James son of George and Mary Shaw of Duckmanton Moor Top privately bapt. 7th Oct.

Thomas son of Robert and Lydia Gee of Duckmanton publicly bapt. 25th Nov.

Mary dau. of John and Mary Cupit of Duckmanton publicly bapt. 30th Dec.

William son of Humphrey and Elizabeth Brookes of Sutton Lane End privately bapt. 30th Dec. 1810, publicly received into the congregation 30th June 1811.

1811

Elizabeth dau. of Thomas and Elizabeth Barber of Calow publicly bapt. 20th Jan.

William son of Paul Unwin junior and Anne his wife of Duckmanton publicly bapt. 3rd Feb.

Hannah dau. of Robert and Elizabeth Brown of New Colliery publicly bapt. 14th April.

Eliza dau. of Peter and Mary Smith of Sutton publicly bapt. 5th May.

William son of Mr Richard Birkett of Long Course and Jane his wife publicly bapt. 20th May.

Jane dau. of Mr Richard Birkett of Long Course and Jane his wife publicly bapt. 20th May.

David son of George and Elizabeth Beresford of Duckmanton publicly bapt. 30th June.

John son of Mr Richard Birkett of Long Course and Jane his wife publicly bapt. 21st July.

Mary dau. of James and Elizabeth Cowley of Duckmanton publicly bapt. 28th July.

Elizabeth dau. of James and Jane Hewitt of Duckmanton publicly bapt. 4th Aug.

Daniel son of David and Helen Gladwin of Sutton born 30th Aug. and publicly bapt. 29th Sept.

Julia Fidler dau. of Sarah Bennett spinster of Duckmanton publicly bapt. 13th Oct.

Dorothy dau. of William and Mary Revill of Duckmanton publicly bapt. 1st Dec.

Joseph son of Joseph and Amy Sales of Duckmanton born 22nd Nov. and publicly bapt. 22nd Dec.

Elizabeth dau. of John and Mary Jepson of Sutton publicly bapt. 25th Dec.

1812

Elizabeth dau. of William and Helen Ward of Duckmanton publicly bapt. 1st Jan.

John son of William and Margaret Turner of Sutton publicly bapt. 1st Jan.

Joseph son of John and Mary Sharman of Sutton publicly bapt. 1st Jan.

Joseph son of Joseph and Elizabeth Heath of Sutton Hagg publicly bapt. 12th Jan.

Sarah dau. of George and Jane Holmes of Duckmanton publicly bapt. 26th Jan.

Joseph son of William and Amy Hewitt of Sutton publicly bapt. 2nd Feb.

Charlotte dau. of James and Frances Watkinson of Sutton publicly bapt. 9th Feb.

Ann dau. of William and Margaret Pearce of Duckmanton bapt. 26th Feb.

Francis son of John and Mary Cooper or Cowper of Duckmanton bapt. 10th May.

Anne dau. of William and Sarah Miles Lloyd of Duckmanton publicly bapt. 24th May.

Millicent dau. of Samuel and Elizabeth Bacon of Duckmanton Moor Top bapt. 31st May.

Maria dau. of Daniel and Tamar Watkinson of Sutton publicly bapt. 14th June.

William son of William and Mary Parker of Duckmanton Moor Top publicly bapt. 28th June.

Julia dau. of Richard and Mary Johnson of Duckmanton privately bapt. 30th
Aug.

George son of James and Hannah Fidler of Sutton Mill privately bapt. 6th Sept.
1812 and publicly received into the congregation 25th Dec. 1814.

Paul son of Paul Unwin junior and Ann his wife of Duckmanton bapt. 12th Nov.

Sarah dau. of Richard and Ann Chapman of Duckmanton bapt. 12th Nov.

Joseph son of George and Sarah Wass of Duckmanton bapt. 23rd Nov.

Sarah dau. of William and Hannah Heath of Sutton bapt. 31st Dec.

N.B. For baptisms subsequent hereto, vide *New Register pursuant to Act of 52
Geo. III.*

BURIALS

1662

Thomas Willson died 29th and bur. 30th Aug.
Nicholas Allatson died 7th and bur. 9th Oct.
Marie dau. of Robert Lorons bur. 19th Nov.
John Gosling died 21st and bur. 22nd Dec.

1663

Joane wife of George Woker died 22nd and bur. 23rd Feb.
Elinn Outrim died 7th and bur. 8th March.
John Glossop died 6th and bur. 7th Nov.

1664

Raph Morly died 21st and bur. 22nd April.
George Leake son of Nicholas, Earl of Scarsdale, died 28th and bur. 29th April.
Edward son of Edward and Elizabeth Arddin died 29th April and bur. 1st May.
Richard son of Nicholas and Mary Redfern died 11th and bur. 12th Oct.

1665

Ralph Richardson senior bur. 1st Jan.
George son of Jeroam Shaw bapt. 30th July and bur. 4th Aug. following.

1667

Dorothie Roberts bur. 17th April.
Robert Batman bur. 22nd April.
Thomas Crosland bur. 5th Aug.
Olive Butcher bur. 5th Aug.
Grace Masey bur. 6th Aug.

John Carr bur. 24th Aug.
George Walker bur. 27th Aug.
John son of John and Mary Bland bapt. 25th and bur. 28th Aug.
Elizabeth Bagshaw bur. 23rd Sept.
Ann dau. of Edward and Elizabeth Arden bur. 26th Oct.

1668

George Douman died 14th and bur. 15th Feb.
Thomas Chantry died 22nd and bur. 23rd April.
Christopher Upton died 5th and bur. 6th Oct.
Mary dau. of Nicholas and Mary Redfern bur. 5th Nov.

1669

Elizabeth Glossop died 25th and bur. 26th Jan.
Mr Oliver Pukerin died 1st and bur. 3rd Feb.
John Hardy bur. 22nd May.
Rodger Noble bur. 25th May.
Betriz Rodgers bur. 17th Oct.
Robert Rodger bur. 19th Oct.
Edward Wilson bur. 12th Nov.

1670

Francis son of William and Mary Scales bur. 6th Jan.
Samuel son of Richard and Mary Whit bur. 25th Jan.
Mr Robert Beveridge bur. 28th Jan.
Grace Gosling bur. 5th May.
John Chapman bur. 20th Aug.
William Watkinson bur. 21st Aug.
Humphrey Hardy bur. 28th Aug.
William Moare bur. 30th Aug.
Mary wife of William Thornally bur. 11th Sept.
Mihel Brett bur. 14th Sept.

1671

Ann wife of Robert Allwood died 27th Jan.

John son of Robert and Elen Hardy born, bapt. and died 28th Jan.

[*No further entries for 1671: page missing.*]

1672

Thomas son of Thomas and Sara Allwood bur. 5th April.
John son of John and Catherin Brett bur. 17th April.
Richard son of Richard and Ann Turner bur. 22nd April.

1673

Nickolas Redfern bur. 9th Feb.
Henry Chantry bur. 30th March.
Mrs Elizabeth Winall wife of Mr Hugh Winall bur. 5th April.
Francis Billbe bur. 18th June.

1675

Richard Shaw bur. 11th March.
William Melor bur. 18th June.
Francis Butcher died 22nd and bur. 23rd Sept.
Joseph Rodgers died 4th and bur. 5th Nov.
Thomas Fretwell died 27th and bur. 29th Dec.

1676

Marie Richardson bur. 19th March.
Robert Bateman bur. 19th Aug.
William Taborner bur. 27th Aug.
Isobel Alken bur. 3rd Oct.
The Lady Mary, dau. to the right hon. Nicholas Leak, Earl of Scarsdale, and the
    Lady Frances his wife, bur. 5th Oct.
Godfrey Sims bur. 17th Dec.

1677

Artor Moare bur. 27th Aug.
Mr Hugh Winall bur. 14th Oct.
John Bamfort bur. 23rd Dec.

1678

Hanna wife of Richard Hawley bur. 19th Jan.
Alse wife of Thomas Marsh bur. 6th April.
Sara dau. of John and Rebeka Allwood bur. 9th May.
Elen wife of John Richardson bur. 2nd July.
Ann Allrin bur. 19th Oct. according to a late Act of Parliament entitled An Act
    for burying in woollen; affidavit under the hand of Thomas Gladwin J.P.
    received 24th Oct. J. Curray, rector.
Elizabeth wife of Henry Carter of the parish of Scarcliffe, bur. at Sutton 1st Dec.
    in woollen; certificate received under the hand of Mr Gladwin J.P. J. Curray,
    rector.

1679

[Blank] Wilson bur. at Sutton 4th Jan. in woollen; certificate received under the
    hand of Mr Gladwin J.P. on Saturday 11th Jan. J. Curray, rector.
Ann Smedley bur. at Sutton 16th Jan. in woollen; certificate received under the
    hand of Mr Gladwin J.P. on Thursday 23rd Jan. J. Curray, rector.
John Bennet bur. 28th Feb. in woollen; certificate received under the hand of Mr
    Gladwin J.P. 6th March. J. Curray, rector.
Joane Laurimer bur. at Sutton 20th June in woollen; certificate received under
    the hand of Mr Burton J.P. 21st June. J. Curray, rector.
William Pratt bur. at Sutton 8th July in woollen; certificate received under the
    hand of Mr Gladwin J.P. dated 12th July. J. Curray, rector.
Hicrome Shaw bur. 31st Oct. in woollen; certificate received under the hand of
    Mr Galdwin J.P. dated 4th Nov. J. Curray, rector.
Ellen Hewis bur. 20th Nov. in woollen; certificate received dated 25th Nov. J.
    Curray, rector.
Samuel son of Henry and Barbara Unwin bur. 17th Dec. according to the
    aforesaid Act; certificate received dated 20th Dec. J. Curray, rector.
Alice Sims bur. 18th Dec. according to the aforesaid Act; certificate received
    under the hand of Mr Gladwin J.P. dated 26th Dec. J. Curray, rector.

Ann Richardson bur. 11th Jan. in woollen; certificate of affidavit received made to Mr Burton 16th Jan. J. Curray, rector.

Sarah Roberts bur. 12th Feb. in woollen; certificate of affidavit received under the hand of Mr Gladwin J.P. 16th Feb. J. Curray, rector.

Ann Hardy widow, of Duckmanton bur. 17th Feb. according to the aforesaid Act; certificate of affidavit received made to Mr Gladwin J.P. dated 23rd Feb. J. Curray, rector.

Ann Seeds a vagrant who died at Duckmanton bur. 1st March according to the aforesaid Act; certificate received 6th March. J. Curray, rector.

Jone Watkinson widow bur. 7th March according to the aforesaid Act; certificate of affidavit received made the day after. J. Curray, rector.

Samuel son of William Woorall of Chesterfield, bur. at Sutton 15th April in woollen; certificate of affidavit received made to Mr Eyre 21st April. J. Curray, rector.

Mary Chapman bur. 8th May in woollen; certificate of affidavit received made 11th May. J. Curray, rector.

Ann Baumforth bur. 4th July according to the aforesaid Act; certificate of affidavit received made 9th July. J. Curray, rector.

Richard Mimmet a traveller who died at Duckmanton bur. 30th July according to the aforesaid Act; certificate of affidavit received made 2nd Aug. J. Curray, rector.

Thomas Allwood of Sutton died 16th and bur. 18th Sept. according to the aforesaid Act; certificate of affidavit received dated 20th Sept. J. Curray, rector.

Jane Fretwell bur. 10th Oct. according to the aforesaid Act; certificate of affidavit dated 22nd Oct. J. Curray, rector.

Henry Carter bur. 18th Oct. in woollen; certificate of affidavit made 25th Oct. J. Curray, rector.

Francis Puckerings bur. at Sutton 25th Oct. according to the aforesaid Act; certificate of affidavit dated 29th Oct. J. Curray, rector.

1681

Isabel Roberts bur. 17th Jan. according to the aforesaid Act; certificate of affidavit made to Mr Gladwyn 21st Jan. J. Curray, rector.

Thomas Hill bur. 17th Jan. according to the aforesaid Act; affidavit dated 24th Jan. J. Curray, rector.

Alice Nelle widow bur. 8th Feb. according to the aforesaid Act; certificate of affidavit received made 13th Feb. J. Curray, rector.

John Haslam son of Edward Haslam bur. at Sutton 1st March according to the aforesaid Act; certificate received from Mr Chadwicke dated 5th March. J. Curray, rector.

Bridget Butcher widow bur. 23rd March according to the aforesaid Act; [certificate received from] Mr Chadwick. J. Curray, rector.

Martha dau. of Edward Haslam bur. 26th March at Sutton according to the aforesaid Act; certificate of affidavit received from Mr Chadwick dated 29th March. J. Curray, rector.

Mary wife of Robert Milner died 28th and bur. 29th March according to the aforesaid Act as appears by certificate from Mr Rishton dated 1st April. J. Curray, rector.

Sarah wife of John Ashbury bur. 30th April according to the aforesaid Act as appears by certificate dated 4th May. J. Curray, rector.

Ann dau. of John and Ann Hallam bur. 28th May according to the aforesaid Act as appears by certificate dated 3rd June. J. Curray, rector.

Elizabeth dau. of James and Elizabeth Taylor bur. 8th Sept. according to the aforesaid Act as appears from a certificate dated 9th Sept. J. Curray, rector.

Thomas Marsh bur. 18th Sept. according to the aforesaid Act as appears by a certificate dated 24th Sept. J. Curray, rector.

Henry Carter senior bur. 28th Sept. according to the aforesaid Act as appears by affidavit made by his son John Carter dated 3rd Oct. J. Curray, rector.

Mary More widow bur. 22nd Dec. according to the aforesaid act.

1682

Thomas Chapman bur. 26th March in woollen.

Robert Fox bur. at Sutton 12th April in woollen.

Francis Hardie child of Robert Hardie bur. 30th Oct. according to the aforesaid Act.

William Outram bur. 24th Nov. in woollen.

Henry Unwin son of Henry and Barbara Unwin bur. 24th Nov. according to the aforesaid Act.

Francis Lech of Bolsover Woodhouse bur. 2nd Dec. at Sutton in wollen.

1683

William Thornally bur. 3rd June according to the aforesaid Act.

Anne dau. of Thomas Chapman bur. 8th June according to the aforesaid Act.

William Sylvester of Duckmanton bur. 27th Oct. in woollen.

Ralph Pickering bur. 30th Nov. in woollen.

Elizabeth dau. of Henry and Barbara Unwin bur. 1st Dec. according to the aforesaid Act.

1684

Benjamin Johnson bur. at Sutton 10th Jan. according to the aforesaid Act.
Elizabeth Chantry widow bur. 26th Feb. according to the aforesaid Act.
Robert son of Robert Allwood bur. 15th April according to the aforesaid Act.
John Finny bur. 26th May according to the aforesaid Act.
Joseph Naylor bur. 23rd June according to the aforesaid Act.
Thomas Butcher bur. 24th June according to the aforesaid Act.
Thomas Freeman gent. bur. 5th Oct. in woollen.
Barbara wife of John Sales of Duckmanton bur. 30th Oct. according to the aforesaid Act.
Sarah Allots bur. 22nd Nov. according to the aforesaid Act.
John son of William and Elizabeth Marsh bur. 27th Nov. in woollen.
John Rogers bur. 23rd Dec. according to the aforesaid Act.

1685

John son of James and Alice Taylor bapt. 27th Feb. and bur. 1st March according to the aforesaid Act.
Bridget wife of John Heath bur. 13th March according to the aforesaid Act.
Elizabeth dau. of Robert Stanley junior and Anne his wife bur. 7th April.
Nickolas Marsh bur. 9th May in woollen.
Richard Hawley bur. 29th Aug. according to the aforesaid Act.
William son of Thomas and Isabel Chapman bur. 26th Sept. according to the aforesaid Act.
Jane wife of Hugh Spooner and her son Edward both bur. 23rd Oct. in woollen.

1686

Ann wife of William Colgreave bur. 26th March according to the aforesaid Act.
Mrs Fitcherandal of Normanton bur. 2nd Aug. according to the aforesaid Act.
Elizabeth wife of John Rogers bur. 21st Nov. according to the aforesaid Act.
Mary wife of Leonard Woodhead bur. 30th Dec. according to the aforesaid Act.

[*Inserted on page facing burials in 1684–7:*]

The Honourable Rich Leake, second son to the Rt. Honble Nicholas, Earl of Scarsdale, and Mrs Mary Mollineux, second daughter to Sir John Mollineux of Teversal in the county of Nottingham, Baronet, were married upon the 6th day of December in the year of our Lord 1680.

Frances, the daughter of the Honble Rich Leake, was born October the 22nd and baptised November the 15th 1681.

Nicholas, the son of the Honble Rich Leake, was born November the 6th and baptised December the 6th 1682.

Lucy, the daughter of the Honble Rich Leake was born February the 14th and baptised March 2nd 1684.

Robert the son of the Honble Rich Leake, was born December 7th and baptised December the 18th 1686.

Mr Leak dyed the 16th and was buried April the 18th 1687.

Madam Leak died February the 25th and was buried March the first 1691.

1687

Robert son of Thomas and Ann Lorans bur. 31st Jan. according to the aforesaid Act.

Mary Chantrey bur. 5th March according to the aforesaid Act.

Francis Flint bur. 24th March according to the aforesaid Act.

Robert son of Francis and Sara Tallents bur. 25th March according to the aforesaid Act.

Lettice dau. of John and Lettice Heath bur. 5th May according to the aforesaid Act.

Mary dau. of Edward and Jone Haslam bur. 9th May according to the aforesaid Act.

Mary wife of Richard Bennett bur. 9th May according to the aforesaid Act.

Richard Babinton bur. 19th May according to the aforesaid Act.

John son of Thomas and Sara Colgreave bur. 26th Nov.

1688

Isabel dau. of Francis and Sara Tallents bur. 6th Jan. according to the aforesaid Act.

Joseph son of Widow Taylor bur. 9th Feb. according to the aforesaid Act.

Jonathan son of John and Elizabeth Shaw bur. 26th Feb. according to the aforesaid Act.

Ann wife of Robert Fox bur. 11th March according to the aforesaid Act.

Roger Gregory bur. 14th March according to the aforesaid Act.

Richard son of John and Elizabeth Shaw bur. 22nd April according to the aforesaid Act.

Mary Dowman bur. 1st June according to the aforesaid Act.

William son of Godfrey and Mary Tallents bur. 3rd June according to the aforesaid Act. The above said William Tallents son of the said Godfrey and Mary Tallents was aged about 12 years when he died, who had lain about one year and seven months visited by the hand of the Almighty with a very strange and miraculous distemper, which was an astonishment to all that beheld him. He was all the time of his sickness endued with almost an unparalleled patience, therefore let all who have any such like grievous distempers pray God would be pleased to endue them with the like patience.

Elizabeth Gregory bur. 26th Nov. according to the aforesaid Act.

1689

Ann dau. of Edward and Joan Haslam bur. 30th May according to the aforesaid Act.

Widow Tarton bur. 13th July according to the aforesaid Act.

Benedictus wife of Francis Roger bur. 13th July.

Mary wife of Simon Ordidge bur. 26th July.

Barbara dau. of Mary Alatson bur. 2nd Aug.

Sara wife of Richard White bur. 6th Oct.

Ellen wife of Simeon Granger bur. 19th Oct.

Mary wife of Mr Metam bur. 6th Nov.

1690

Ann Roger widow bur. 18th Jan.

William Richardson of Normanton bur. 26th Jan.

Thomas Lorans bur. 31st Jan.

William son of Francis and Sara Tallents bur. 11th Feb.

Ann dau. of Robert Fox bur. 8th March.

Mary wife of William Shaw bur. 16th March.

Lettice wife of John Heath bur. 22nd March.

Ann wife of William Richardson bur. 26th March.

Mr Robert Beveridge bur. 17th April.

Mary wife of Thomas Thornaly bur. 19th April.

Mary Alatson bur. 26th April.

Dorothy wife of Godfrey Flint bur. 27th May.
Mary dau. of Godfrey and Mary Shipston bur. 12th Oct.
Elizabeth wife of William Marsh bur. 30th Nov.

1691

Sara wife of Thomas Colgreave bur. 18th Jan.
Robert Standley bur. 29th Jan.
Jane wife of Robert Standley bur. 28th Feb.
Samuel son of Thomas Colgreave bur. 12th May.

1692

Ralph Richardson bur. 22nd Feb.
John Heath bur. 13th May.
Samuel Milner bur. 19th May.
Mary dau. of Robert and Ann Standley bur. 19th May.
Robert Milner bur. 4th June.
Catherine dau. of Henry and Sarah Carter bur. 3rd July.
Mr Henry Carter bur. 31st Aug.
Isabel Butcher bur. 2nd Dec.

1693

Elizabeth Unwin bur. 8th July.
Mary Thiselton bur. 8th July.
Joseph son of Joseph and Ann Allwood bur. 14th July.
William Walker bur. 21st July.
Isabel Baumfort bur. 13th Aug.
Robert Nailor bur. 3rd Sept.
Marget Roberts bur. 15th Sept.
Thomas son of Samuel and Susanah Steemson bur. 11th Nov.

1694

Widow Fox bur. 7th March.
Francis son of Francis and Ann Richardson [alias] Gregory bur. 11th Sept.
Ann wife of Henry Fern bur. 2nd Dec.

George Ashbury bur. 2nd Dec.

1695

Sara Scales bur. 11th March.
Mary dau. of Thomas and Ann Colier bur. 13th March.
Catherine Finney bur. 30th Sept.
Mr John Currey, rector of this church bur. 13th Nov.

1696

Robert son of Robert Butcher bur. 11th Feb.
Edward Bennett bur. 1st April.
Thomas Fox bur. 4th April.
Mr James Mettam bur. 10th April.
Joan wife of William Baumfort bur. 8th Nov.

1697

Suzanna Vesley bur. 7th Jan.
Sara Turton bur. 2nd Feb.
Mary Shaw bur. 6th Feb.
Peter Vicerstaff bur. 18th Feb.
Alice Thornally bur. 13th March.
Richard White bur. 28th March.
Francis son of Philip and Catherine Tallents bur. 8th May.
Thomas son of John and Elizabeth Shaw bur. 2nd June.
John Allwood bur. 12th June.
Elizabeth wife of Edward Ardin bur. 1st July.
John Milner bur. 6th Aug.
Mary Whiteland bur. 22nd Oct.
Thomas Noble bur. 24th Oct.
Anne wife of Richard Turner bur. 9th Nov.

1698

Sarah Turner bur. 13th Jan.
Thomas Vessey bur. 13th March.

William son of William Dowman bur. 8th May.
Frances dau. of William Colgreave of Bolsover Woodhouse bur. at Sutton 17th
    May.
Henry Unwin senior bur. 28th June.
Margrett wife of Revell Shaw bur. 16th July.
Anne Hill widow bur. 22nd July.
Ann Noble widow bur. 27th Nov.

1699

Francis Rodger bur. 2nd March.
Elizabeth Sampson a stranger bur. 2nd March.
Robert Peace bur. 3rd March.
George Wild bur. 14th March.
Mr Charles Wayne bur. 18th April.
Richard Hallam a stranger bur. 22nd May.
Elizabeth dau. of Ralph Heathcoate bur. 2nd June.
William son of John Barker bur. 24th Aug.
Francis Rodger bur. 21st Sept.

1700

Frances Jones bur. 21st Jan.
John son of James Brailsford bur. 20th Feb.
Christopher Upton bur. 18th March.
Joseph son of Joseph Alwood of Heath bur. 25th May.
Robert Hardy senior bur. 12th June.
Samuel Stevenson bur. 2nd July.
Alice Butcher widow bur. 9th Sept.
Elizabeth dau. of William Wingfield bur. 26th Sept.
Edward Haslam bur. 1st Nov.
Mary dau. of John Wood bur. 10th Nov.
Anne wife of John Lievesley bur. 10th Dec.

1701

Elizabeth dau. of Thomas and Mary Bennett bur. 31st Jan.
Francis Richardson bur. 7th Feb.
Elizabeth wife of John Shaw bur. 20th July.

Francis son of Godfrey Shipston bur. 28th July.

Elizabeth Outram widow bur. 19th Aug.

Francis Turner bur. 16th Sept.

Sarah Alwood widow bur. 20th Sept.

Mary dau. of Robert Stevenson bur. 25th Sept.

A copy of this Register was delivered at the Bishop's Visitation at Chesterfield 4th Oct.

Elizabeth dau. of Ralph Heathcoate, rector of this church, and his wife Elizabeth bur. 11th Oct.

Anne dau. of John Shaw bur. 22nd Oct.

John son of John Onyon bur. 30th Oct.

1702

Richard Turner bur. 28th Jan.

Anne Hornbuckle of Heath widow bur. at Sutton 7th March.

Mary Cousin bur. 16th April.

Abigail dau. of Ralph Heathcoate, rector of this church, and his wife Elizabeth bur. 20th April.

1703

George son of Ralph Heathcoate, rector of this church, and Elizabeth his wife, bur. 4th Jan.

Edward Arderne bur. 26th May.

Mrs Eleanor Horton widow bur. 13th Sept.

1704

Mary wife of John Castle bur. 26th Feb.

John Ashbury bur. 15th March.

Alice dau. of Robert Butcher bur. 15th May.

Francis son of Samuel Tallents bur. 12th June.

Barbara wife of Henry Unwin bur. 13th Aug.

Henry Ferne bur. 14th Nov.

Anthony Upton bur. 19th Nov.

Godfrey Tallents Senior bur. 20th Dec.

Robert Allwood of Heath bur. at Sutton 29th Dec.

1705

Alice Taberner widow bur. 8th Jan.
Mr Charles Freeman bur. 5th April.
William son of Robert Stanley bur. 27th April.

A copy of this Register was delivered at the Bishop's Visitation at Chesterfield 16th May.

Mary dau. of Robert Ferne bur. 6th Aug.

1706

Samuel Unwin bur. 30th Jan.
John son of John Christian bur. 25th Feb.
Mary wife of Godfrey Shipston bur. 15th March.
Frances Tallents bur. 30th April.
Ruth wife of Matthew Wostendale of Ryely in the parish of Scartcliffe bur. 12th May.
Mary Marsh widow bur. 20th May.
Samuel son of Henry Unwin bur. 24th May.
Thomas son of John Stevenson bur. 14th June.
John Lievesley bur. 25th June.
Elizabeth dau. of John Christian bur. 28th Sept.
Sarah dau. of Thomas Lawrence bur. 5th Dec.
Elizabeth dau. of Thomas Hardy bur. 15th Dec.

1707

Mary wife of George Widdowson bur. 6th March.
Thomas Chapman bur. 9th May.
Jacob son of Michael Brett bur. 2nd July.
Samuel Piererpoint Esq. of Old-Coates in the parish of Heath bur. at Sutton 8th Sept.
Richard Hawley bur. 16th Sept.
Arthur Nalson bur. 8th Oct.

1708

Mary Turner widow bur. 26th Jan.

Francis Widdowson bur. 12th April.

Anne dau. of Francis Hawkins of the parish of Chesterfield bur. at Sutton 28th
   May.

*A copy of this Register was delivered at the Bishop's Visitation at Chesterfield
   10th June.*

William Roberts senior bur. 6th Sept.

Godfrey Richardson bur. 10th Sept. [*This entry appears to be crossed out.*]

Elizabeth dau. of Nicholas Marsh bur. 13th Nov.

Elizabeth Naylor widow bur. 14th Dec.

1709

John Brett bur. 1st March.

Joseph son of Francis Tallents junior bur. 19th June.

Richard Bennett bur. 14th Aug.

Francis son of widow Richardson bur. 20th Sept.

John son of John Babington of Calow bur. 29th Sept.

1710

Edward son of Edward Haslam bur. 25th July.

Jane dau. of George Doeman bur. 7th Nov.

George Turner bur. 17th Nov.

1711

Michael son of Michael Brett bur. 16th Feb.

Robert Butcher bur. 25th March.

Dorathy Littilwood bur. 6th April.

Ann Cleton bur. 12th April.

Catherine Bret widow bur. 13th April.

Ann dau. of William and Ann Watkinson bur. 14th Nov.

1712

[*Blank*] Bennet widow bur. 29th Jan.
Matthew Wossendale bur. 25th July.
William Marsh bur. 7th Sept.
Mary wife of John Scales bur. 13th Oct.

1713

Mrs Elizabeth Freeman of Heath bur. 6th Jan.
William Richardson senior bur. 31st March.
Anne dau. of George and Jane Doeman bur. 8th April.
Michael Brett a poor man bur. 12th Nov.
Elizabeth Walker bur. 29th Nov.

1714

Elizabeth Butcher bur. 12th Feb.
William Winfield bur. 23rd March [aged 66].
Francis Lawrence bur. 18th May.
Margaret dau. of Edward and Jane Haslam bur. 10th June.

A copy of this Register delivered at the Bishop's Visitation at Chesterfield 17th June.

William son of Edward and Jane Haslam bur. 2nd July.
Jane wife of Edward Haslam bur. 30th Sept.

1715

Thomas Lawrence bur. 13th March.
William Shaw bur. 13th March.
Anne wife of Godfrey Flint bur. 18th May.
Robert Clarke bur. 30th May.
Jerom Shaw a poor man bur. 27th Sept.

[*There are no burial entries between 1716 and March 1732; eight pages left empty should have been filled in. The following entries have been inserted*

1716

Godfrey Shipston bur. 16th April.
Jonathan Swallow bur. 30th May.
Elizabeth Hardy bur. 17th Oct.
Robert Stephenson bur. 20th Nov.

1717

Henry Unwin bur. 29th March.
Widow Hardy bur. 10th Aug.
Robert Fern bur. 15th Sept.

1718

John Haslam bur. 6th Jan.
William Peace bur. 11th Aug.

1719

John Madin bur. 14th March.
John Turner bur. 25th April.

1727

William Marsden bur. 5th Aug.
Catherine wife of Francis Flint bur. 22nd Aug.
Ellen wife of Samuel Dowker bur. 15th Sept.

1728

Samuel Tallents bur. 7th Jan.
Barbara Finney bur. 12th Jan.
Job son of William and Mary Butcher bur. 3rd March.

Anne wife of William Plant bur. 29th April.
John Wingfield bur. 8th Nov.

1729

Thomas Rawlins bur. 23rd Sept.
George Doeman bur. 26th Oct.
John Hodgkinson bur. 9th Dec.
Thomas Collier bur. 28th Dec.

1730

Anne Clark bur. 1st March.
Mr Robert Jones bur. 12th March.
John Woodhead bur. 12th April.
William Richardson bur. 26th July.
Catherine Johnson an infant bur. 2nd Oct.
William Frith son of John and Mary Frith bur. 18th Nov.
John son of John Hall bur. 15th Dec.

1731

Mary Richardson bur. 8th Feb.
Robert son of Richard and Ann Johnson bur. 6th Oct.

1732

Elizabeth Brett bur. 30th March.
William Richardson junior bur. 3rd Feb.
Alice Bamforth bur. 3rd Feb.
Isaac Brett bur. 5th March
Moses Mosely bur. 19th March.

[At this point entries in the register resume.]

Thomas son of Thomas and Mary Cantrell bur. [*Day omitted*] April.
Joan wife of John Pogmore bur. 21st June.
Elizabeth dau. of John and Mary Turner bur. 30th July.
Hannah dau. of Henry and Elizabeth Rawlins bur. 31st July.
John Scales bur. 24th Aug.
John Holmes [freemason] bur. 3rd Oct. [aged 43].
Dorothy dau. of Thomas and Dorothy Taylor bur. 1st Nov.
Mary wife of Nicholas Marsh bur. 26th Dec.
Godfrey Tallents bur. 29th Dec.

1733

Ann Bennett bur. 22nd Jan.
Frances Brett bur. 8th Feb.
Mary Bennett bur. 28th March.
Ellen wife of William Woodhead bur. 21st April.
Grace dau. of Catherine Holmes bur. 22nd April [aged 2 months].
Alexander Clark Bur. 27th May.
Robert Butcher bur. 26th June.
Thomas Bennett bur. 23rd Dec.

1734

Elizabeth dau. of Ellen Palmer bur. 22nd Jan. [aged 18 months].
Elizabeth wife of Francis Watkinson bur. 5th April.
Martha wife of John Stephenson bur. 21st Aug.

1735

Revel Shaw bur. 24th Feb.
Mary Johnson bur. 27th May.
William Marsden bur. 15th June.
Anne Watkinson bur. 8th Aug.
Godfrey Stanley bur. 31st Oct.

1736

Francis Flint bur. 14th Jan.

Catherine Tallents bur. 12th May.

Margory wife of Robert Hardy bur. 14th June.

Mary Tallents bur. 20th June.

Elizabeth Gardiner [maiden lady, sister of wife of Rev. Stephen Ward] bur. 31st July.

The Right Honourable Nicholas, Earl of Scarsdale, bur. 4th Aug.

Edward son of Anne Tallents bur. 22nd Sept. [aged 11 months].

John son of Francis and Elizabeth Butcher bur. 8th Oct.

1737

William Widowson bur. 7th Jan.

John Frith bur. 26th Jan.

Alice Widowson bur. 27th Jan.

Catherine Holmes bur. 29th Jan.

John Eyre bur. 27th March.

Nicholas Marsh junior bur. 15th April.

Ann Butcher bur. 17th May.

Hannah dau. of Henry and Elizabeth Rawlin bur. 24th July.

Michael son of John and Sarah Unwin bur. 31st July.

1738

John son of Sarah Stork bur. 28th Jan. [aged 1 month].

Anne Marsden bur. 3rd Feb.

Joseph Ashbury bur. 1st May.

Grace Turner bur. 7th May.

Francis Butcher bur. 4th July.

James Brailsford and Judith his wife both bur. 16th Sept.

James Haslam bur. 16th Nov.

1739

Anne Shaw bur. 14th Feb.

Elizabeth wife of Thomas Stanley bur. 3rd April.

William Unwin bur. 10th April.

Elizabeth Butcher bur. 15th June.

Anne Vessey bur. 3rd Aug.

1740

Benedicta wife of Richard White bur. 3rd Feb.
Anne Unwin bur. 13th Oct.

1741

Francis Butcher bur. 9th March.
Thomas son of Thomas and Elizabeth Vessey bur. 21st June.

1742

[William son of John and Jane Hewitt bur. 12th Feb. aged 15 years].
Thomas Lowe bur. 22nd Feb.
Willoughby Roberts bur. 28th March.
Robert Briggs bur. 28th Dec.
Mary wife of John [*Blank*] bur. 14th May.
Sarah wife of Francis Wingfield bur. 12th June.

1743

Mary Grundy bur. 29th March.
Thomas Wingfield bur. 14th May.
James son of Joshua and Anne Daybanke bur. 25th June.
Frances Stevenson bur. 29th Sept.

1744

Edward son of Edward and Ann Stanley bur. 25th May [aged less than 1 year].

1745

Anne White bur. 13th May.
Elizabeth Clarke bur. 16th May.
Robert son of William and Mary Peace bur. 14th June [aged less than 2 years].
William Lowe bur. 17th June.
Anne wife of John Wood bur. 26th June.

1746

Elizabeth dau. of Joseph and Anne Newton bur. 10th April [aged 7 months].

Temperance wife of Edmund Reddish bur. 5th April.

Sarah wife of John Unwin bur. 3rd May.

Elizabeth wife of Henry Rawling bur. [9th] June.

Robert Ferne bur. 8th Nov.

Elizabeth dau. of Sampson and Frances Johnson bur. 16th Nov. [aged 2 years 8 months].

Jane Bennett [wife of Ralph Bennett] bur. 20th Nov. [aged 51].

1747

Elizabeth White bur. 1st Jan.

Richard Shaw bur. 6th March.

John Unwin bur. 20th March.

Mr George Cowlishaw bur. 9th April.

Lydia Booth bur. [*Date missing*].

Elizabeth dau. of John and Jane Hewitt bur. 5th July.

Mary Cousen bur. 29th Aug. [aged 80].

William Wingfield bur. 9th Oct.

Joseph Pogmore bur. 18th Nov.

John Shaw bur. 14th Dec. [aged 63].

1748

Sarah Roberts bur. 17th Jan.

Elizabeth Woodard bur. 15th May.

Elizabeth Bomford bur. 11th Sept.

Catherine Finney bur. 16th Sept.

Stephen son of Edward and Ann Stanley bur. 23rd Sept.

John Wood bur. 17th Nov.

1749

James Wingfield bur. 16th Jan.

Anne Stanley bur. 3rd Feb.

Anne Kirk bur. 16th Feb.

Joseph Wragg bur. 20th March.

1749

Mary Fern bur. 28th June.
John Pulteney bur. 3rd Nov.
Thomas Rodgers bur. 27th Dec.

1750

Peter Glossop bur. 8th April.
Mr Samuel Ward [son of Rev. Stephen Ward] bur. 6th May.
The Reverend Mr Stephen Ward, rector of Sutton-cum-Duckmanton, bur. 12th
    May.
William son of Edward and Ann Stanley bur. 20th May.
Elizabeth dau. of William and Anne Barlow bur. 25th Nov.
Alice Johnson bur. 13th Dec.
Anne Lawrence bur. 24th Dec.

1751

Mary dau. of Thomas and Ellen Ferne bur. 20th March.
Elizabeth dau. of Michael and Mary Scales bur. 12th May.
Jane Doeman bur. 30th May.
Jane dau. of Edward and Susannah Woodhead bur. 23rd Aug.
John Pogmore bur. 9th Oct.
Elizabeth Lowe bur. 13th Oct.

1752

John Cutt bur. 2nd Jan. [aged 69].
Nicholas Marsh bur. 5th Jan.
Sarah Coe bur. 19th Jan.
James son of Godfrey and Mary Flint bur. 15th March.
Elizabeth Mellor bur. 20th May.
Ralph son of Ralph and Mary Bennett bur. 14th Aug.
Thomas Cousen bur. 20th Sept. [aged 74].
Martha Marsh bur. 22nd Dec.
Jane Slater bur. 25th Dec.

1753

Elizabeth Rodgers bur. 6th Jan.
Elizabeth Vessey bur. 24th April.
Elizabeth Butcher bur. 24th April.
Mrs Lydia Johnston [housekeeper to Godfrey Clarke] bur. 28th April [aged 53].
Thomas Stanley bur. 26th July.
Francis Richardson bur. 29th July.
Robert Frith bur. 30th Nov.
Henry Rawling bur. 23rd Dec. [aged 49].

1754

Robert Ferne bur. 20th May.
Thomas Shaw bur. 21st July.
Joseph White bur. 7th Aug.
John Lawrence bur. 8th Aug. [aged 63].
Joseph son of James and Elizbeth Wilson bur. 13th Sept.

1755

Ellen dau. of Peter and Anne Tallents bur. 25th March.
Joseph Newton bur. 15th May.
Anne dau. of Godfrey Clarke Esq. and Anne his wife bur. 25th May.
Anne dau. of Samuel and Margaret Swift bur. 30th May.
Mary Ashbury bur. 31st Dec.

1756

Martha Tallents bur. 21st June.
John Madin bur. 16th July.
Margaret wife of Samuel Swift bur. 27th Oct.
Edward Stanley bur. 19th Dec.

1757

John son of Samuel and Margaret Swift bur. 27th Jan.
Sarah Beane bur. 17th Feb.

Anne Scales bur. 27th Feb.

Deliver my soul O Lord from lying lips and from deceitful tongues! The prayer of Frans. Tallents 14th March 1757. Philalethes.

Mr John Mott bur. 19th March.
John Renshaw bur. 15th April.
Lydia wife of Edmund Reddish bur. 4th July.
Alice wife of Thomas Wingfield bur. 8th July.
Alice wife of Jo. Wood bur. 17th July.

1758

Richard Newton bur. 8th Feb. [aged 20].
Thomas an infant son of John and Elizabeth Lowe bur. 2nd March.
Henry Rollins bur. 30th April [aged 20].
John Hewit bur. 5th May.
Jane Cutt bur. 26th May [aged 76].
Thomas infant son of William and Elizabeth Woodhead bur. 1st July.
Alice infant dau. of John and Sarah Saunderson bur. 5th Sept.
Elizabeth wife of Francis Rogers of Duckmanton bur. 6th Sept.
Mary Bennett widow of Duckmanton bur. 15th Nov.
John Bennett of Duckmanton bur. 26th Dec.

1759

Sarah dau. of Francis and Sarah Nalson of Duckmanton bur. 17th Jan.
Francis Tallents of Sutton bur. 9th March.
Thomas Stanley of Duckmanton bur. 4th June.
Elizabeth wife of John Lowe bur. 13th June.
Lydia wife of Joseph Lowe bur. 23rd Sept.
John Stevenson of Duckmanton bur. 26th Sept.
John Swallow of Sutton bur. 23rd Oct.

1760

Sarah Flint of Duckmanton bur. 3rd Jan.
George son of George and Elizabeth Hewit of Sutton bur. 4th Jan.
Francis Tallents of Sutton bur. 6th Jan.

Ann wife of William Plant bur. 24th Feb.

Ann dau. of John and Elizabeth Mott bur. 9th April [aged 8 months].

Francis Rodgers of Duckmanton bur. 24th Aug. [aged 68].

Thomas Engley of Sutton bur. 3rd Sept. [aged 60].

James son of William Peace of Duckmanton bur. 11th Nov. [aged 21].

Mary dau. of John Bomfort bur. 12th Nov.

1761

Elizabeth dau. of Thomas and Hannah Butcher of Duckmanton bur. 1st March.

Mary dau. of George and Elizabeth Brett bur. 22nd March.

Elizabeth dau. of George and Elizabeth Brett bur. 26th March.

Sarah dau. of William and Ann Shaw bur. 12th April.

John son of William and Sarah Witney bur. 1st May.

Margaret Tomlinson of Duckmanton widow bur. 2nd May.

Mary w. of Michael Scales of Duckmanton bur. 5th May.

Jane Palmer widow of Duckmanton bur. 26th May.

Mary dau. of Ann Tallents widow of Sutton bur. 19th July.

1762

Joseph Ashbury of Duckmanton bur. 31st Jan.

Joseph infant son of Joseph and Ann Ashbury bur. 3rd Feb.

Ann wife of Francis Nalson senior bur. 4th Feb.

William Woodhead of Duckmanton bur. 3rd March.

James Swallow of Duckmanton bur. 23rd March.

Elizabeth wife of Thomas Swallow bur. 28th March.

Thomas Swallow of Duckmanton bur. 9th April.

Thomas White bur. 14th April.

William infant son of Richard and Mary Marsh of Sutton bur. 18th April.

Mary Frost of Duckmanton bur. 25th April.

Elizabeth Brett widow of Duckmanton bur. 6th June.

Robert Thornley butler [died 31st July] bur. 3rd Aug. [aged 77].

1763

Mary Stevenson bur. 19th Jan.

Francis Watkinson bur. 4th Feb. [aged 82].

Daniel Kirk bur. 27th Feb.

Esau Butcher infant [twin] son of Thomas and Hannah Butcher bur. 27th Feb.
Hannah Butcher bur. 27th Feb.
Mary wife of John Dawson bur. 13th March.
Ann dau. of George and Elizabeth Brett bur. 12th June.

1764

Elizabeth wife of Joseph Mellars bur. 3rd Feb.
Mary Frith widow bur. 15th March.
Abigail Doeman widow bur. 16th March.
Joseph son of Joseph and Elizabeth Bennett [of Long Course] bur. 31st March [aged 37].
Thomas Taylor bur. 5th April.
Elizabeth wife of Joseph Bennett [of Long Course] bur. 25th May [aged 70].
Francis Nelson bur. 28th Oct.

1765

Richard Johnson bur. 12th March.
Ann wife of John Wood bur. 13th May.
Joseph Hodgkinson bur. 27th June.
Alice dau. of George and Elizabeth Britt bur. 15th Aug.
Elizabeth Wingfield widow bur. 24th Oct.
Edward Hodgkinson [died 23rd] and bur. 25th Oct. [aged 43].
Peter Ashbury bur. 6th Nov. aged 4.
Godfrey Glossop bur. 10th Nov.
Frances dau. of William and Ann Barlow bur. 2nd Dec.
Grace wife of Thomas Rodgers bur. 24th Dec.

1766

Edward Lawrence bur. 26th Jan.
Jonathan Swallow bur. 6th Feb.
John Bennett bur. 9th Feb. [aged 60].
Peter Ashbury bur. 22nd May [aged 64].
Hellen wife of Joseph Hodgkinson bur. 30th May [aged 71].
John Maden bur. 13th June.
Elizabeth Perkin bur. 18th June.

1767

Richard White of Duckmanton bur. 2nd Feb.
Ann dau. of John and Mary Cox bur. 11th Feb.
Francis Septimus son of John and Ann Wood bur. 10th March.
George Bennett of Duckmanton bur. 27th April.
James Allen bur. 8th July.
Sarah dau. of Thomas and Mary Lievesley bur. 25th Aug.
Elizabeth wife of Robert Richardson bur. 30th Aug.
Thomas Rodgers bur. 15th Nov.

1768

Aaron son of George and Elizabeth Brett bur. 28th Feb.
John Tompson bur. 17th March.
Mary wife of Benjamin Lawrence bur. 30th March.
John son of Robert and Ann Hewitt bur. 24th June.
Mary wife of Joshua Swallow bur. 25th June.
Mary wife of John Wood bur. 11th Sept.
Joshua Swallow of Sutton bur. 21st Sept.
William Plant of Duckmanton bur. 29th Sept.
Thomas Marsh of Sutton bur. 18th Dec.
Joseph son of Edward and Ann Hodgkinson bur. 23rd Dec. [aged 2].

1769

William Brett bur. 8th Jan.
Elizabeth Shields bur. 11th Jan.
Ann wife of Jonathan Gardiner bur. 17th Jan.
Samuel Grundy bur. 30th Jan.
Mary Renshaw widow bur. 9th Feb.
Francis Winfield bur. 21st Feb.
Francis son of John and Mary Rivel bur. 2nd March.
John Slater bur. 5th July.
Mary wife of Joseph Law bur. 23rd July.
Thomas Cantril bur. 2nd Aug.
Mary Bennet bur. 12th Nov.
Richard son of Samuel and Mary Johnson bur. 24th Nov.
John Mott bur. 30th Dec. [aged 45].

1770

Mary dau. of John and Mary Parkin bur. 27th Jan.

Elizabeth dau. of John and Mary Parkin bur. 3rd Feb.

Henry Unwin of Sutton bur. 18th Feb.

Margaret dau. of Sarah Scales bur. 31st April.

Sarah wife of James Newton bur. 7th May.

Joseph Hodgkinson of Duckmanton bur. 27th May [aged 75].

Joseph Bennet [of Long Course] bur. 11th June [aged 69].

Mary Watkinson widow bur. 3rd Aug.

James son of Elizabeth and James Swallow bur. 13th Oct.

James son of Robert and Ann Hewit bur. 6th Nov.

1771

Jane dau. of William and Mary Peace bur. 3rd Feb.

Christopher Wilson bur. 8th Feb.

Godfrey son of Godfrey Flint bur. 26th April.

Edmund Raddish bur. 10th May.

Leonard son of Edward and Susanna Woodhead bur. 11th June.

Mary Wingfield bur. 15th June [aged 26].

Samuel son of William and Elizabeth Woodhead bur. 20th June.

Anne dau. of William and Ann Booker bur. 16th July.

Susan dau. of John and Mary Lowe bur. 26th July.

Deborah dau. of Godfrey and Mary Flint bur. 31st July.

Susannah dau. of Edward and Ann Hodgkinson bur. 3rd Aug. [aged 5 months].

Sarah Frith widow bur. 21st Aug.

William son of Thomas and Hannah Butcher bur. 6th Oct.

Joseph Lowe bur. 10th Oct.

Anne dau. of John and Mary Bennet bur. 3rd Oct.

Jacob son of Thomas and Hannah Butcher bur. 20th Oct.

Elizabeth dau. of Richard and Mary Marsh bur. 6th Nov. [aged 22].

1772

John son of John and Mary Parkin bur. 19th Jan.

Jane Hewit widow bur. 26th Feb.

Hannah wife of Thomas Butcher bur. 8th March.

Francis son of Thomas and Hannah Butcher bur. 7th April.

John Lievesley bur. 24th May.

Hannah dau. of William and Esther Frost bur. 31st May.
Thomas Fern bur. 9th June.
Elizabeth dau. of Hannah Fox widow bur. 8th Sept.
Catharine Tallents bur. 9th Sept.
Benjamin Lawrence bur. 5th Oct.
Mary wife of Thomas Bennet bur. 22nd Nov. [aged 21].

1773

Nevil Wilkes bur. 23rd Jan.
Ellen Stevenson widow bur. 4th April.
Francis Butcher bur. 27th April.
Hannah Froggat bur. 13th June.
William son of John and Anne Wood bur. 22nd June.
Mary wife of William Newham bur. 21st Nov.
John Stafford bur. 3rd Dec.
Gertrude Patrick bur. 23rd Dec.

1774

Mary Spray widow bur. 11th Jan.
Mary wife of John Cox bur. 16th Jan.
Elizabeth Shaw widow bur. 6th March.
Charles Wood bur. 8th March.
John Glosop of Duckmanton bur. 10th Dec. [aged 45].

1775

Sarah dau. of John and Mary Parkin bur. 28th March.
Ann dau. of William and Elizabeth Milward bur. 7th July.
Jane dau. of Richard Radish and his first wife bur. 7th Sept.
Richard Marsh of Sutton bur. 31st Oct.
Ann Johnson of Duckmanton bur. 18th Nov.

1776

Thomas Sales of Duckmanton bur. 3rd March [aged 67].
Ruth infant dau. of Thomas and Mary White bur. 23rd March.

Mary wife of Samuel Pattinson bur. 7th May.
Elizabeth wife of Thomas Reddish bur. 23rd July.
Jane dau. of Robert and Ann Hewit bur. 28th Oct.
Anne dau. of Edward and Ann Hodgkinson bur. 15th Nov.
Joseph son of William and Ann Booker bur. 18th Nov.

1777

Mary widow of John Bennet bur. 18th Jan.
William infant son of James and Ellen Plant bur. 27th Feb. [aged 11 weeks].
Rebecca Lawrence widow bur. 30th March.
The Reverend Mr John Denton, rector of Sutton-cum-Duckmanton, died 2nd
    May and bur. 5th May in the parish church of Sutton.
James Tallents bur. 22nd May.
Anne Ashbury spinster bur. 2nd June.
Hannah dau. of Paul and Mary Unwin bur. 5th Sept.
Mary dau. of Benjamin and Mary Rodgers bur. 20th Oct.
Ann Newton widow bur. 21st Dec.

1778

Elizabeth wife of William Milward bur. 3rd Jan.
Ann dau. of Thomas and Elizabeth Renshaw bur. 10th March.
Mary wife of Godfrey Flint bur. 16th March.
James infant son of William and Elizabeth Peace bur. 29th April.
William Bennet of Sutton bur. 15th July.
Elizabeth wife of John Patrick bur. 21st July.
William son of William and Anne Shaw bur. 16th Aug.
Hannah dau. of Thomas and Sarah Scales bur. 23rd Aug.
Mary wife of Thomas Reddish bur. 10th Sept.
Joseph Unwin of Sutton bur. 11th Nov. [aged 78].

1779

Joseph Lievesley bur. 8th Feb. aged 73.
Mary wife of William Peace senior bur. 30th June.
Benjamin infant son of Benjamin and Mary Rodgers bur. 10th July.
Elizabeth Ashbury spinster, housekeeper to the late Godfrey Clarke Esq. bur.
    21st Aug.

William son of James and Ann Wingfield bur. 15th Sept.

Ann wife of John Frisby of Bon Burk, parish of Cuckney, Notts., bur. 4th Oct.

James son of James and Elizabeth Swallow bur. 4th Oct.

James illegitimate infant son of Mary Davenport bur. 13th Oct.

Thomas son of Thomas and Grace Rodgers bur. 14th Dec. aged 24.

Thomas son of John and Elizabeth Hopkinson bur. 29th Dec. aged 1.

1780

William Peace widower bur. 7th March aged 73.

Thomas Butcher widower bur. 10th March.

Mary Marsh wife of John Marsh of Sutton bur. 19th March aged 60.

Mary Cantrell widow bur. 27th March aged 80.

Mary wife of Samuel Johnson bur. 15th May aged 43.

William infant son of Benjamin and Mary Rodgers bur. 15th May.

Robert Richardson *alias* Gregory bur. 24th May.

Susannah infant dau. of James and Ellen Plant bur. 24th Oct.

1781

Ann Tallents widow of Sutton bur. 6th Jan.

Thomas Mellors widower of Duckmanton bur. 7th Jan.

Anne Unwin widow bur. 24th Jan. aged 84.

John Renshaw bur. 1st Feb. aged 64.

Mary Goodwin of Staveley parish bur. 2nd March aged 54.

Mary infant dau. of Jos. and Benedicta Parker bur. 14th May.

Sarah Frith bur. 26th May aged 21.

Thomas son of John and Mary Wood bur. 14th July aged 7.

Ann Ashbury widow bur. 15th Aug. aged 47.

Michael Scales bur. 8th Oct.

Hannah infant dau. of Benjamin and Mary Rodgers bur. 12th Oct.

Hannah Fox widow bur. 17th Dec.

Richard son of Charles and Hannah Hudson bur. 18th Dec.

1782

Dolly wife of George Clarkson bur. 15th Feb.

Reuben spurious son of Mary Green bur. 11th May.

Ralph Bennett bur. 3rd July.

William Newham bur. 14th Nov.
Rebecca dau. of William Watkinson bur. 8th Dec.

1783

Ann wife of William Barlow bur. 17th Jan.
Ann dau. of James Plant bur. 6th Feb.
Richard Rodgers bur. 24th Feb.
Dolly Unwin widow bur. 23rd March [aged 73].
Ann wife of Francis Fern bur. 27th April.
Mary Pogmore widow bur. 2nd June aged 89.

Act for every burial 3d.

Ellen dau. of John and Ann Frith bur. 4th Nov.
Godfrey Flint of Sutton bur. 7th Dec.

1784

Thomas Kirk bur. at Chesterfield 22nd Jan.
Mary wife of Thomas Pogmore bur. 13th July.
Francis Rodgers son of late Richard Rodgers bur. 10th Oct.
John Bennitt bur. 15th Nov.

1785

*Inspected 8th Jan. 1785 for year ending Oct. 1st. Burials 4, duty 1s. By J.
Bower, Collector of Duties, Chesterfield.*

Mary Bennitt widow bur. 28th April.
Joseph son of Joseph and Benedicta Parker bur. 26th Aug.
Elizabeth wife of Joseph Webster bur. 7th Oct.
Joseph Standley bur. 16th Nov.
Ann Woodhead wife of Edward Woodhead bur. 16th Nov.
Hannah dau. of William Sales bur. 21st Nov.

1786

Esther wife of William Frost bur. 6th Jan.
Mary dau. of Mr Inglet bur. 14th Jan.
Charles Hadfield a pauper bur. 11th Feb.

Paid the above to 14th Feb. 1786.

Ann infant dau. of Benjamin Rodgers and Mary his wife bapt. 13th and bur.
    22nd Feb.
Sarah Swallow widow bur. 5th March aged 93.
Ann dau. of John Pogmore and his wife bur. 6th March.
Edward Woodhead bur. 3rd April.
Thomas son of John Pogmore and his wife bur. 2nd May.
William Stalks a pauper bur. 18th Aug.
George Needham a pauper bur. 21st Sept.
Elizabeth dau. of Jarvase and Elizabeth Johnson bur. 7th Nov.
John Shaw of Sutton bur. 21st Nov.

Paid the above to Mr Bower 11th Dec.

Ann wife of Robert Hewitt bur. 17th Dec.

1787

George Dicken of Sutton bur. 9th May.
James Wingfield a pauper bur. 14th May.

Paid the above to Mr Bower.

1788

Ann infant dau. of Thomas and Elizabeth Wragg bur. Jan. 31st.
Hannah wife of William Rudderforth bur. 3rd Feb. [aged 55].
Ann Rodgers widow bur. 9th March.
Lydia wife of William Renshaw bur. 11th March.
Elizabeth Malem a pauper bur. 17th March.
Ellen Hewitt a pauper bur. 20th April.
Sarah dau. of Thomas Bennett bur. 23rd April.
George son of Joseph Green bur. 3rd June.

Elizabeth wife of Henry Hodgkinson bur. 3rd Aug.
Sarah dau. of Richard and Hannah Marsh bur. 24th Sept.
William son of William Barlow bur. 29th Sept.
William son of William Renshaw bur. 25th Nov.

1789

Elizabeth wife of William Peace bur. 2nd Jan.
Ann wife of John Frith bur. 6th Jan.
James infant son of Henry Hodgkinson bur. 15th Jan.

The above settled with Mr Bower 17th Jan.

Ann wife of Peter Talents bur. 26th Feb.
Ellen Fern widow, a pauper bur. 5th March.
Ellen dau. of Benjamin Rodgers bur. 6th March.
Sarah dau. of Charles [and Hannah] Hudson bur. 8th March.
John son of William [and Lydia] Renshaw bur. 22nd March.
Susannah Woodhead widow bur. 12th June.
John son of Humphrey and Mary Belfit bur. 31st July.
Mary dau. of Humphrey and Mary Belfit bur. 28th Aug.
Thomas Pogmore a pauper bur. 7th Sept.
Sampson Johnson bur. 23rd Oct. [aged 82].
Richard son of Richard Marsh bur. 27th Oct.

The above paid to Mr Bower 2nd Jan. 1790.

1790

Godfrey Tallents bur. 1st Feb. aged 85.
John Dawson a pauper bur. 21st Feb.
Elizabeth dau. of John Marsh bur. 21st Feb. [aged 7 months].
John Renshaw in the Sick Club bur. 28th Feb.
[Blank] dau. of Benjamin Rodgers and his wife bur. 3rd April.
Ann Mary dau. of John and Mary Sculthorpe bur. 12th Sept. [aged 7].

Paid the above to Mr Bower 14th Oct.

John Marsh bur. 2nd Dec. [aged 81].
Thomas Bennett son of widow Bennett a pauper bur. 18th Dec.

1791

Mary Green bur. 15th Feb.

Charlotte dau. of Richard Reddish and his wife [Mary] a pauper bur. 14th April.

Sarah Ashbury widow bur. 26th April.

Hannah Tallents widow bur. 1st May.

Benedicta dau. of Richard Reddish [and his wife Mary] a pauper bur. 3rd May.

Ann wife of James Hardwick bur. 15th May.

Martha infant dau. of Benjamin and Mary Rodgers of Duckmanton bur. 18th June.

Frances widow of Sampson Johnson bur. 28th June [aged 78].

A copy of this Register was delivered at the Visitation at Chesterfield 5th July.

John son of Thomas [and Anne] Bennett bur. 3rd Aug.

John Patrick schoolmaster bur. 23rd Aug. aged 80.

Paid duty for the above funerals for year ending 1st Oct. 1791.

Ann Lievesley widow of Joseph Lievesley bur. 7th Nov. [aged 82].

Mary dau. of Humphrey and Mary Belfit bur. 7th Nov.

John infant son of William and Ann Barlow bur. 28th Nov.

Ann Bennett widow of Duckmanton bur. 8th Dec.

Rebecca infant dau. of David and Mary Britt bur. 20th Dec.

John [son of Sampson and Frances] Johnson of Duckmanton bur. 20th Dec. [aged 57].

1792

Joseph Parker of Moor Top bur. 14th Jan. aged 46.

Thomas Rawling of Sutton bur. 7th March aged 48.

John infant son of Mary Taylor bur. 3rd April.

Paid Mr Bower the duty up to 1st Oct.

William Watkinson of Sutton a pauper, bur. 18th Nov.

Isabella Sharman of Sutton bur. 3rd Dec.

1793

Mary Pearce of Duckmanton bur. 4th Jan. aged 18.

Thomas twin son of Thomas and Mary Lievesley bur. 30th Jan.

Edward son of William and Ann Cutt of Duckmanton bur. 2nd March.

Mary Allwood of Duckmanton bur. 28th April aged 15.

Benjamin Rodgers of Duckmanton bur. 18th June aged 44.

William son of William and Ann Cutt of Duckmanton bur. 21st July.

Elizabeth Woodhead wife of William Woodhead of Duckmanton bur. 15th Oct.
    [aged 67].

William Woodhead husband of the said Elizabeth bur. 24th Oct. aged 76.

1794

Martha Frith of Duckmanton bur. 26th March [aged 15].

Paid Mr Bower duty up to 1st Oct. 1794.

Duty ceased.

Edmund twin son of Edmund and Ann Firn of Nottingham bur. 12th Nov.

1795

William Shaw of Duckmanton Moor Top bur. 29th Jan. aged 78.

Ann dau. of John and Mary Sculthorpe now of Brimington bur. 5th March aged
    1.

Samuel son of John and Hannah Pogmore bur. 15th March aged 5.

Thomas Renshaw of Duckmanton Moor Top bur. 2nd April aged 69.

Ann dau. of Thomas and Elizabeth Wragg of Bolsover bur. 28th May.

Mary wife of Richard Wood of Duckmanton bur. 3rd June.

Sarah dau. of John and Elizabeth Hopkinson of North Wingfield bur. 14th June.

A copy of this Register was delivered at the Visitation up to 1st July.

Thomas Wingfield of Duckmanton bur. 17th July aged 63.

William Firn of Duckmanton bur. 10th Sept. aged 68.

Sarah wife of John Sanderson of Calow bur. 18th Oct. aged 70.

Edward Hodgkinson junior of Duckmanton bur. 19th Nov. aged 22.

1796

Elizabeth Renshaw of Hasland widow of the late John Renshaw of Woodnook bur. 14th Jan. aged 66.

Ann dau. of Thomas and Elizabeth Stevenson of Long Course bur. 15th March aged 5 years 11 months.

Mary dau. of Richard and Mary Wood of Duckmanton bur. 23rd April.

William Pearce of Duckmanton bur. 29th April aged 58.

Ann wife of Samuel Pattison of Sutton bur. 15th May aged 65.

William son of Humphrey and Mary Belfit of Calow bur. 14th June aged 9.

Hannah dau. of Robert and Sarah Dicken of Sutton bur. 28th Aug. aged 3.

Ann infant dau. of David and Mary Britt of Sutton bur. 14th Nov.

Elizabeth Renshaw widow of late Thomas Renshaw of Moor Top bur. 16th Nov. aged 71.

Elizabeth dau. of John and Ann Hodgkinson of Duckmanton bur. 26th Nov. aged 2.

William son of Joseph and Hannah Cantrell of Moor Top bur. 15th Dec. aged 12.

Mary wife of David Britt of Sutton bur. 22nd Dec. aged 37.

William Frost of Duckmanton bur. 26th Dec. aged 88.

1797

Mrs Hannah Hewitt bur. 12th Jan. aged 77.

Samuel Swift of Sutton bur. 23rd May aged 78.

Ann Wingfield widow of Duckmanton bur. 30th May aged 82.

Mary dau. of Thomas Bennett of Duckmanton bur. 26th Aug. aged 32.

1798

Mary illegitimate infant dau. of Mary White of Sutton, spinster bur. 15th Jan. [aged 13 days].

John Woodhead of Duckmanton bur. 26th March aged 47. N.B. He was one of the Chesterfield Troop of the Derbyshire Volunteer Cavalry and the first funeral in that Troop. The Troop attended the funeral and he was interred with the customary military honours.

John Wood of Duckmanton bur. 29th April aged 74.

Thomas Farnsworth Firn infant son of Elizabeth Firn of Duckmanton spinster bur. 26th Aug.

[Sketch in register shows the location of a grave at the junction of the North and Cross Alleys in the church.]

William Rodgers, parish apprentice to Charles Hudson, killed by a stroke from a horse, bur. 22nd Oct. aged 13.

Joseph Rodgers late of Duckmanton but now of Barlow Lees bur. at Sutton 22nd Nov. aged 32.

Edward Hodgkinson late of Duckmanton but now of Sutton bur. 12th Dec. aged 68.

Joseph Hall of Duckmanton Moor Top bur. 27th Dec.

1799

Richard Marsh of Sutton bur. 2nd Jan.

George Britt of Duckmanton bur. 15th Jan. aged 84.

Margaret Hall wife of the above Joseph Hall bur. 2nd Feb. aged 85.

Thomas Bennett schoolmaster of Duckmanton bur. 3rd March aged 65.

Elizabeth wife of Joseph Woodhead of Duckmanton bur. 29th May aged 37.

Joseph Woodhead, nephew to Charles Hudson, bur. 6th June aged 26.

Elizabeth Green wife of Joseph Green of Hasland but late of Sutton bur. 19th July aged 46.

Mr George Wragg late of Duckmanton but now of Bolsover bur. in Sutton Church 26th July aged 67.

[Sketch in register shows location of the grave in the North Alley and near the Scarsdale tomb.]

Elizabeth Allwood of Duckmanton bur. 15th Aug. aged 16.

Abraham infant son of Moses Britt of Duckmanton bur. 19th Sept.

Mary wife of Thomas White late of Duckmanton now of Sutton bur. 12th Nov. aged 63.

John Swallow of Duckmanton bur. 28th Dec.

1800

John Unwin son of Paul and Mary Unwin of Duckmanton bur. 29th Jan.

Hannah Taylor single woman of Duckmanton bur. 2nd March.

Joseph infant son of William and Ann Cutt of Duckmanton bur. 29th April.

Elizabeth Plant of Duckmanton widow bur. 26th May aged 87.

Thomas Wingfield of Duckmanton (hanged himself – Coroner's verdict – lunacy) bur. 13th June aged 42.

Mary Bennett widow of John Benett of Far Duckmanton bur. 3rd Aug. aged 77.

Ann Shaw widow of Moor Top bur. 17th Aug. aged 69.

A copy of this register delivered at the Visitation up to 20th Aug.

George infant son of John and Ann Hodgkinson of Duckmanton bur. 31st Aug.
aged 10 months – smallpox.

Ann dau. of William and Ann Cutt of Duckmanton bur. 7th Sept. aged 2 –
smallpox.

Elizabeth dau. of Samuel and Margaret Lievesley of Duckmanton bur. 26th Sept.
aged 1 – consumption.

1801

Jonathan Adlington son of John Adlington of Calow bur. 21st June aged 36 –
consumption.

Elizabeth dau. of the late Thomas Wingfield of Duckmanton bur. 7th Aug. aged
37 – fits.

Mary Pearce wife of William Pearce of Duckmanton bur. 20th Aug. aged 21 –
consumption.

Hannah infant dau. of David Gladwin of Sutton bur. 18th Oct. aged 1 week –
convulsions.

Richard Reddage of Duckmanton bur. 12th Nov. aged 73 – decay of nature.

John Woodhead son of John Woodhead of Duckmanton bur. 7th Dec. aged 11
– fever.

1802

Richard Rodgers of Mappleton formerly of Duckmanton bur. in church 9th Jan.
aged 34 – accident.

[Sketch in register shows location of grave in the Cross Alley.]

Edward Woodhead of Duckmanton bur. 9th Feb. aged 49 – consumption.

Elizabeth wife of James Newton of Duckmanton bur. 1st March aged 61.

Mary Marsh of Sutton bur. 23rd March aged 78 – decay of nature.

William infant son of Thomas Shaw bur. 6th June aged ¼ year – convulsions.

Marianne dau. of Robert [and Hannah] Lievesley of [Wakefield] Leeds bur. 31st
Aug. aged 14 – consumption.

William Milward junior of Chesterfield bur. 8th Sept. aged 31 – fever.

Sarah wife of Thomas Sales of Duckmanton bur. 21st Nov. aged 58 – consumption.

James infant son of John and Mary Sculthorpe of Chesterfield bur. 23rd Nov. aged 6 months – convulsions.

1803

Peter Tallants formerly of Sutton but late of Darley bur. 5th Jan. aged 88 – old age.

George son of Moses Britt late of Duckmanton killed by a cart wheel, bur. 8th April aged 12 – accident.

Ann Hodgkinson widow of the late Edward Hodgkinson bur. 17th April aged 68 – paralytic stroke.

Mary Sales widow of Duckmanton bur. 8th May aged 85 – old age.

Sarah dau. of George Beresford bur. 23rd May aged 1 – fever or influenza.

Mary Marsh late housekeeper to William Woodhead of Duckmanton bur. 25th Sept. – dropsy.

Ann Shaw wife of Thomas Shaw of Duckmanton Moor Top bur. 9th Oct. aged 25 – dropsy.

Nanny dau. of Robert and Sarah Frith of Duckmanton bur. 22nd Oct. aged 1½ years – chicken pox and whooping cough.

William son of Daniel and Thamar Watkinson of Sutton bur. 30th Oct. aged 1½ years – whooping cough.

Joseph Marsh of Sutton bur. 3rd Dec. aged 39 – paralytic stroke.

John infant son of Richard and Elizabeth Barlow of Duckmanton bur. 16th Dec. aged 5 weeks.

1804

Mary wife of John Lowe of Newdale bur. 8th Jan. aged 75 – old age.

Ann wife of Joseph Lievesley of Duckmanton bur. 15th March aged 70.

Eleanor dau. of John and Jane Marsh of Sutton died 17th and bur. 19th March aged 18¾ years – inflammatory rheumatism and consumption.

Ann Tallents of Sutton, widow of Francis Tallents formerly clerk of this parish, bur. 29th April aged 91 – paralytic and old age.

Mary dau. of Richard and Ann Chapman of Duckmanton bur. 31st May aged 11 – paralytic stroke.

Charles Hudson of Sutton bur. 3rd June – pleurisy and consumption.

Robert Hewitt of Duckmanton bur. 16th Sept. aged 73 – decay of nature.

John Lowe bachelor of Duckmanton bur. 12th Nov. aged 33 – dropsy.

1805

Robert son of Robert Woodruff of Duckmanton New Colliery bur. 11th Jan. aged 2.

Richard Barlow of Duckmanton bur. 20th Feb. aged 23 – epidemic fever. N.B. He was a volunteer in the Bolsover, Sutton and Scarcliffe Volunteer Infantry and the Company attended the funeral and interred him with the customary military honours.

Elizabeth Britt widow of George Britt of Duckmanton bur. 24th Feb. aged 78 – decay of nature.

John Revill of Duckmanton bur. 25th Feb. aged 72 – dropsy.

Samuel Johnson of Duckmanton Moor Top bur. 28th March aged 70 – rheumatism and cramp.

Jane wife of John Marsh of Sutton schoolmaster and parish clerk bur. 9th May aged 52 – dropsy. N.B. She was afflicted with the dropsy about 9 years.

A copy of this Register delivered at Chesterfield 4th Sept. 1805.

Susannah Smith wife of Mr Smith of Pilsley late of Sutton bur. 3rd Oct. aged 56 – dropsy.

Anne wife of John Pogmore of Common bur. 3rd Oct. aged 66 – asthma.

Elizabeth widow of Thomas Wingfield of Duckmanton bur. 11th Dec. aged 70 – decay of nature.

1806

Sarah wife of Francis Nelson of Duckmanton bur. 1st Jan. aged 84 – decay of nature.

Mrs Helen Kirk widow bur. at Chesterfield 5th Feb. – dropsy.

Mary Heath widow bur. 18th March aged 74 – natural decay.

Francis Nelson of Duckmanton bur. 2nd May aged 74 – dropsy.

Thomas White of Sutton bur. 21st May aged 68 – killed by a tree falling on him.

Francis Firn junior of Duckmanton bur. 26th June aged 25 – consumption.

Mrs Alice Lowe of Calow bur. 4th July aged 53 – pleurisy, fever etc.

George son of Robert Woodruff of Duckmanton New Colliery bur. 22nd Aug. aged 1½ years.

Joseph Lievesley formerly of Bolsover but late of Duckmanton bur. 19th Oct.

aged 68.

John Pearce of Duckmanton bur. 26th Dec. aged 26 – consumption. With military honours as a Volunteer. [N.B. He was a Volunteer with the Bolsover, Sutton and Scarcliffe Volunteer Infantry and the Company interred him with full military honours.]

1807

John Sculthorpe bur. 8th April aged 59 – dropsy.

Dorothy Watkinson bur. 10th April aged 82 – old age.

Mrs Ann Hayward of Duckmanton bur. 24th April aged 50 – apoplectic fit.

Francis son of James and Elizabeth Cowley of Duckmanton bur. 25th April aged 3 – decline.

Ann dau. of William [and Sarah] Turner of Duckmanton New Colliery bur. 7th May aged ¾ year – decline.

Thomas Reddish of Duckmanton bur. 8th May aged 25 – decline.

William Johnson of Duckmanton bur. 21st July aged 30 – fever.

William Rotherforth of Duckmanton bur. 18th Dec. aged 71.

1808

Sophia dau. of William and Sarah Lloyd of Duckmanton bur. 6th March aged 1 year 11 months – influenza.

William son of Samuel Bacon of Moor Top bur. 16th March aged ½ year.

George son of Richard Chapman of Duckmanton bur. 16th March aged ¾ year.

John Godber of Duckmanton bur. 6th July aged 79.

Mrs Ann Wragg of Duckmanton bur. 27th July aged 79. Interred over Mr Wragg [in Church].

Catharine Fearne now of Totley late of Duckmanton bur. 5th Aug. aged 83.

Ann infant dau. of Samuel Bacon of Moor Top bur. 8th Oct.

William Milward bur. 10th Nov. aged 79 – dropsy.

1809

Hannah wife of John Bowler bur. 1st Jan. aged 88 – decay of nature.

John son of Robert and Lydia Gee bur. 5th Feb. aged 1 – smallpox.

Ann dau. of Robert and Lydia Gee bur. 27th Feb. aged 3 – smallpox.

[Blank] son of Richard and Ann Chapman bur. 28th Feb. aged 1 week.

Robert Hayward of Duckmanton bur. 7th May aged 44 – burst blood vessel.

Elizabeth wife of Joseph Nelson of Duckmanton bur. 14th May aged 45 – consumption.

James Fidler of Sutton Mill bur. 18th May aged 75 – decay of nature.

John Frith late of Duckmanton bur. 16th July aged 83 – dropsy.

Sarah wife of Sampson Johnson of Duckmanton bur. 10th Oct aged 78 – decay of nature.

Elizabeth wife of John Lowe of Duckmanton Moor bur. 1st Nov. aged 75 – asthma and old age.

James son of William Pogmore of Duckmanton Moor bur. 11th Dec. aged 3 – measles.

Abraham Frost of Duckmanton bur. 29th Dec. aged 52 – suddenly.

1810

Anne dau. of Thomas and Elizabeth Barber late of Duckmanton now of Calow bur. 21st Jan. aged 3 – inflammation of the lungs.

Hannah dau. of William and Hannah Meakin bur. 28th Jan. aged 11 months – convulsions.

Joseph infant son of Humphrey Brookes bur. 2nd Feb. aged 2 days.

Jane wife of James Newton of Duckmanton bur. 13th Feb. aged 80 – old age.

Jasper son of Jasper Whitcomb of New Works bur. 15th March aged 4 – smallpox.

George son of Stephen and Sarah Thompson of Moor Top bur. 29th March aged 10 months – smallpox.

William son of Humphrey and Elizabeth Brookes bur. 1st April aged 2 years 4 months – smallpox.

John son of William and Jane Robinson of Duckmanton bur. 31st May aged 1 – teeth.

Ann wife of William Booker of Duckmanton bur. 16th June aged 65 – fever.

Joseph Nixon of Duckmanton bur. 15th July aged 44 – dropsy.

Francis son of Godfrey and Grace Flint of Calow bur. 13th Aug. aged 12 – fever.

Martha dau. of Robert and Sarah Frith of Duckmanton bur. 28th Aug. aged 15 – consumption.

A copy of this Register was delivered at Chesterfield 20th Sept. 1810 from Lady Day 1805 to Lady Day 1810.

James infant son of George and Mary Shaw of Duckmanton Moor Top bur. 21st Oct. aged 3 weeks.

Mary Reddish now of Staveley bur. at Sutton 26th Dec. aged 47 – fever.

1811

Ann Sales bur. 1st Jan. aged 29 – fever.

Hannah dau. of William and Mary Harvey of Duckmanton New Colliery bur. 21st Jan. aged 4 – fever.

George son of said William and Mary Harvey bur. 23rd Jan. aged 6 months – fever.

John Lowe of Duckmanton Moor bur. 24th Jan. aged 86 – old age.

Mary Steel dau. of John Hodgkinson of Duckmanton bur. 6th March aged 24 – consumption.

Mr Joseph Smith of Pilsley late of Sutton bur. 12th April aged 78 – old age.

Mary Twells bur. 12th July aged 19 – consumption.

Samuel Stanley late of Staveley but formerly of Duckmanton bur. 12th Oct. aged 57 – inflammation.

Helen dau. of James Plant junior of Duckmanton bur. 7th Nov. aged 1¼ years.

1812

Anne dau. of George Beresford of Duckmanton bur. 25th Jan. aged 8 – fever.

William son of George Beresford of Duckmanton bur. 3rd Feb. aged 2 – fever.

Joseph son of Thomas and Hannah Cantrell of Moor Top bur. 26th Feb. aged 1 year 7 months – convulsions.

Thomas son of Robert and Helen Lievesley of Duckmanton bur. 29th Feb. aged 2 – fever.

Elizabeth dau. of Robert and Helen Lievesley of Duckmanton bur. 7th March aged 3¾ years – fever.

Thomas son of Ann Reddage spinster of Duckmanton bur. 18th March aged 3 – fever.

Ann dau. of William and Margaret Pearce of Duckmanton bur. 16th April aged 2 months – convulsions.

Francis Firn of Duckmanton bur. 11th Oct. aged 71 – decay of nature.

Obadiah Bunting of Duckmanton bur. 26th Oct. aged 78 – decay of nature.

Mrs Sarah Dicken wife of Mr Robert Dicken of Sutton bur. 31st Dec. aged 60 – dropsy.

N.B. For burials subsequent hereto vide *New Register pursuant to Act of 52 Geo. III.*

1st January 1827

The day and year above written was the first time of George Marsh performing duty as clerk of the parish of Sutton-cum-Duckmanton, and was appointed to the said office by the Revd William Bagnall, curate of the said parish, at a meeting held at Duckmanton School on the tenth of the same month, and Richard Johnson was appointed schoolmaster at the same time.

Of the time of the deaths of such persons of Mr Clarke's family as came to the knowledge of J. Marsh, Parish Clerk.

Godfrey Clarke Esq. died at London, 30th March 1774, and interred at Brampton, 16th April following, aged 60.

Godfrey Bagnall Clarke Esq. (His son) M.P. for the County of Derby, died at London 26th December 1774, and was interred at Brampton, 7th January 1775, aged 33.

Gilbert Clarke Esq. (His 2nd son) died at London [*Blank*] 1786, and was interred at Brampton [*Blank*] August following.

Mrs Sarah Price-Clarke (daughter of the abovesaid Godfrey Clarke Esq.) wife of Job Hart Price Clarke Esq., died at Exeter in Devonshire 23rd November 1801, and was interred in the Chancel of Exeter Cathedral.

Godfrey Price Clarke (son of the abovesaid Job Hart Price Clarke by the said Sarah his wife) died at their seat at Ulcomb, near Maidstone in Kent, [*Blank*] 180[2], and was interred in Ulcomb Church the [*Blank*] 180[2], aged [*Blank*].

August 28th 1791

The day and year above written, after morning prayer, John Marsh was appointed clerk of the parish of Sutton-cum-Duckmanton, by the Revd Mr Bourne, rector of said parish.

Nicholas Marsh last accompts being constable of
Sutton-cum-Duckmanton for the year 1784

Disbursements: 27. Paid Joseph Woodhead and Obadiah Bunting concerning sheep wash, 1s. 4d. each, 2s. 8d. 28. Paid H. Heath his bill 1s. 3d. 29. Paid for 2 dozen of sparrow heads 8d. 30. Paid William Fern for being pinder 10s. 0d. 31. Paid Sam. Bennett 2s. 6d. 32. Paid Samuel Johnson and Thomas Bennett 13s. 6d. 33. My day going to Chesterfield – due to me £1 12s. 1d. Rec. of Paul Unwin, overseer, see his accompts for the year 1784/5.

Scarcity

In the summer of 1796, a little before harvest, corn was supposed to be very scarce and wheat was sold at three guineas per load of 3 bushels. In London the quartern loaf sold for 15 pence halfpenny. The country was alarmed, fearing bread could not be procured to supply the inhabitants; the magistrates and principal gentlemen particularly requested the use of coarse bread only, and in general set the example themselves by forbidding the use of puddings and white bread in their families; they also recommended potatoes to be mixed with flour to make bread of. Government ordered returns from every parish of the quantity of corn produced from the preceding crop; and allowed great bounties on the importation of foreign corn into England. But it pleased God to send a plentiful harvest, which, together with the great quantity imported, discovered the scarcity (which was more artificial than real) to be chiefly owing to the corn factors, who monopolized all the corn they could get, into their own hands; buying it of the farmers before they could set it down in the market; and keeping it in magazines till great quantities were spoiled: After harvest wheat soon got down to a guinea per load, and many corn factors' names appeared (as bankrupts) in the Gazette every week. May it prove a timely warning to all succeeding factors and may they learn from thence that: 'Wherein men deal proudly, God is above them!'.

May 31st 1662
Richard White, Churchwarden

1662 October 12 day gathered 6 houses, 1 being burned within the parish of Saint Martin's, Charles Titford and the rest, the sum of five shillings, six pence.

November 2 day gathered for Colwich in the County of Staford the sum of three shillings, seven pence.

1663 May the 3 day gathered for three four and six houses that was burned in Hexham in the county of Northumberland the sum of four shillings and five pence.

1680 August the 6th, collected by Virtue of a Brief for a fire at Weston in the parish of Bulkington, co. Warwick, seven shillings and ten pence.

1681 June the 5th, collected by Virtue of a Brief for a fire at Duxford in Cambridgeshire, five shillings and six pence.

1684 August the 1st, received then of Mr Currey for Westminster briefe, the sum of £0 4s. 8d. I say received by me. Sam. Elwis.

Febr. 26th 1684. Rec. then of Mr Currey for Cawston breife the sume of £11 4s. For Ely breife the sume of £0 4s. 6d. For Alrewas briefe the sume of £0 4s. 0d. I say received then by me, Sam. Elwis.

Aprill 30th 1685. Rec. of Mr Currey, Minister of Sutton-cum-Duckmanton, the sum of four shillings and three pence for St Bridget in Chester, by me, Arthur Fox, Collector.

September 9th 1685. Paid unto Arthur Fox by Godfrey Richardson, Churchwarden, Lilleshall, Sawsden and Market Deeping Breives, the whole sume being 8 shillings and two pence. This is a true copy of Mr Fox's acquittance, J. Curray.

Apprentices

1784: On 6th May, John Swallow put to J. Plant. On 13th May, James Taylor son of Hannah Taylor, put to Mr Jos. Woodhead. On 4th July, Elizabeth Wilmot a girl, put to Mr Thomas Sales.

1786: On 18th May, Godfrey Middleton son of [Blank] Middleton, put to Obadiah Bunting.

1787: On 12th April, William Hewitt put to Mr R. Dicken. On 21st April, Sarah Hewitt put to Jos. Lievesley. On 30th May, John Hewitt put to Mr. Stevenson. Matthew Fox put apprentice to W. Kirk.

1813: On 17th April, Eleanor Sheppard daughter of Samuel Sheppard put to Mr William Birkett. On 17th April, Mary Sheppard daughter of Samuel Sheppard put to Edward Johnson, Far Duckmanton.

1822: On April 15th, Martha Rodgers daughter of Lucy Rodgers of Calow put to Mr William Woodhead of Duckmanton. William Pearce, Overseer. On April 15th, William Cooper son of late George Cooper of Inkersell put to Mr White of Sutton. Sarah Lievesley daughter of Ann Lievesley (*alias* Wright) put to Mr Middleton. William Jepson son of John Jepson put to Mr Kirk.

MARRIAGES

1663

Godfrey Flinte and Dorothy Allotson mar. 5th Feb.
John Hille and Ann Booth mar. 18th May.
George Wright and Ann Murphin mar. 16th June.
William Scales and Marie More mar. 27th Aug.
Edward Willson and Ann Cooke mar. 10th Sept.

1664

Howin Litherland and Sarah Tuder mar. 10th March.
Richard Bennett and Mary Bradshaw mar. 7th June.
Nicholas Richardson and Marie Tovely mar. 21st June.

1665

William More and Mary Flint mar. 10th Oct.

1666

William Walker and Elizabeth Marsh mar. 27th Feb.
Gilberd Baker and Isabell Stanley mar. 2nd Oct.

1667

John Fisher and Mary Fox mar. 24th June.

1669

William Marsh and Elizabeth Walker mar. 17th May.

1670

Thomas Noble and Ann Deane mar. 24th Jan.

1671

William Jonson and Sara Stanley mar. 17th Jan.

1673

Ralph Richardson and Isabel Hay mar. 21st Jan.

1676

Thomas Poynton and Ann Stanley mar. 8th May.
Samuel Stevenson and Susanor Iles mar. 28th Sept.
John Allwood and Rebecka Outram mar. 28th Nov.

1679

Henry Unwin and Barbara Walker mar. 29th May.

1681

Arthur Nalsen and Sara Taborner mar. 12th Dec.

1683

Robert Cooke of the parish of Staveley and Ann Richardson of Duckmanton mar. Tuesday 18th Sept.

Robert Stanley of Duckmanton and Ann Stubbinge of Whittington, having first obtained a licence, were married in the parish church of Chesterfield 19th December 1683, according to a certificate directed to me by Mr J. Lobley, vicar of Chesterfield. Registered by me, John Curray.

1684

Godfrey Wheatcroft of Chesterfield and Ann Beveridge of Sutton mar. at Sutton 5th Feb.

George Chantrey of the parish of Dronfield and Lydia White mar. at Sutton 19th Aug.

1685

William Shaw and Mary Brett mar. 30th Nov.

1686

John Frith and Elin Flint mar. 29th June.

Thomas Colgreave and Sara Roger mar. 11th Nov.

1687

William Baumfort and Jone Butcher mar. 2nd Feb.

George Hodgskinson and Ann Ferne mar. 18th April.

Godfrey Shipston and Mary Richardson mar. 1st June.

George Walker and Barbara Hill mar. 21st June.

Thomas Yong and Sara Allwood mar. 4th July.

1689

Robert Eastland and Sarah Arderne mar. 2nd Feb.

William Bennet and Ann Marsh mar. 1st April.

Francis Widdeson and Alice Butcher mar. 1st Oct.

Thomas Shaw and Elizabeth Allwood mar. 19th Nov.

1692

Thomas Rogers and Ann Woodhead mar. 8th Feb.

Francis Butcher and Elizabeth Dowman mar. 17th May.

1693

Thomas Padison and Alice Bennet mar. 15th Jan.
William Hadfield and Gertrude Hodson mar. 20th June.

1694

John Lievesley and Ann Bilbey mar. 2nd June.
James Brailsford and Sara Charnell mar. 6th Nov.
George Dowman and Jane Woodhead mar. 10th Nov.
George Ashbury and Jane Baker mar. 13th Nov.

1695

Thomas Marsh and Lydia Ashbury mar. 4th Feb.
Roger Hewitt and Elizabeth Outram mar. 21st May.
Thomas Wilde and Mary Brett mar. 1st June.
Joshua Dowker and Ruth White mar. 25th Aug.
John Scales and Mary Naylor mar. 4th Nov.

1696

Robert Hardy and Elizabeth White mar. 5th May.
George Slack and Mary Barnes mar. 27th Oct.

1697

Joseph Alletson and Jane Bilby mar. 15th June.

1698

Thomas Gill of Harwood Grange and Elizabeth Tallents of this parish mar. 10th
    Feb.
John Barker and Isabell Stubing, both of this parish, mar. 13th Feb.

1699

Revell Shaw and Anne Holmes, both of this parish, mar. 2nd Feb.

John Unwin and Sarah Stevenson, both of this parish, mar. 18th May.

John Bradshaw of the parish of Brampton and Hannah Bilby of this parish mar. 1st Dec.

1700

John Eyre and Elizabeth Upton widow mar. 1st Oct.

1701

Nicholas Holmes and Isabel Silcock, both of this parish, mar. 30th Oct.

1702

John Lievesley and Mary Longdale, both of this parish, mar. 14th Jan.

John Naylor of Chesterfield and Mary Tallents of Sutton mar. 15th Jan.

Henry Holdsworth of Warsop and Isabel Wilmot of this parish mar. 2nd June.

1703

William Roberts and Sarah Godber, both of this parish, mar. 21st Jan.

Mathew Parker of Bolsover and Mary Widdowson of this parish mar. 27th July.

Robert Butcher and Anne Burton, both (poor) of this parish, mar. 17th Aug.

1704

George Clark and Ann Richardson widow, both of this parish, mar. 10th Feb.

John Bennett and Mary Scales, both of this parish, mar. 4th Feb.

A copy of this Register was delivered in at the Bishop's Visitation at Chesterfield 16th May 1705.

1706

John Stevenson and Mary Shaw, both of this parish, mar. 29th April.

Godfrey Fooler of the parish of Bakewell and Mary Chapman of this parish mar. 2nd Oct.

1707

Francis Marsh and Martha Jeffrey, both of this parish, mar. at Sutton 29th Dec.

1708

Edward Tournay of Caneby and Anne Booth of Lincoln mar. at Sutton 24th Aug.

A copy of this Register was delivered in at the Bishop's Visitation at Chesterfield 10th June 1708.

1709

John Cowsell of the parish of Syson in the county of Lincoln and Jane Hardy of this parish mar. 10th Nov.

William Marsden and Abigail Doeman of this parish mar. 21st Nov.

1710

Francis Slater of the parish of South Normanton and Jane Unwin of this parish mar. 16th Jan.

John Glossop and Anne Turner, both of this parish, mar. 4th May.

John Darby of the parish of Bolsover and Mary Pawson of this parish mar. 6th June.

John Lievesley of the parish of Staveley and Elizabeth Roberts of this parish mar. 11th June.

1712

Jervase Newball and Dorothy Dowker mar. 14th July.

1713

Francis Nelson and Anne Green, both of this parish, mar. 11th May.

A copy of this register was delivered in at the Bishop's Visitation 17th June 1714.

1715

Nathaniel Bradshaw of Bolsover and Anne Dowker of this parish mar. 2nd Feb.
Humphrey Smail and Hannah Barker both of the parish of Bolsover mar. 28th April.
Thomas May and Margaret Bennet mar. 15th May.

[Entries for 1716–30 are taken from the bishop's transcripts at Lichfield.]

1716

Thomas Shaw and Elizabeth Streson, both of this parish, mar. 20th Nov.
Samuel Newton of the town and county of Nottingham and Elizabeth Flint of the parish of Crytch in this county mar. 7th Sept.
John Walker and Mary Sybrock both of the parish of Bolsover mar. 9th Dec.

1718

Godfrey Flint of the parish of Chesterfield and Elizabeth Tallents of this parish mar. 9th Dec.

1719

John Mott and Susanna Christian, both of this parish, mar. 2nd Jan.

1727

Samuel Fidler and Sarah Oldfield mar. 7th April.
Charles Alwood and Barbara Cosins mar. 15th June.

Timothy Pigott and Elizabeth Wilson mar. 17th June.
Benjamin Pogmore and ... Ratcliff mar. 19th June.

1728

John Stevens and Elizabeth Allizon mar. 9th May.

1729

William Plant and Ann Green were mar. [*No date*].
John Machey and Martha Holms mar. 28th Aug.
Thomas Cantrell and Mary Bagguley mar. [*No date*].

1730

Joseph Armstrong and Mary Bingham mar. 2nd Nov.

1733

Joseph Milward and Anne Bingham mar. 29th Jan.
Edward Dickinson and Ellen Matrix mar. 1st May.
George Darby and Ruth Johnson mar. 24th July.

1734

Richard Alcock and Elizabeth Mitchell mar. 28th Jan.
Isaac Jenkinson and Mary Johnson mar. 13th May.
John Johnson and Mary Hay mar. 15th Aug.
Edward Slack and Martha Thompson mar. 4th Sept.
Richard Cope and Frances Shaw mar. 26th Oct.

1735

Matthew Cheniry and Anne Willmott mar. 28th April.
Cornelius Alcroft and Elizabeth Johnson mar. 4th May.

1736

John Dawson and Mary Stephenson mar. 19th Sept.
Story White and Elizabeth Fentham mar. 2nd Nov.
Godfrey Tallents and Martha Stocks mar. 30th Nov.
William Frost and Esther Hind mar. 24th Dec.
Thomas Middleton and Mary Roberts mar. 28th Dec.

1737

William Hodgkinson and Elizabeth Kitchen mar. 13th April.
John Bennett and Ann Marshall mar. 1st Aug.
Charles Hatfield and Elizabeth Renshaw mar. 22nd Sept.
Joseph Shelley and Elizabeth Cutt mar. 27th Oct.
Thomas Rhodes and Mary Ince mar. 26th Dec.

1738

William Stephenson and Catherine Marsh mar. 13th Feb.
John Allwood and Mary Christian mar. 6th April.
William Newham and Mary Cutt mar. 3rd May.
Martin Radcliffe and Grace Hall mar. 29th Dec.

1739

Richard Hardwick and Elizabeth Charlesworth mar. 30th Jan.
Ralph Tagg and Mary Unwin mar. 28th Feb.
Samuel Taylor and Mary Turner mar. 13th Aug.

1740

Paul Unwin and Ann Hodgkinson mar. 19th May.
Joseph Drable and Anne Cree mar. 11th June.
Joseph Holmes and Elizabeth Allison mar. 28th Sept.
William Marsh and Anne Hopkins mar. 30th Sept.
William Harrison and Frances Stanful mar. 4th Dec.
William Charlesworth and Elizabeth Beely mar. 30th Dec.

1741

John Drable and Mary Cree mar. 19th May.

1742

John Fisher and Anne Mellors mar. 26th Dec.

1743

Thomas Mitchell and Anne Bacon mar. 2nd Jan.
Benjamin Rhodes and Alice Cousen mar. 20th July.

1744

Benjamin Lawrence and Mary Clarke mar. 2nd Jan.
John Lievesley and Sarah Nixon mar. 3rd Jan.
Francis Nelson and Sarah Frith mar. 10th April.
Edmund Reddish and Temperance Vessey mar. 18th April.
Edward Jefferies and Mary Lee mar. 20th Sept.

1745

Francis Sims and Elizabeth Chapman mar. 31st Jan.
John Crosby and Sarah Snowden mar. 4th Sept.
John Haslam and Ellen Mitchell mar. 11th Nov.

1746

William Shaw and Anne Lowe mar. April [*Day not given*].
Richard Marsh and Mary Swallow mar. 14th May.
Thomas Pogmore and Mary Whitehead mar. 27th May.
Jonathan Charlesworth and Jane Hallam mar. 11th Nov.

1747

Thomas Pogmore and Mary Mather mar. 2nd March.

John Patrick and Elizabeth Lievesley mar. 19th April.
Michael Woodard and Elizabeth Stevenson mar. 14th Nov.

1748

William Barlow and Ann Shaw mar. 12th April.
George Brett and Elizabeth Hodgkinson mar. 13th April.
Thomas Renshaw and Elizabeth Brailsford mar. 2nd June.
William Whitehead and Anne Gaskin mar. 7th Nov.
James Richardson and Lidya Andrews mar. 13th Nov.
William Armstrong and Elizabeth Beane mar. 29th Nov.

1749

William Crofts and Anne Webster mar. 15th Jan.
John Lowe and Elizabeth Shaw mar. 24th Oct.
Thomas Holmes and Anne Jackson mar. 20th Nov.
Joseph Bennett and Elizabeth Roome mar. 27th Dec.

1750

John Mettam and Elizabeth Martin mar. 11th Jan.
John Davenport and Elizabeth Wilson mar. 2nd Feb.
Samuel Stubbing and Ann Shooter mar. 12th Feb.

1751

Thomas Cousen and Ann Lilleyman mar. 16th April.

1754

James Wilson and Elizabeth Nelson of Bolsover mar. 7th Jan.
Thomas Wingfield and Alice Richardson, both of this parish, mar. 25th Feb.

REGISTER OF MARRIAGES
1754–1812

1754

Joseph Hall and Margaret Tomlinson, both of this parish, mar. 17th June (according to the late Act of Parliament).

1755

William Beane of Heath and Sarah Glossop of this parish mar. 3rd June (according to the late Act of Parliament).

Edward Bentley of Heath and Elizabeth Collier of this parish mar. 11th Aug. (according to the late Act of Parliament).

John Lowe and Elizabeth Tye, both of this parish, mar. 25th Sept. (according to the late Act of Parliament).

Edmund Reddish and Elizabeth Spray, both of this parish, mar. 29th Dec. by licence.

1758

John Mott and Elizabeth Barlow, both of this parish, mar. by licence 16th Nov. by J. Denton, curate.

1759

John Lowe widower and Mary Siddon spinster both of this parish mar. 29th Oct. by J. Denton, curate.

Joseph Ashbury and Ann Rodgers, both of this parish, mar. by licence 1st Nov. by J. Denton, curate.

John Glossop and Sarah Glossop a minor, both of this parish, mar. 7th Nov. by J. Denton, curate.

1760

William Bell and Elizabeth Barge, both of this parish, mar. 21st July by John Bourne, curate of Heath.

Edward Hodgkinson and Ann Lievesley, both of this parish, mar. 2nd Sept. by J. Denton, curate

Edward Milns of Rotherham and Sarah Plant of this parish mar. 24th Sept. by John Denton, curate.

Samuel Parker of Middleton (Youlgreave) and Hannah Garrat of this parish mar. 11th Nov. by J. Denton, curate.

1761

William Bean of Heath and Elizabeth Fletcher of this parish mar. 1st Jan. by J. Denton, curate.

Thomas Bennet and Ann Unwin minor, both of this parish, mar. 15th Jan. by John Denton, curate.

Joseph Lowe widower and Mary Wilson, both of this parish, mar. 23rd March by John Denton, curate.

William Parkin and Catherine Bowler, both of this parish, mar. 2nd Aug. by John Denton, curate.

1762

John Scothern and Jane Lowe, both of this parish, mar. 12th April by J. Denton, curate.

Samuel Johnson, blacksmith, of this parish and Mary Hatfield of Chesterfield mar. 12th May by William Garthwaite, curate.

Thomas White, farmer, and Mary Dawson, both of this parish, mar. 25th May by William Garthwaite, curate.

1763

John Bowler and Hannah Swallow widow, both of this parish, mar. 24th Jan. by J. Denton, curate.

Joseph Mellars and Elizabeth Say, both of this parish, mar. 9th May by J. Denton, curate.

John Lievesley and Dorothy Pearce, both of this parish, mar. 25th Oct. by J. Denton, curate.

Godfrey Tallents widower and Hannah Hills, both of this parish, mar. by licence 10th Nov. by Seth Ellis.

Joseph Morton of Barlbro' and Ann Plant of this parish mar. 18th Oct. by J. Denton, curate.

William Plant widower and Elizabeth Fern widow, both of this parish, mar. 18th Dec. by J. Denton, curate.

1765

Robert Hewitt and Ann Steemson, both of this parish, mar. 1st Jan. by J. Denton, curate.

William Booker and Ann Nalson, both of this parish, mar. 29th Jan. by J. Denton, curate.

Peter Tallents and Lydia Clay, both of this parish, mar. by licence 18th June by J. Denton, curate.

James Rhodes of Bolsover and Sarah Tallents of this parish mar. 10th July by J. Denton, curate.

Thomas Lievesley and Mary Bennet, both of this parish, mar. 24th Oct. by J. Denton, curate.

John Cox of Chesterfield and Mary Pearce of this parish mar. 12th Nov. by J. Denton, curate.

Joseph Mellars widower and Martha Tatton both of this parish, mar. 1st Dec. by J. Denton, curate.

1766

Samuel Unwin of Bolsover and Mary Mellars of this parish mar. 7th Jan. by J. Denton, curate.

Tristam Ridgway of Staveley and Mary Swift of this parish mar. by licence 7th May by J. Denton, curate.

John Froggot of Chesterfield and Prisilla Beatmore of this parish mar. by licence 1st July by William Richardson, curate.

William Rotherforth of Bolsover and Hannah Swallow of this parish mar. 9th Sept. by J. Denton, curate.

John Wood widower and Mary Froggat, both of this parish, mar. 22nd Sept. by J. Denton, curate.

Richard Sharman and Isabel Booer, both of this parish, mar. 13th Nov. by J. Denton, curate.

1768

Thomas Kirk of Rotherham and Ellen Hodgkinson of this parish mar. by licence 24th Jan. by J. Denton, curate.

Joseph Parker of Chesterfield and Benedicta Rodgers (minor) of this parish mar. by licence 16th Feb. by J. Denton, curate.

James Fidler and Mary Glossop, both of this parish, mar. by licence 13th May by J. Denton, curate.

Gervase Madley of Barlbro' and Mary Milward of this parish mar. by licence 25th July by J. Denton, curate.

1769

Obadiah Bunting and Ann Lawrence, both of this parish, mar. by licence 5th Jan. by J. Denton, curate.

William Bennet and Hannah Milward, both of this parish, mar. 9th Feb. by J. Denton, curate.

James Plant, farmer, and Ellen Woodhead, both of this parish, mar. by licence 7th Dec. by J. Denton, curate.

Ephraim Fisher of Ault Hucknall and Sarah Sharman of this parish mar. by licence 28th Dec. by J. Denton, curate.

1770

James Swallow and Elizabeth Froggat, both of this parish, mar. 4th Jan. by J. Denton, curate.

John Mayland of Brampton and Elizabeth Fern of this parish mar. 18th June by J. Denton, curate.

William Milward and Elizabeth Rollins, both of this parish, mar. by licence 11th July by J. Denton, curate.

Luke Firth of North Wingfield and Ellen Dawson of this parish mar. by licence 13th Sept. by J. Denton, curate.

John Wood widower and Mary Cantrel, both of this parish, mar. 13th Nov. by J. Denton, curate.

Thomas Green and Elizabeth Parramour, both of this parish, mar. 27th Nov. by J. Denton, curate.

Edward Woodhead of Barlbro' and Ann Tallents of this parish mar. 1st Jan. by
J. Denton, curate.

Benjamin Lawrence and Mary Palfreman, both of this parish, mar. 1st April by
J. Denton, curate.

Thomas Bennett and Mary Maron, both of this parish, mar. by licence 28th April
by J. Denton, curate.

Francis Hudson and Elizabeth Frith, both of this parish, mar. by licence 6th Aug.
by J. Denton, curate.

George Warder and Ann Bull, both of this parish, mar. by licence 9th April by
J. Denton, curate.

Thomas Reddish and Elizabeth Stox, both of this parish, mar. 27th July by J.
Denton, curate.

Paul Unwin and Mary Reddish, both of this parish, mar. by licence 10th Nov.
by J. Denton, curate.

Charles Hudson and Hannah Tallents, both of this parish, mar. 14th Dec. by J.
Denton, curate.

John Gervis of North Wingfield and Anne Fern of this parish mar. 19th April by
J. Denton, curate.

John Johnson of Ault Hucknall and Mary Bennet of this parish mar. 28th June
by J. Denton, curate.

Thomas Allern of Bolsover and Ann Frith of this parish mar. 28th June by J.
Denton, curate.

Samuel Johnson and Sarah Whitney, both of this parish, mar. by licence 29th
June by J. Denton, curate.

Joseph Horton of St Martin's, Leicester, and Mary Lievesley of this parish mar.
by licence 30th June by J. Denton, curate.

George Clarkson of Chesterfield and Dorothy Lievesley widow of this parish
mar. by licence 13th Oct. by J. Denton, rector.

Joseph Giles and Frances Shaw, both of this parish, mar. by licence 21st Dec.
by J. Denton, rector.

Joshua Hulley of Staveley and Catherine Fern of this parish mar. 27th Dec. by
J. Denton, rector.

William Pearce and Betty Mitchell, both of this parish, mar. by licence 29th
  Dec. by J. Denton, rector.

1774

Thomas Allwood of Chesterfield and Jane Woodhead of this parish mar. by li-
  cence 31st Jan. by J. Denton, rector.
George Swift of Staveley and Sarah Jacson of this parish mar. 31st Jan. by John
  Denton, rector.
Robert Hernshaw and Elizabeth Middleton mar. 1st Feb. by John Denton, rector.
Joshua Andrew of Staveley and Mary Lawrence of this parish mar. by licence
  18th Sept. by J. Denton, rector.
William Kent of Sheffield and Anne Bennet mar. 28th Nov. by J. Denton, rector.

1775

Samuel Hodkin of Barlbro' and Ann Watkinson of this parish mar. 13th March
  by J. Denton, rector.
George Cox of Eckington and Ann Rodgers of this parish mar. by licence 2nd
  Nov. by J. Denton, rector.
Thomas Pogmore and Mary Hall, both of this parish, mar. 14th Dec. by J.
  Denton, rector.

1776

Gervas Johnson and Elizabeth Barlow, both of this parish, mar. by licence 27th
  May by John Robinson, curate of Bolsover.
Thomas Sales and Sarah Glossop widow, both of this parish, mar. by licence
  23rd Dec. by Joseph Ashbridge, curate. (Joseph Ashbridge curate *pro tem-*
  pore.)

1777

William Cutts of this parish and Ann Dean of Bolsover mar. 5th May by J.
  Ashbridge, curate.
James Cree and Mary Fern, both of this parish, mar. 19th Aug. by J. Ashbridge,
  curate.

John Renshaw and Elizabeth Fearne, both of this parish, mar. 19th Aug. by J. Ashbridge, curate.

Joseph Furness of Norton and Elizabeth Watkinson of this parish mar. 18th July by J. Ashbridge, curate.

John Smith of Harthill and Elizabeth Johnson of this parish mar. by licence 2nd Nov. by J. Ashbridge, curate.

1778

John Hopkinson and Elizabeth Lowe, both of this parish, mar. 17th Nov. by J. Ashbridge, curate.

Thomas Reddish and Margaret Gratton, both of this parish, mar. 23rd Dec. by J. Ashbridge, curate.

William Glossop of Staveley and Anne Lowe of this parish mar. by licence 29th Dec. by J. Ashbridge, curate.

1779

Joseph Woodhead and Elizabeth Bennet (by consent of guardians), both of this parish, mar. by licence 13th April by J. Ashbridge, curate.

Joseph Green and Elizabeth Renshaw, both of this parish, mar. 17th June by John Bourne, rector.

Hugh Heath and Hannah Bennet, both of this parish, mar. 7th July by J. Ashbridge, curate.

Joseph Keeton of North Wingfield and Elizabeth Askew of this parish mar. 12th July by J. Ashbridge, curate.

1780

Samuel Pattinson and Ann Marsh, both of this parish, mar. 29th June by J. Ashbridge, curate.

George Askey and Ann Shaw, both of this parish, mar. 28th June by J. Ashbridge, curate.

John Marsh (age 20, with consent of father) and Jane Thomas (age 20, with consent of father), both of this parish, mar. by licence 23rd July by J. Ashbridge, curate.

1781

Benjamin Brentall (age 20, with consent of father) and Margaret Bennet (age 18, with consent of guardians), both of this parish, mar. by licence 19th June by J. Ashbridge, curate.

William Barlow and Martha Bennett, both of this parish, mar. 1st Oct. by J. Ashbridge, curate.

Joseph Wilson of Bolsover and Betty Malam of this parish mar. by licence 27th Dec. by J. Ashbridge, curate.

1782

William Renshaw and Lydia Reddish, both of this parish, mar. 31st Jan. by J. Ashbridge, curate.

George Dicken of this parish and Mary Green of Scarcliffe mar. by licence 10th Feb. by John Bourne.

Robert Crofts and Mary Dewis, both of this parish, mar. 7th March by J. Ashbridge, curate.

1783

Samuel Gill and Sarah Rodgers, both of this parish, mar. 21st April by J. Ashbridge, curate.

Richard Marsh and Hannah Frith, both of this parish, mar. 29th June by Thomas Field (minister).

William Rodgers and Ann Thornley, both of this parish, mar. 21st July by John Bourne, rector.

1784

Humphry Belfit of Wingerworth and Mary Johnson of this parish mar. 2nd May by John Bourne.

William Hawley of this parish and Elizabeth Ball of North Wingfield mar. 27th Sept. by J. Ashbridge, curate.

Joseph Nelson and Elizabeth Whitaker, both of this parish, mar. 23rd Nov. by J. Ashbridge, curate.

Robert Dicken and Sarah Wilcockson, both of this parish, mar. by licence 10th July by John Bourne.

Robert Berry and Frances Palfreyman, both of this parish, mar. by licence 6th March by John Bourne.

Robert Walker of Bolsover and Ann Barlow of this parish mar. 28th March by J. Ashbridge, curate.

1786

Richard Rollison and Mary Scales, both of this parish, mar. 23rd Jan. by J. Ashbridge, curate.

John Pogmore and Hannah Ashton, both of this parish, mar. 17th Oct. by J. Ashbridge, curate.

John Coup of Scarcliffe and Sarah Makinson of this parish mar. 17th Oct. by J. Ashbridge, curate.

John Hodgkinson and Ann Bell, both of this parish, mar. 30th Oct. by J. Ashbridge, curate.

John Poolsmith and Martha Adlington, both of this parish, mar. by licence 4th Dec. by J. Ashbridge, curate.

1787

William Banks and Mary Watkinson, both of this parish, mar. by licence 1st Feb. by J. Ashbridge, curate.

Benjamin Goodwin and Ann Butcher, both of this parish, mar. 3rd June by J. Bourne, rector.

John Bretnall and Sarah Rodgers, both of this parish, mar. 27th Aug. by J. Ashbridge, curate.

Thomas Wragg and Elizabeth Woodhead, both of this parish, mar. by licence 3rd Dec. by John Bourne.

Thomas Hayes and Ann Hardy, both of this parish, mar. 25th Dec. by J. Ashbridge, curate.

Joseph Rodgers and Ann Johnson, both of this parish, mar. 31st Dec. by J. Ashbridge, curate.

1788

John Pogmore and Ann Siddon, both of this parish, mar. 21st April by J. Ashbridge, curate.

William Meakin and Hannah Swallow, both of this parish, mar. by licence 18th Aug. by J. Ashbridge, curate.

1789

Roger Wilmot of Darley and Catherine Fearne, a minor, by consent of her guardians, both of this parish, mar. by licence 20th April by J. Ashbridge, curate.

Thomas Stevenson and Elizabeth Bunting (a minor, by consent of her parents), both of this parish, mar. by licence 9th June by J. Ashbridge, curate.

William Cooper of Tibshelf and Elizabeth Booker of this parish mar. 15th June by J. Ashbridge, curate.

John Godber of Chesterfield and Ann Sailes of this parish mar. by licence 18th June by John Bourne.

1790

William Dalton of Dronfield and Ann Lievesley of this parish mar. by licence 11th Jan. by J. Ashbridge, curate.

James Newton widower and Elizabeth Swallow widow, both of this parish, mar. 1st Feb. by J. Ashbridge, curate.

Samuel Reeve and Rebecca Hopkinson, both of this parish, mar. 15th Feb. by J. Ashbridge, curate.

1791

Joseph Richardson of Clowne and Elizabeth Swallow of this parish mar. 15th Sept. by J. Ashbridge, curate.

1792

Joshua Ashley of Chesterfield and Ann Sharman of this parish mar. 9th Jan. by J. Ashbridge, curate.

Thomas Ford of Morton and Hellen Woodhead of this parish mar. by licence 1st May by John Bourne.

James Hardwick widower and Sarah Hill, both of this parish, mar. by licence 25th Oct. by J. Ashbridge, curate.

George Wright of Mansfield and Lydia Pogmore of this parish mar. 29th Oct. by J. Ashbridge, curate.

1793

Godfrey Flint shoemaker and Grace Rodgers, both of this parish, mar. 13th Sept. by J. Ashbridge, curate.

John Sharman and Mary Wells, both of this parish, mar. 24th Feb. by J. Ashbridge, curate.

John Parker of North Wingfield and Sarah Smith of this parish mar. by licence 31st March by John Bourne.

1794

George Beresford and Elizabeth Lievesley, both of this parish, mar. by licence 31st March by John Bourne.

William Baggeley of Bolsover and Ann Fern of this parish mar. 2nd June by J. Ashbridge, curate.

1795

David Gladwin and Ellen Bennett, both of this parish, mar. 6th April by J. Ashbridge, curate.

1796

Richard Wood widower and Mary Rodgers widow, both of this parish, mar. 5th Sept. by J. Ashbridge, curate.

George Goodall of Ault Hucknall and Anne Revell of this parish mar. 28th Nov. by J. Ashbridge, curate.

John Fletcher of Ecclesfield and Mary Kirk of this parish mar. by licence 13th Dec. by J. Ashbridge, curate.

1797

John Northedge of Bolsover and Ann Swallow of this parish mar. 27th Nov. by
B.B. Nickolls, officiating minister.

1798

John Spence and Sarah Heath, both of this parish, mar. by licence 29th Aug. by
John Bourne.

William Pearce and Mary Cooper, both of this parish, mar. 7th Nov. by J.
Ashbridge, officiating minister.

1799

Henry Hodgkinson and Amy Sharman, both of this parish, mar. by licence 3rd
Jan. by Thomas Field.

Ralph Deakin and Margaret Dawson, both of this parish, mar. by licence 25th
March by Joseph Ashbridge, officiating minister.

Stephen Glossop and Sarah Grey, both of this parish, mar. 25th March by Joseph
Ashbridge, officiating minister.

Thomas Cantrell and Hannah Holland, both of this parish, mar. 21st Oct. by
Joseph Ashbridge, officiating minister.

James Hewitt and Jane Cooper, both of this parish, mar. 25th Nov. by Joseph
Ashbridge, officiating minister.

1800

James Shepherd of North Wingfield and Mary White of this parish mar. 14th
April by Jos. Ashbridge.

William Ferne and Anne Goodwin (otherwise Ferne), both of this parish, mar.
by licence 13th Aug. by John Bourne.

James Plant junior and Mary Smith, both of this parish, mar. by licence 24th
Dec. by J. Ashbridge.

1801

Thomas Barber and Elizabeth Unwin, both of this parish, mar. 1st Jan. by J. Ashbridge.

Richard Brooks of Eastwood, Notts., and Anna Houldsworth of this parish mar. 11th May by J. Ashbridge.

Thomas Shaw, tailor, and Ann Tetley, both of this parish, mar. 13th Nov. by J. Ashbridge.

1802

Joshua Davidson and Hannah Lievesley, both of this parish, mar. 1st Dec. by J. Ashbridge (curate for the time).

1803

Robert Lievesley, sawyer, and Helen Reddage, both of this parish, mar. 24th Jan. by J. Ashbridge.

Francis Bunting of North Wingfield and Lydia Hodgkinson of this parish mar. by licence 2nd June by Thomas Field.

1804

George Wright of Ashover and Keturah Pearce of this parish mar. 9th Jan. by J. Ashbridge.

Robert Hardy of Eckington and Elizabeth North of this parish mar. by licence 11th Jan. by Thomas Field.

William Pearce and Margaret Woodhead (a minor), both of this parish, mar. by licence 17th April by John Bourne, rector.

Joseph Sales and Amey Brailsford, both of this parish, mar. 3rd Dec. by J. Ashbridge.

1805

Joseph Heath and Elizabeth Redfern, both of this parish, mar. by licence 10th Jan. by J. Bourne, rector.

Thomas Sales widower and Ann Wingfield widow, both of this parish, mar. 26th Jan. by J. Ashbridge.

Francis Bentley and Hannah Marsh widow, both of this parish, mar. 15th April by J. Ashbridge.

Robert Gee and Lydia Booker, both of this parish, mar. 16th Dec. by J. Ashbridge.

1806

Jeremiah Greatorex widower of North Wingfield and Ann Barlow of this parish, aged 22, mar. by licence 18th Oct. by J. Ashbridge.

Paul Unwin and Ann Sales, both of this parish, mar. 3rd Nov. by Simon Mountfort.

Samuel Bacon and Elizabeth Cantrell, both of this parish, mar. 24th Nov. by Simon Mountfort.

Charles Watts and Martha Barlow, both of this parish, mar. 1st Dec. by Simon Mountfort.

Humphrey Brookes and Elizabeth Pogmore, both of this parish, mar. 9th Dec. by Simon Mountfort.

1807

William Mellor of Chesterfield and Elizabeth Kirk of this parish mar. by licence 16th March by Simon Mountfort.

1808

William Sales of this parish and Ann Tomlinson widow of Dronfield mar. 9th May by Simon Mountfort.

John Barlow of Staveley and Maria Redferne of this parish mar. 20th June by Simon Mountfort.

John Marsh widower and Sarah Rotherforth widow, both of this parish, mar. by licence by Simon Mountfort.

1809

George Shipman and Elizabeth Mason, both of this parish, mar. 9th Jan. by J. Ashbridge, curate *pro tempore*.

William Hewitt and Amy Johnson, both of this parish, mar. 2nd Feb. by Simon Mountfort.

Samuel Eastwood and Susannah Bell, both of this parish, mar. 6th Nov. by G. Sampson.

George Dicken, aged 25, of Bolsover and Elizabeth Dicken, aged 20 (with consent of father), of this parish mar. by licence 23rd Nov. by G. Sampson.

1810

Robert Brown and Elizabeth Whitcomb, both of this parish, mar. 1st Oct. by G. Whitehead, minister.

William Taylor of Handsworth and Mary Britt of this parish mar. by licence 16th Oct. by G. Whitehead.

1811

William Ward and Helen Nelson, both of this parish, mar. 18th Feb. by J.L. Sisson A.B., curate.

Samuel Hopkinson widower aged 40 and upwards of Dronfield and Sarah Plant spinster aged 30 and upwards of this parish mar. by licence 18th March by J.L. Sisson, curate.

William Dicken bachelor aged 25 of this parish and Ann Dicken spinster aged 27 and upwards of Tideswell mar. by licence by J.L. Sisson, curate.

George Wass and Sarah Nixon, both of this parish, mar. 13th Sept. by J.L. Sisson, curate.

William Smith and Elizabeth Thornely, both of this parish, mar. 26th Nov. by Joseph Ashbridge A.M.

1812

George Dicken aged 25 of Tideswell and Margaret Dicken of this parish mar. by licence 25th May by R. Heathcote, curate.

James Gregory and Bridget Poolsmith, both of this parish, mar. 2nd Nov. by W.C. Tinsley, officiating minister.

Richard Haywood of Pleasley and Sarah Whitehead of this parish mar. 30th Nov. by W.C. Tinsley.

REGISTER OF BAPTISMS
1813–37

1813

Mary dau. of William and Helen Ward (Nelson) of Duckmanton, labourer, bapt. 21st Jan. by W.C. Tinsley, curate of Bolsover.

Joseph son of George and Sarah Wass (Nixon) of Duckmanton, labourer, bapt. 31st Jan. by W.C. Tinsley.

Maria dau. of Hezekiah and Alice Saviere (King) of Duckmanton Furnace, labourer, bapt. 31st Jan. by W.C. Tinsley.

James son of Humphrey and Elizabeth Brookes (Pogmore) of Sutton, labourer, bapt. 7th Feb. by W.C. Tinsley.

Thomas son of Thomas and Hannah Cantrell (Holland) of Duckmanton Moor Top, labourer, bapt. 14th Feb. by W.C. Tinsley.

Ann illegitimate child of Jane Hewitt spinster of Duckmanton bapt. 11th March by W.C. Tinsley.

Joseph illegitimate child of Ann Reddish spinster of Duckmanton bapt. 14th March by W.C. Tinsley.

Mary Ann dau. of Thomas and Elizabeth Barber (Unwin) of Calow, labourer, bapt. 28th March by Ralph Heathcote.

Samuel son of Samuel and Catherine Renshaw (Greaves) of Duckmanton Moor Top, farmer, bapt. 11th April by Ralph Heathcote.

Elizabeth dau. of Robert and Lydia Gee (Booker) of Duckmanton, labourer, bapt. 18th April by Ralph Heathcote.

Rebekah dau. of Thomas and Lydia Parker (Eastwood) of Calow, labourer, bapt. 18th April by Ralph Heathcote.

James son of William and Margaret Pearce (Woodhead) of Duckmanton, farmer, bapt. 25th April by Ralph Heathcote.

William son of Robert and Helen Lievesley (Reddish) of Duckmanton, wheelwright, bapt. 25th April by Ralph Heathcote.

Amy dau. of Samuel and Mary Johnson (Clayton) of Duckmanton Moor Top, blacksmith, bapt. 2nd May by Ralph Heathcote.

William son of James and Jane Hewitt (Cowper) of Duckmanton, cordwainer, bapt. 9th May by W.C. Tinsley.

Ruth dau. of John and Mary Sharman (Wells) of Sutton, gardener, bapt. 6th June by Ralph Heathcote.

Samuel son of Samuel and Mary Unwin (Woodhead) of Duckmanton Furnace, labourer, bapt. 6th June by Ralph Heathcote.

Elizabeth dau. of James and Elizabeth Cowley (Firn) of Duckmanton, labourer, bapt. 13th June by Ralph Heathcote.

Alfred son of John and Sarah Bennett (Sales) of Middle Duckmanton, tailor, bapt. 27th June by W.C. Tinsley.

Elizabeth dau. of Richard and Jane Birkett (Marshall) of Duckmanton, farmer, bapt. 12th July by W.C. Tinsley.

Sarah dau. of George and Mary Shaw (Freeman) of Duckmanton Moor Top, labourer, bapt. 25th July by W.C. Tinsley.

Hannah dau. of George and Elizabeth Beresford (Lievesley) of Duckmanton, labourer, bapt. 28th Aug. by Ralph Heathcote.

Susannah dau. of James and Mary Plant (Smith) of Duckmanton, farmer, bapt. 12th Sept. by Ralph Heathcote.

Alexander son of Benjamin and Elizabeth Marsden (Thorpe) of Duckmanton, wheelwright, bapt. 3rd Oct. by W.C. Tinsley.

Abner son of Benjamin and Elizabeth Marsden (Thorpe) of Duckmanton, wheelwright, bapt. 3rd Oct. by W.C. Tinsley.

Jane dau. of John and Mary Marsh (Bentley) of Sutton, farmer, bapt. 31st Oct. by Ralph Heathcote.

John son of Thomas and Mary Bennett (widow Hawkins, maiden name Eastwood) of Duckmanton, labourer, bapt. 21st Nov. by Ralph Heathcote.

Joseph son of Samuel and Elizabeth Bacon (Cantrell) of Duckmanton Moor Top, collier, bapt. 13th Dec. by Ralph Heathcote.

George son of Joseph and Amy Sales (Brailsford) of Duckmanton, labourer, bapt. 26th Dec. by Ralph Heathcote.

1814

Thomas son of George and Sarah Wass (Nixon) of Duckmanton, labourer, bapt. 16th Jan. by T.B. Lucas.

Charles son of John and Mary Cooper (Parker) of Duckmanton, labourer, bapt. 20th March by Ralph Heathcote.

Anne dau. of William and Amy Hewitt (Johnson) of Sutton, labourer, bapt. 20th March by Ralph Heathcote.

Mary dau. of William and Sarah Turner of Duckmanton, moulder at Iron Furnace, bapt. 30th March at Chesterfield according to certificate received by Rev. G. Bossley, vicar.

Joseph Dicken-Wilcockson son of Mary Ann Dicken spinster of Sutton, bapt. 5th April at Brimington by Rev. Thomas Field.

Mary dau. of Thomas and Catherine Todd (Barlow) of Duckmanton, moulder at Iron Furnace, bapt. 10th May at Chesterfield by Rev. G. Bossley, vicar.

Robert son of William and Mary Parker (Herrod) of Duckmanton, farmer, bapt. 26th June by Ralph Heathcote.

George son of John and Mary Jepson (Spray) of Sutton, labourer, bapt. 3rd July by Ralph Heathcote.

Amy dau. of William and Mary Revill (Miles) of Duckmanton, labourer, bapt. 3rd July by Ralph Heathcote.

John son of Hezekiah and Alice Saviere (King) of Duckmanton Furnace, labourer, bapt. 14th July by George Hall, curate.

James son of David and Helen Gladwin (Bennett) of Sutton, farmer, bapt. 18th July by Joseph Ashbridge.

William son of George and Jane Blanksby (Eastwood) of Duckmanton Works, moulder, bapt. 31st July by Ralph Heathcote.

Ann dau. of John and Grace Wingfield (mason) of Duckmanton, labourer, bapt. 13th Aug. by J. Ashbridge.

Horatio son of William and Jane Robinson of Duckmanton Furnace, moulder, bapt. 14th Aug. by W. Carlisle, rector.

Margaret dau. of William and Margaret Turner (Crofts) of Sutton, farmer, bapt. 11th Sept. by Ralph Heathcote.

Eliza dau. of Joseph and Elizabeth Heath of Sutton Hagg, blacksmith, bapt. 12th Sept. by J. Ashbridge.

John son of William and Hannah Heath (Sales) of Calow, blacksmith, bapt. 9th Oct. by Ralph Heathcote.

Elizabeth dau. of Francis and Dorothy Whitworth (Watkinson) of Sutton, labourer, bapt. 20th Nov. by Ralph Heathcote.

Jasper son of James and Hannah Fidler (Beardmore) of Sutton Mill, miller, bapt. 25th Dec. by Ralph Heathcote.

1815

Eliza dau. of Mary Meakin spinster of Sutton bapt. 1st Jan. by Ralph Heathcote.

James son of George and Jane Holmes (Coulson) of Duckmanton, coalminer, bapt. 1st Jan. by Ralph Heathcote.

Joseph son of Robert and Helen Lievesley (Reddish) of Duckmanton, wheelwright, bapt. 5th Feb. by Ralph Heathcote.

Elizabeth dau. of William and Mary Chapman (Dean) of Duckmanton, coalminer, bapt. 12th Feb. at Bolsover.

Hannah dau. of William and Mary Harvey (Wright) of Duckmanton Furnace, labourer, bapt. 19th March by Ralph Heathcote.

William illegitimate son of Elizabeth Meakin of Duckmanton bapt. 19th March by Ralph Heathcote.

Frances dau. of Richard and Jane Birkett (Marshall) of Duckmanton, bapt. 22nd March by J. Ashbridge.

Benjamin son of John and Mary Sharman (Wells) of Sutton, labourer, bapt. 25th March by J. Ashbridge.

Henry son of John and Mary Marsh (Bentley) of Sutton, farmer, bapt. 30th April by J. Ashbridge.

William son of Ann Lievesley, pauper of Duckmanton, bapt. 4th June by Ralph Heathcote.

William son of Thomas and Hannah Barlow (Frith) of Duckmanton, husband-man, bapt. 11th June by Ralph Heathcote.

William son of John and Esther Wingfield (Harrison) of Duckmanton, labourer, bapt. 17th June by J. Ashbridge.

Leonard son of William and Margaret Pearce (Woodhead) of Duckmanton, farmer, bapt. 26th July by J. Ashbridge.

Mary dau. of James and Mary Plant (Smith) of Duckmanton, farmer, bapt. 26th July by J. Ashbridge.

Sarah dau. of Richard and Elizabeth Charlesworth (Kenyon) of Duckmanton, mason, bapt. 30th July by Ralph Heathcote.

Samuel son of Edward and Hannah Boot (Day) of Sutton, framework knitter, bapt. 13th Aug. by Ralph Heathcote.

Joseph son of William and Anne Howard (Lievesley) of Duckmanton, hus-bandman, bapt. 10th Sept. by Ralph Heathcote.

John son of William and Helen Ward (Nelson) of Duckmanton Moor Top, collier, bapt. 25th Oct. by Ralph Heathcote.

William son of Samuel and Elizabeth Bacon (Cantrell) of Duckmanton Moor Top, collier, bapt. 29th Oct. by Ralph Heathcote.

Joseph son of Thomas and Hannah Cantrell (Holland) of Duckmanton Moor Top, labourer, bapt. 3rd Dec. by Ralph Heathcote.

Robert son of John and Mary Cooper (Parker) of Duckmanton, labourer, bapt. 10th Dec. by Ralph Heathcote.

1816

Francis Eyre son of David Caleb and Ann Brett (Eyre) of Sutton, farmer, bapt. 14th Jan. by Ralph Heathcote.

William son of Samuel and Mary Unwin (Woodhead) of Duckmanton Furnace, labourer, bapt. 4th Feb. by Ralph Heathcote.

Elizabeth dau. of Joseph and Amy Sales (Brailsford) of Duckmanton, labourer, bapt. 10th Feb. by J. Ashbridge.

Hannah dau. of Thomas and Rebekah Woodhead (Woodhead) of Duckmanton Furnace, labourer, bapt. 10th March by Ralph Heathcote.

Hannah dau. of Thomas and Katherine Todd (Barlow) of Duckmanton Furnace, moulder, bapt. 10th March by Ralph Heathcote.

Robert son of William and Amy Hewitt (Johnson) of Sutton, labourer, bapt. 24th March by Ralph Heathcote.

Grace dau. of Hezekiah and Alice Saviere (King) of Duckmanton Furnace, labourer, bapt. 2nd April by Joseph Ashbridge.

Samuel son of Paul Unwin junior and Ann Unwin (Sales) of Duckmanton, labourer, bapt. 9th April by Joseph Ashbridge.

Ann dau. of John and Sarah Bennett (Sales) of Duckmanton, tailor, bapt. 9th April by Joseph Ashbridge.

Ann dau. of George and Jane Blanksby (Eastwood) of Duckmanton Furnace, labourer, bapt. 21st April by Ralph Heathcote.

Joseph son of Samuel and Catherine Renshaw (Greaves) of Duckmanton Moor Top, farmer, bapt. 12th May by T.B. Lucas.

Joseph son of Benjamin and Elizabeth Marsden (Thorpe) of Duckmanton Moor Top, wheelwright, bapt. 2nd June by Thomas Field, Brampton.

Sarah dau. of Robert and Lydia Gee (Booker) of Duckmanton, labourer, bapt. 18th Sept. by T.B. Lucas.

Jane dau. of William and Margaret Turner (Crofts) of Sutton, farmer, bapt. 6th Oct. by T.B. Lucas.

Ann dau. of Hugh and Sarah Heath (Lowe) of Sutton, blacksmith, bapt. 10th Nov. by T.B. Lucas.

Luke son of William and Mary Parker (Herrod) of Duckmanton, farmer, bapt. 26th Nov. by T.B. Lucas.

Mary dau. of Robert and Ellen Lievesley (Reddish) of Duckmanton, wheelwright, bapt. 1st Dec. by T.B. Lucas.

Ann dau. of Richard and Jane Birkett (Marshall) of Duckmanton, farmer, bapt. 15th Dec. by T.B. Lucas.

Henry son of John and Mary Jepson (Spray) of Sutton, labourer, bapt. 22nd Dec. by T.B. Lucas.

1817

Mary dau. of John and Esther Wingfield (Harrison) of Duckmanton, labourer, bapt. 11th Jan. by T.B. Lucas.

Hannah dau. of William and Hannah Heath (Sales) of Calow, blacksmith, bapt. 12th Jan. by T.B. Lucas.

Ann dau. of William and Mary Chapman (Dean) of Duckmanton, coalminer, bapt. 24th Jan. by T.B. Lucas.

Jane dau.of George and Jane Holmes (Coulson) of Duckmanton, coalminer, bapt. 29th Jan. by T.B. Lucas.

Amy dau. of David and Helen Gladwin (Bennett) of Sutton, farmer, bapt. 9th March by T.B. Lucas.

Charles son of Charles and Priscilla Hemson (Roome) of Sutton, under-gardener, bapt. 9th March by T.B. Lucas.

Sarah dau. of John and Mary Cooper (Parker) of Duckmanton, labourer, bapt. 30th March by T.B. Lucas.

Samuel son of Samuel and Elizabeth Bacon (Cantrell) of Duckmanton Moor Top, collier, bapt. 9th April by T.B. Lucas.

Robert son of James and Jane Hewitt (Cowper) of Duckmanton, cordwainer, bapt. 14th April by T.B. Lucas.

Anne dau. of Thomas and Hannah Barlow (Frith) of Duckmanton, labourer, bapt. 14th April by T.B. Lucas.

James son of John and Mary Marsh (Bentley) of Sutton, farmer, bapt. 11th May by T.B. Lucas.

Thomas son of William and Sarah Turner (Coates) of Duckmanton Furnace, moulder, bapt. 1st June by T.B. Lucas.

Isabell dau. of Robert and Ann Stevens (Gregory) Sutton, gardener to Marquis of Ormonde, bapt. 22nd June by T.B. Lucas.

Hannah dau. of James and Hannah Fidler (Beardmore) of Sutton Mill, miller, bapt. 29th June by T.B. Lucas.

George son of Richard and Elizabeth Charlesworth of Duckmanton, mason, bapt. 30th July by T.B. Lucas.

Richard Woodhead son of William and Margaret Pearce (Woodhead) of Duckmanton, farmer, bapt. 30th July by T.B. Lucas.

Elizabeth dau. of Henry and Sarah Revill (Lievesley) of Duckmanton, labourer, bapt. 5th Oct. by T.B. Lucas.

John son of Humphrey and Elizabeth Brookes (Pogmore) of Duckmanton, labourer, bapt. 1st Dec. by T.B. Lucas.

Rosanna dau. of Hezekiah and Alice Saviere (King) of Duckmanton Furnace, labourer, bapt. 21st Dec. by T.B. Lucas.

1818

Anne dau. of Paul and Anne Unwin (Sales) of Duckmanton, labourer, bapt. 1st Jan. by T.B. Lucas.

George son of George and Jane Blanksby (Eastwood) of Duckmanton Furnace, labourer, bapt. 11th Jan. by T.B. Lucas.

James son of Thomas and Mary Bennett (Eastwood) of Duckmanton, labourer, bapt. 3rd Feb. by T.B. Lucas.

Esther dau. of John and Mary Sharman (Wells) of Sutton, labourer, bapt. 15th Feb. by T.B. Lucas.

Mary dau. of William and Amy Hewitt (Johnson) of Sutton, labourer, bapt. 1st March by T.B. Lucas.

William son of Charles and Martha Watts (Barlow) of Duckmanton, labourer, bapt. 8th March by T.B. Lucas.

Mary Ann dau. of David Caleb and Ann Britt (Eyre) of Sutton, farmer, bapt. 29th March by Ralph Heathcote.

John son of Joseph and Amy Sales (Brailsford) of Duckmanton, labourer, bapt. 4th April by T.B. Lucas.

Mary dau. of William and Sarah Lievesley (Frith) of Duckmanton, butcher, bapt. 4th April by T.B. Lucas.

Jemima dau. of Benjamin and Elizabeth Marsden (Thorpe) of Duckmanton Moor Top, wheelwright, bapt. 14th June by T.B. Lucas.

William son of Hugh and Sarah Heath (Lowe) of Sutton, blacksmith, bapt. 5th July by T.B. Lucas.

Sophia dau. of William and Sarah Lloyd (D'Ewis) of Duckmanton, labourer, bapt. 11th Aug. by T.B. Lucas.

James son of William and Ann Lievesley of Duckmanton, labourer, bapt. 30th Aug. by T.B. Lucas. N.B. Her husband had absconded and she had the child in his absence.

Mary dau. of William and Elizabeth Britt (Britt) of Duckmanton, farmer, bapt. 1st Sept. by T.B. Lucas.

Rebecca dau. of Thomas and Rebecca Woodhead of Duckmanton Furnace, labourer, bapt. 13th Sept. by T.B. Lucas.

George son of Samuel and Mary Unwin (Woodhead) of Duckmanton Furnace, labourer, bapt. 18th Oct. by T.B. Lucas.

John son of William and Ann Hayward (Lievesley) of Bakewell, now at Duckmanton, labourer, bapt. 25th Oct. by T.B. Lucas.

Charlotte dau. of John and Charlotte Meakin (Saxilby) of Sutton, labourer, bapt. 25th Oct. by T.B. Lucas.

James son of William and Mary Revill (Mills) of Duckmanton, labourer, bapt. 26th Oct. by T.B. Lucas.

Mary dau. of Samuel and Mary Johnson (Clayton) of Duckmanton Moor Top, blacksmith, bapt. 6th Dec. by T.B. Lucas.

Martha dau. of Samuel and Catharine Renshaw (Greaves) of Duckmanton Moor Top, farmer, bapt. 29th Dec. by T.B. Lucas.

Henry son of John and Mary Cooper (Parker) of Duckmanton, labourer, bapt. 25th Jan. by T.B. Lucas.

Joseph (posthumous) son of late Thomas and Helen Cooke (Bamford) of Far Duckmanton, labourer, bapt. 23rd Feb. by T.B. Lucas.

Ann dau. of Henry and Elizabeth Cutt (Wragg) of Inkersall, at present at Sutton, glazier, bapt. 21st March by T.B. Lucas.

George son of Elizabeth Meakin, spinster of Duckmanton bapt. 8th April by T.B. Lucas.

John son of Humphrey and Elizabeth Brookes (Pogmore) of Duckmanton Moor, labourer, bapt. 18th April by T.B. Lucas.

Richard son of William and Mary Chapman (Dean) of Duckmanton, coalminer, bapt. 19th April by T.B. Lucas.

Robert son of Elizabeth Pearce, spinster of Duckmanton, bapt. 19th April by T.B. Lucas.

Joseph son of John and Mary Jepson (Spray) of Sutton, labourer, bapt. 9th May by T.B. Lucas.

Rebecca dau. of Richard and Jane Birkett (Marshall) of Long Course, farmer, bapt. 6th June by T.B. Lucas.

William son of Robert and Lydia Gee (Booker) of Duckmanton, labourer, bapt. 20th June by T.B. Lucas.

Mary dau. of John and Mary Marsh (Bentley) of Sutton, farmer, bapt. 27th June by T.B. Lucas.

Hannah dau. of Thomas and Hannah Cantrell (Holland) of Duckmanton Moor Top, labourer, bapt. 25th July by T.B. Lucas.

William son of William and Sarah Lievesley (Frith) of Duckmanton, butcher, bapt. 2nd Aug. by J. Ashbridge.

James son of Julia Ann Taylor, spinster of Sutton bapt. 22nd Aug. by T.B. Lucas.

Sarah dau. of Thomas and Hannah Barlow (Frith) of Duckmanton, labourer, bapt. 12th Sept. by T.B. Lucas.

Sarah dau. of Joseph and Elizabeth Horton (Newton) of Sutton, schoolmaster, bapt. 3rd Oct. by T.B. Lucas.

James son of James Plant junior and Mary Plant (Smith) of Duckmanton, farmer, bapt. 21st Oct. by T.B. Lucas.

Ann dau. of James and Hannah Fidler (Beardmore) of Sutton Mill, miller and farmer, bapt. 24th Oct. by T.B. Lucas.

Harriet dau. of John and Elizabeth Flint (Sheppard) of Sutton, labourer, bapt. 24th Oct. by T.B. Lucas.

Charlotte dau. of William and Jane Wragg (Saxelby) of Sutton, mason, bapt. 11th Nov. by T.B. Lucas.

Joseph son of Thomas and Sarah Slack (Barlow) of Duckmanton, labourer, bapt. 12th Dec. by T.B. Lucas.

Ann dau. of William and Hannah Heath (Sales) of Sutton, blacksmith, bapt. 19th Dec. by T.B. Lucas.

1820

George son of George and Jane Blanksby (Eastwood) of Duckmanton, labourer, bapt. 16th Jan. by T.B. Lucas.

Mary dau. of Richard and Elizabeth Charlesworth (Kenyon) of Duckmanton, mason, bapt. 1st Feb. by Rev. W. Carlisle, rector.

Mary dau. of Thomas and Mary Bennett (Eastwood) of Duckmanton, labourer, bapt. 29th March by T.B. Lucas.

Samuel son of John and Mary Cooper (Parker) of Duckmanton, labourer, bapt. 22nd April by T.B. Lucas.

Helen dau. of Mary Wilcockson spinster of Brampton, bapt. 7th May by T.B. Lucas.

Elizabeth dau. of Hezekiah and Alice Saviere (King) of Duckmanton Furnace, labourer, bapt. 7th May by T.B. Lucas.

Sarah dau. of George and Elizabeth White (Smith) of Duckmanton, labourer, bapt. 19th May by T.B. Lucas.

Sarah dau. of William and Sarah Turner (Coates) of Duckmanton Furnace, moulder, bapt. 21st May by T.B. Lucas.

Mary dau. of Paul and Anne Unwin (Sales) of Duckmanton, labourer, bapt. 23rd May by T.B. Lucas.

Septimus son of Humphrey and Elizabeth Brookes (Pogmore) of Sutton, labourer, bapt. 7th June by T.B. Lucas.

Caleb son of David Caleb and Ann Britt (Eyre) of Sutton, farmer, bapt. 11th June by T.B. Lucas.

Sarah dau. of William and Amy Hewitt (Johnson) of Sutton, labourer, bapt. 18th June by T.B. Lucas.

Amy dau. of Joseph and Amy Sales (Brailsford) of Duckmanton, labourer, bapt. 29th June by T.B. Lucas.

Ellen dau. of John and Mary Sharman (Wells) of Sutton, labourer, bapt. 9th July by Ralph Heathcote.

Edward son of William and Margaret Pearce (Woodhead) of Duckmanton, farmer, bapt. 30th Aug. by T.B. Lucas.

George son of William and Elizabeth Britt (Britt) of Duckmanton, farmer, bapt. 30th Aug. by T.B. Lucas.

Mary dau. of Henry and Elizabeth Cutt (Wragg) of Inkersall, at present at Sutton, glazier, bapt. 17th Sept. by T.B. Lucas.

William son of James and Grace Blanksby (Whitcomb) of Duckmanton Furnace, labourer, bapt. 24th Sept. by T.B. Lucas.

Caroline dau. of Benjamin and Elizabeth Marsden (Thorpe) of Duckmanton Moor Top, wheelwright, bapt. 21st Oct. at Chesterfield by Rev. Mr Hall.

Hannah dau. of Mary Taylor, spinster now at Duckmanton, bapt. 29th Oct. by T.B. Lucas.

Matthew son of Matthew and Mary Charlton (Bower) of Duckmanton Moor Top, butcher, bapt. 10th Dec. by T.B. Lucas.

1821

Sarah dau. of Thomas and Charlotte Lievesley (Ward) late of Sheffield, now at Duckmanton, labourer, bapt. 1st Jan. by T.B. Lucas.

Sarah dau. of Thomas and Rebecca Woodhead (Woodhead) of Duckmanton Furnace, labourer, bapt. 11th March by T.B. Lucas.

John Newton son of Joseph and Elizabeth Horton (Newton) of Sutton, schoolmaster, bapt. 11th March by T.B. Lucas.

Emma dau. of William and Mary Chapman (Dean) of Duckmanton, coalminer, bapt. 29th April by T.B. Lucas.

Mary dau. of William and Elizabeth Davison (Cantrell) of Duckmanton Moor Top, labourer, bapt. 13th May by the Rev. Mr Wagstaff.

William son of Henry and Sarah Revill (Lievesley) of Duckmanton, labourer, bapt. 29th July by T.B. Lucas.

Ann dau. of Joseph and Hannah Jarvis (Cooper) of Duckmanton, labourer, bapt. 29th July by T.B. Lucas.

George son of Charles and Martha Eastwood (Wheelhouse) of Duckmanton Furnace, bapt. 2nd Sept. by T.B. Lucas.

Matthew son of John and Mary Jepson (Spray) of Sutton, labourer, bapt. 21st Oct. by T.B. Lucas.

John son of Hugh and Sarah Heath (Lowe) of Calow, blacksmith, bapt. 21st Oct. by T.B. Lucas.

Richard son of Thomas and Hannah Barlow (Frith) of Duckmanton, labourer, bapt. 13th Nov. by T.B. Lucas.

John son of William and Sarah Lievesley (Frith) of Duckmanton, Butcher, bapt. 13th Nov. by T.B. Lucas.

Ann dau. of Thomas and Mary Bennett (Eastwood) of Duckmanton, labourer, bapt. 13th Nov. by T.B. Lucas.

Benjamin son of Benjamin and Elizabeth Marsden (Thorpe) of Duckmanton Moor Top, wheelwright, bapt. 18th Nov. by T.B. Lucas.

Ann dau. of William and Ann Rodgers (Renshaw) of Sutton, under-gamekeeper, bapt. 25th Dec. by T.B. Lucas.

Mary dau. of James and Hannah Fidler (Beardmore) of Sutton Mill, miller and farmer, bapt. 3rd Feb. by Rev. W. Williams.

Isaac son of John and Mary Walker (Walker) of Duckmanton Furnace, labourer, bapt. 23rd Feb. by T.B. Lucas.

Hannah dau. of Paul and Ann Unwin (Sales) of Duckmanton, labourer, bapt. 18th March by T.B. Lucas.

John son of Thomas and Hannah Cantrell (Holland) of Duckmanton Moor Top, labourer, bapt. 31st March by T.B. Lucas.

Thomas son of Thomas and Charlotte Lievesley (Ward) of Duckmanton, labourer, bapt. 28th April by T.B. Lucas.

Benjamin illegitimate son of Helen Cooke (Bamford) of Far Duckmanton, widow, bapt. 28th March at Bolsover by W.C. Tinsley.

George son of Robert and Lydia Gee (Booker) of Duckmanton, labourer, bapt. 27th May by T.B. Lucas.

Elizabeth dau. of Richard and Elizabeth Charlesworth of Duckmanton, mason, bapt. 23rd June by T.B. Lucas.

Mary dau. of John and Mary Cooper (Parker) of Duckmanton, labourer, bapt. 4th Aug. by T.B. Lucas.

Elizabeth dau. of David Caleb and Anne Britt (Eyre) of Sutton, farmer, bapt. 18th Aug. by T.B. Lucas.

Edward son of Joseph and Amy Sales (Brailsford) of Duckmanton, labourer, bapt. 18th Aug. by T.B. Lucas.

George son of Humphrey and Elizabeth Brookes (Pogmore) of Sutton, labourer, bapt. 28th Oct. by T.B. Lucas.

Mary dau. of Joseph and Elizabeth Horton (Newton) of Sutton, schoolmaster, bapt. 3rd Nov. by T.B. Lucas.

Charles son of John and Mary Jepson (Spray) of Sutton, labourer, bapt. 17th Nov. by T.B. Lucas.

William son of William and Elizabeth Britt (Britt) of Duckmanton, farmer, bapt. 29th Nov. by T.B. Lucas.

Mary dau. of James and Grace Blanksby (Whitcomb) of Duckmanton Furnace, labourer, bapt. 8th Dec. by T.B. Lucas.

1823

William son of John and Alice Johnson (Varley) of Duckmanton, labourer, bapt. 9th Jan. by T.B. Lucas.

Elizabeth dau. of William and Elizabeth Davison (Cantrell) of Duckmanton Moor Top, labourer, privately bapt. at Chesterfield by Rev. Mr Hill.

Ann dau. of Thomas and Martha Clarke (Shaw) of Duckmanton Moor Top, labourer, bapt. 19th Jan. by T.B. Lucas.

George son of Hezekiah and Alice Saviere (King) of Duckmanton Furnace, labourer, bapt. 23rd Feb. by Rev. Mr Fields, vicar of Brimington.

Mary dau. of William and Mary Chapman (Dean) of Duckmanton, coalminer, bapt. 30th March by T.B. Lucas.

Josiah Timmis son of Benjamin and Harriet Smith (Timmis) of Duckmanton Moor Top, iron master, bapt. 30th March by T.B. Lucas, curate.

Frances dau. of Richard and Jane Birkett (Marshall) of Long Course, farmer, bapt. 11th May by A. Auriol Barker.

Elizabeth dau. of William and Amy Hewitt (Johnson) of Sutton, labourer, bapt. 18th May by A.A. Barker.

Sarah illegitimate dau. of Anne Riggot, spinster of Duckmanton bapt. 15th June by A.A. Barker.

John son of John and Hannah Nixon (Britt) of Normanton bapt. 20th July by A.A. Barker.

Jane illegitimate dau. of Anne Taylor, spinster of Duckmanton bapt. 3rd Aug. by A.A. Barker.

Frederick son of Joseph and Elizabeth Horton (Newton) of Sutton, schoolmaster, bapt. 21st Sept. by A.A. Barker, curate.

Eliza dau. of Thomas and Rebecca Woodhead (Woodhead) of Duckmanton Furnace, labourer, bapt. 28th Sept. by A.A. Barker.

George son of Solomon and Rebecca Wickdom (Harvey) of Duckmanton Furnace, labourer, bapt. 5th Oct. by A.A. Barker.

James son of Ann Barber widow of Duckmanton bapt. 19th Oct. by A.A. Barker.

Joseph posthumous son of late Joseph and Hannah Jarvis (Cooper) of Duckmanton, labourer, bapt. 2nd Nov. by A.A. Barker.

Joseph son of Hugh and Sarah Heath (Lowe) of Calow, blacksmith, bapt. 16th Nov. by Mr Arnold.

James son of Charles and Martha Eastwood (Wheelhouse) of Duckmanton Furnace, labourer, bapt. 23rd Nov. by A.A. Barker.

Elizabeth dau. of Samuel and Mary Unwin of Duckmanton Furnace, labourer, bapt. 23rd Nov. by A.A. Barker.

Hannah dau. of John and Sarah Bennett (Sales) of Duckmanton, tailor, bapt. 23rd Nov. by A.A. Barker.

George son of William and Hannah Heath (Sales) of Sutton, blacksmith, privately bapt. 1st Dec. by J.Ashbridge.

Ellen twin of the above, dau. of William and Hannah Heath (Sales) privately bapt. 1st Dec. by J. Ashbridge.

William son of Joseph and Anne Plant (Waller) of Duckmanton, farmer, bapt. 23rd Dec. by A.A. Barker.

1824

Ann dau. of John and Ann Revill (Pogmore) of Duckmanton, labourer, bapt. 3rd Feb. by A.A. Barker.

Joseph son of William and Ann Rodgers (Renshaw) of Sutton, under-game-keeper, bapt. 22nd Feb. by A.A. Barker.

Richard son of George and Ellen Marsh (Frith) of Sutton, tailor, privately bapt. 17th March by J. Ashbridge.

Thomas son of Thomas and Hannah Barlow (Frith) of Duckmanton, labourer, bapt. 30th March by A.A. Barker.

Elizabeth dau. of Sam and Elizabeth Lievesley (Meakin) of Duckmanton, labourer, bapt. 10th April by A.A. Barker.

Sarah dau. of John and Sarah Sales (Hewitt) of Duckmanton, butcher, 5th May by A.A. Barker.

Joseph son of James and Hannah Fidler (Beardmore) of Sutton Mill, miller and farmer, bapt. 7th May by A.A. Barker.

Thomas son of Thomas and Mary Bennett (Eastwood) of Duckmanton, labourer, bapt. 16th May by A.A. Barker.

Charlotte dau. of Joseph and Amy Sales (Brailsford) of Duckmanton, labourer, bapt. 4th July by A.A. Barker.

Thomas illegitimate son of Mary Jarvis, spinster of Duckmanton bapt. 25th July by George Alderson, curate.

Richard son of Richard and Elizabeth Charlesworth of Duckmanton, mason, bapt. 30th Aug. by G. Alderson.

Herbert son of John and Mary Walker of Duckmanton Furnace, labourer, bapt. 30th Aug. by G. Alderson.

Anne dau. of William and Sarah Lievesley (Frith) of Duckmanton, labourer, bapt. 19th Sept. by G. Alderson.

Stephen son of John and Mary Jepson (Spray) of Sutton, labourer, bapt. 3rd Oct. by G. Alderson.

Elizabeth dau. of Paul and Ann Unwin (Sales) of Duckmanton, labourer, bapt. 17th Oct. by G. Alderson.

Hannah illegitimate dau. of Rhoda Wheelhouse of Duckmanton Furnace bapt. 21st Oct. by G. Alderson.

John son of John and Alice Johnson (Varley) of Duckmanton, labourer, bapt. 19th Dec. by G. Alderson.

1825

Thomas son of Hugh and Sarah Heath (Lowe) of Calow, blacksmith, bapt. 9th Jan. by G. Alderson.

Sarah dau. of James and Grace Blanksby (Whitcomb) of Duckmanton Furnace, labourer, bapt. 23rd Jan. by G. Alderson.

John Pepper son of Thomas and Sarah Wragg (Pepper) of Sutton, farmer, bapt. 27th Jan. by G. Alderson.

William son of William and Elizabeth Davison (Cantrell) of Duckmanton Moor Top, labourer, privately bapt. 30th Jan. by Rev. Mr Knox of Chesterfield.

Ann dau. of John and Sarah Sales (Hewitt) of Duckmanton, butcher, bapt. 2nd Feb. by G. Alderson.

William son of John and Elizabeth Flint (Sheppard) of Sutton, labourer, bapt. 20th Feb. by G. Alderson.

Ellen dau. of Joseph and Ann Plant (Waller) of Duckmanton, farmer, bapt. 7th March by G. Alderson.

William son of John and Jane Wood (Johnson) of Duckmanton, labourer, bapt. 28th March by G. Alderson.

Sarah dau. of Solomon and Rebecca Wickdom (Harvey) of Duckmanton Furnace, labourer, bapt. 30th March by G. Alderson.

Hannah dau. of David Caleb and Anne Britt (Eyre) of Sutton, farmer, bapt. 17th April by G. Alderson.

Anne dau. of William and Mary Watkinson (Platts) of Sutton, labourer, bapt. 7th May by G. Alderson.

Mary dau. of Thomas and Martha Clarke (Shaw) of Duckmanton Moor Top, labourer, bapt. 16th May by G. Alderson.

Sarah dau. of James and Anne Booth of Duckmanton, shoemaker, bapt. 26th June by G. Alderson.

George illegitimate son of Ann Watts, *pro tempore* Duckmanton, spinster bapt. 3rd July by G. Alderson.

William son of William and Mary Chapman (Dean) of Duckmanton, coalminer, bapt. 5th Sept. by G. Alderson.

Sarah dau. of Joseph and Ann Nixon (Smith) of Duckmanton, labourer, bapt. 12th Sept. by G. Alderson.

Emma dau. of John and Sarah Bennett (Sales) of Duckmanton, tailor, bapt. 25th Sept. by G. Alderson.

George son of Hezekiah and Alice Saviere (King) of Duckmanton Furnace, labourer, bapt. 21st Nov. by G. Alderson.

1826

Herbert son of William and Margaret Pearce (Woodhead) of Duckmanton, farmer, bapt. 2nd Jan. by G. Alderson.

Samuel son of Charles and Martha Eastwood (Wheelhouse) of Duckmanton Furnace, labourer, bapt. 10th Jan, by G. Alderson.

Mary dau. of William and Hannah Heath (Sales) of Sutton, blacksmith, bapt. 29th Jan. by G. Alderson.

Harriot dau. of Thomas and Rebecca Woodhead (Woodhead) of Duckmanton Furnace, labourer, bapt. 7th Feb. by G. Alderson.

Ann illegitimate dau. of Rhoda Wheelhouse of Duckmanton Furnace bapt. 7th Feb. by G. Alderson.

Sarah dau. of Aaron and Ann Jarvis of Chesterfield, coachmaker, bapt. 19th March by G. Alderson.

Richard son of Joseph and Elizabeth Horton (Newton) of Sutton, schoolmaster, bapt. 2nd April by G. Alderson.

Esther dau. of John and Alice Johnson of Duckmanton, labourer, bapt. 3rd April by G. Alderson.

Martha dau. of Thomas and Mary Bennett of Duckmanton, labourer, bapt. 23rd April by G. Alderson.

Ann illegitimate dau. of Jane Beresford spinster of Duckmanton bapt. 30th April by G. Alderson.

Mary dau. of John and Ann Revill of Duckmanton, labourer, bapt. 15th May by G. Alderson.

William son of John and Sarah Sales of Duckmanton, butcher, bapt. 28th May by G. Alderson.

Elizabeth dau. of Richard and Elizabeth Charlesworth of Bolsover Lane, mason, bapt. 29th May G. Alderson.

Frances dau. of Thomas and Hannah Barlow of Duckmanton, labourer, bapt. 30th July by Rev. Cragg.

Charles son of John and Jane Wood of Duckmanton, labourer, bapt. 17th Sept. by Rev. W. Carlisle, rector.

Charles son of James and Hannah Fidler of Sutton Mill, miller, bapt. 21st Oct. by William Badnall, curate.

Charles son of Thomas and Sarah Meakin of Duckmanton, wheelwright, bapt. 7th Nov. by William Badnall.

Thomas son of George and Mary Robinson of Duckmanton, blacksmith, bapt. 13th Nov. by W. Badnall.

Sarah dau. of Moses and Ann Turner of Duckmanton, moulder, bapt. 11th Dec. by W. Badnall.

1827

Ellen dau. of William and Ellen Ward of Duckmanton, labourer, bapt. 15th Jan. by W. Badnall.

Jane dau. of William and Elizabeth Davison of Duckmanton Moor Top, labourer, bapt. 24th Feb. by W. Badnall.

Ann dau. of Thomas and Ann Reddish of Duckmanton, labourer, bapt. 4th March by John Hand.

Joseph son of William and Sarah Lievesley (Frith) of Duckmanton, labourer, bapt. 1st April by W. Badnall.

George son of Thomas and Maria Watkinson (Sheppard) of Sutton, shoemaker, bapt. 13th May by W. Badnall.

William son of Sampson and Hannah Johnson of Far Duckmanton, farmer, bapt. 14th May by W. Badnall.

Henry son of Henry and Sarah Revill (Lievesley) of Duckmanton, labourer, bapt. 15th July by W.C. Tinsley of Bolsover.

Emma dau. of William and Hannah Taylor of Duckmanton Furnace, moulder, bapt. 23rd July by W. Badnall.

Eliza dau. of William and Mary Chapman (Dean) of Middle Duckmanton, coalminer, bapt. 1st Aug. by W. Badnall.

Elizabeth dau. of John and Alice Johnson (Varley) of Middle Duckmanton, labourer, bapt. 2nd Sept. by Samuel Revell.

Sarah dau. of Thomas and Martha Clarke (Shaw) of Duckmanton Moor Top, labourer, privately bapt. 10th Sept. by Rev. T. Fields.

Mary dau. of Joseph and Mary Reddish of Duckmanton, labourer, bapt. 16th Sept. by S. Revell.

Charles son of Charles and Martha Eastwood of Duckmanton Furnace, labourer, bapt. 14th Oct. by S. Revell.

Abraham son of David Caleb and Ann Britt (Eyre) of Sutton, farmer, bapt. 14th Oct. by S. Revell.

George son of Paul and Ann Unwin (Sales) of Duckmanton, labourer, bapt. 28th Oct. by S. Revell.

Sarah dau. of William and Ann Pirsglove (Lievesley) of Duckmanton, labourer, bapt. 30th Oct. by S. Revell.

John son of John and Sarah Bennett (Sales) of Duckmanton, tailor, bapt. 30th Dec. by S. Revell.

1828

Matthew son of John and Mary Cooper (Parker) of Duckmanton, labourer, bapt. by S. Revell.

Mary dau. of Robert and Lydia Gee (Booker) of Duckmanton, labourer, bapt. 2nd March. by S. Revell.

Elizabeth dau. of James and Grace Blanksby of Duckmanton Furnace, labourer, bapt. 16th March by S. Revell.

Abraham illegitimate son of Rhoda Wheelhouse of Far Duckmanton bapt. 23rd March by S. Revell.

Mary dau. of Joseph and Elizabeth Bennett of Far Duckmanton, labourer, bapt. 30th March by S. Revell.

Benjamin son of Joseph and Ann Plant (Waller) of Duckmanton, farmer, bapt. 11th April by Rev. S. Foxlowe.

Mary dau. of John and Elizabeth Godfrey of Duckmanton, labourer, bapt. 27th April by S. Revell.

Ann dau. of Thomas and Rebecca Woodhead (Woodhead) of Duckmanton Furnace, labourer, bapt. 8th June by S. Revell.

William illegitimate son of Amy Sharman spinster of Sutton bapt. 25th July by S. Revell.

Elizabeth illegitimate dau. of Mary Jarvis spinster of Duckmanton bapt. 17th Aug. by S. Revell.

Hannah dau. of John and Ann Revell (Pogmore) of Duckmanton, labourer, bapt. 31st Aug. by S. Revell.

Margaret dau. of Thomas and Mary Nix (Turner) of Sutton, farmer, bapt. 12th Oct. by S. Revell.

Harriot dau. of William and Hannah Heath (Sales) of Sutton, blacksmith, bapt. 12th Oct. by S. Revell.

Herbert illegitimate son of Frances Johnson spinster of Far Duckmanton bapt. 12th Oct. by S. Revell.

Hannah dau. of Thomas and Martha Clarke (Shaw) of Duckmanton Moor Top, labourer, bapt. 9th Nov. by S. Revell.

John son of John and Sarah Sales (Hewitt) of Duckmanton, butcher, bapt. 21st Dec. by Rev. S. Foxlowe.

Ann dau. of Joseph and Mary Reddish (Atkin) of Duckmanton, labourer, bapt. 28th Dec. by S. Revell.

1829

Paul and Matthew twin sons of Thomas and Mary Bennett of Duckmanton, labourer, bapt. 4th Jan. by S. Revell.

John Henry son of George and Ellen Marsh (Frith) of Sutton, tailor, bapt. 11th Jan. by S. Revell.

Joseph son of Matthew and Sarah Oates (Barlow) of Duckmanton, victualler, bapt. 25th Jan. by S. Revell.

Sydney son of Thomas and Maria Watkinson (Sheppard) of Sutton, shoemaker, bapt. 8th Feb. by S. Revell.

Eliza dau. of Solomon and Rebecca Whitcombe (Harvey) of Duckmanton Furnace, labourer, bapt. 9th May by S. Revell.

John son of George and Mary Robinson (Walker) of Duckmanton, blacksmith, bapt. 28th June by S. Revell.

John son of William and Elizabeth Bennett (Machin) of Duckmanton, labourer, bapt. 29th June by S. Revell.

Sandom son of William and Betty Davison (Cantrell) of Duckmanton Moor Top, labourer, bapt. 12th July by S. Revell.

Peggy dau. of William and Sarah Lievesley (Frith) of Duckmanton, labourer, bapt. 12th July by S. Revell.

William son of George and Ann Shaw (Harvey) of Duckmanton Moor, labourer, bapt. 26th July by S. Revell.

Eliza dau. of William and Ann Rodgers (Renshaw) of Sutton, gamekeeper, bapt. 4th Oct. by S. Revell.

Ann dau. of John and Mary Frith (Fearne) of Duckmanton, labourer, bapt. 5th Oct. by S. Revell.

Hannah and Martha twin daus. of Thomas and Hannah Barlow (Frith) of Duckmanton, labourer, bapt. 11th Oct. by S. Revell.

Mary Ann dau. of Samuel and Elizabeth Leivesley (Makin) of Duckmanton, labourer, bapt. 16th Oct. by S. Revell.

John son of William and Ann Pirslove (Lievesley) of Duckmanton, labourer, bapt. 25th Oct. by S. Revell.

Peter son of Alsop and Hannah Smith (Eyre) of Sutton, farmer, bapt. 4th Nov. by J. Ashbridge.

1830

John son of William and Mary Chapman (Dean) of Middle Duckmanton, coalminer, bapt. 28th March by S. Revell.

William illegitimate son of Rhoda Wheelhouse spinster of Far Duckmanton bapt. 25th April by S. Revell.

William son of George and Mary Revell of Far Duckmanton, labourer, bapt. 16th May by S. Revell.

Edward son of John and Alice Johnson (Varlow) of Middle Duckmanton, labourer, bapt. 16th May by S. Revell.

Joe son of Joseph and Elizabeth Bennett of Far Duckmanton, labourer, bapt. 27th June by S. Revell.

George son of William and Amy Wood (Sharman) of Sutton, labourer, bapt. 25th July by S. Revell.

John son of Thomas and Amy Gelstrap of Duckmanton Furnace, labourer, bapt. 29th Aug. by S. Revell.

Ellen dau. of John and Elizabeth Godfrey of Duckmanton, labourer, bapt. 29th Aug. by S. Revell.

Grace dau. of Thomas and Rebecca Woodhead of Duckmanton Furnace, labourer, bapt. 19th Sept. by S. Revell.

Daniel son of Thomas and Maria Watkinson (Sheppard) of Sutton, shoemaker, bapt. 3rd Oct. by S. Revell.

Sarah dau. of Robert and Hannah Taylor of Sutton, labourer, bapt. 17th Oct. by S. Revell.

Elizabeth dau. of Hugh and Elizabeth Heath (Lowe) of Calow, blacksmith, bapt. 5th Dec. by S. Revell.

Hannah illegitimate dau. of Jane Beresford spinster of Duckmanton bapt. 12th Dec. by S. Revell.

1831

Hannah dau. of Joseph and Ann Plant (Waller) of Duckmanton, farmer, bapt. 20th Feb. by S. Revell.

John son of Joseph and Mary Reddish (Atkin) of Duckmanton, labourer, bapt. 24th April by S. Revell.

Elizabeth dau. of Thomas and Sarah Wragg (Pepper) of Sutton Mill, miller and farmer, bapt. 24th April by S. Revell.

William son of John and Mary Jepson (Oakley) of Sutton, labourer, bapt. 24th April by S. Revell.

Henry son of Solomon and Rebecca Whitcombe (Harvey) of Duckmanton Furnace, labourer, bapt. 29th May by S. Revell.

Luke son of Thomas and Mary Bennett (Eastwood) of Duckmanton, labourer, bapt. 26th June by J.W. Luch, curate.

Hannah dau. of William and Ann Pirsglove (Lievesley) of Duckmanton, labourer, bapt. 26th June by S. Revell.

Bernard illegitimate son of Charlotte Watkinson spinster of Sutton bapt. 14th Aug. by S. Revell.

Thomas son of William and Hannah Ordish of Sutton, gamekeeper, bapt. 4th Sept. by S. Revell.

Rhoda Marinna dau. of William and Betty Davison (Cantrell) of Duckmanton Moor Top, coalminer, bapt. 4th Sept. by S. Revell.

Elizabeth dau. of William and Sarah Lievesley (Frith) of Duckmanton, labourer, bapt. 11th Sept. by S. Revell.

George son of Thomas and Martha Clarke (Shaw) of Duckmanton Moor Top, labourer, bapt. 16th Oct. by S. Revell.

John son of Thomas and Sarah Meakin of Duckmanton, wheelwright, bapt. 16th Oct. by S. Revell.

Elizabeth dau. of Alsop and Hannah Smith (Eyre) of Sutton, farmer, bapt. 30th Oct. by S. Revell.

Emma illegitimate dau. of Rhoda Wheelhouse spinster of Far Duckmanton bapt. 8th Jan. by S. Revell.

Elizabeth dau. of William and Elizabeth Bennett (Machin) of Duckmanton, labourer, bapt. 22nd Jan. by S. Revell.

Joseph son of Paul and Ann Unwin (Sales) of Duckmanton, labourer, bapt. 22nd Jan. by S. Revell.

Joseph son of Thomas and Hannah Barlow (Frith) of Duckmanton, labourer, bapt. 26th Feb. by S. Revell.

Elizabeth dau. of John and Sarah Sales (Hewitt) of Duckmanton, labourer, bapt. 26th Feb. by S. Revell.

Hebron son of Daniel and Hannah Piggin of Sutton, brickmaker, bapt. 11th March by S. Revell.

William son of William and Hannah Heath (Sales) of Sutton, blacksmith, bapt. 25th March by S. Revell.

Tamer dau. of Thomas and Maria Watkinson (Sheppard) of Sutton, shoemaker, bapt. 22nd April by S. Revell.

John son of William and Ann Cooper of Duckmanton, moulder, bapt. 13th May by S. Revell.

George son of George and Mary Revell of Far Duckmanton, labourer, bapt. 11th June by Rev. Fletcher.

Jemima dau. of William and Mary Chapman (Dean) of Middle Duckmanton, coalminer, bapt. 17th June by S. Revell.

Ann dau. of John and Mary Cooper (Parker) of Duckmanton, labourer, bapt. 8th July by S. Revell.

Ann dau. of John and Alice Johnson (Varlow) of Duckmanton, labourer, bapt. 15th July by S. Revell.

George son of William and Amy Wood (Sharman) of Sutton, labourer, bapt. 29th July by S. Revell.

Ellen illegitimate dau. of Ann Hewitt spinster of Sutton bapt. 26th Aug. by S. Revell.

Ellen dau. of Thomas and Rebecca Woodhead of Duckmanton Furnace, labourer, bapt. 26th Aug. by S. Revell.

Patience dau. of John and Ann White (Hibbard) of Sutton, farmer, bapt. 4th Sept. by S. Revell.

Eliza illegitimate dau. of Ruth Sharman spinster of Sutton bapt. 16th Sept. by S. Revell.

William son of Joseph and Elizabeth Bennett of Far Duckmanton, labourer, bapt. 2nd Dec. by S. Revell.

George illegitimate son of Ann Lievesley widow of Duckmanton bapt. 1st Jan. by S. Revell.

Eliza dau. of Joseph and Mary Tansley (Unwin) of Duckmanton Furnace, blacksmith, bapt. 13th Jan. by S. Revell.

Eliza dau. of David Caleb and Ann Britt (Eyre) of Sutton, farmer, bapt. 28th Jan. by S. Revell.

George son of George and Ann Holmes of Duckmanton, labourer, bapt. 24th March by S. Revell.

Samuel son of William and Hannah Shaw (Brailsford) of Duckmanton Moor, labourer, bapt. 21st April by S. Revell.

Ann dau. of Charles and Martha Eastwood of Duckmanton Furnace, moulder, bapt. 5th May by S. Revell.

William son of Charles and Martha Eastwood of Duckmanton Furnace, moulder, bapt. 5th May by S. Revell.

William son of Robert and Hannah Taylor of Sutton, labourer, bapt. 5th May by S. Revell.

Emma illegitimate dau. of Sarah Heath spinster of Sutton bapt. 12th May by S. Revell.

John son of John and Ann Revell (Pogmore) of Duckmanton, labourer, bapt. 2nd June by S. Revell.

John son of Solomon and Rebecca Whitcombe (Harvey) of Duckmanton Furnace, labourer, bapt. 9th June by S. Revell.

John son of William and Harriot Brookes (Sheppard) of Duckmanton Moor, labourer, bapt. 30th June by S. Revell.

Thomas son of Thomas and Sarah Wragg (Pepper) of Sutton Mill, miller and farmer, privately bapt. 11th July by John Knight, minister of Bolsover.

Frances dau. of Joseph and Ann Plant (Waller) of Duckmanton, labourer, bapt. 14th July by S. Revell.

Charles son of Luke and Jane Plats (Coulson) of Duckmanton, labourer, bapt. 28th July by S. Revell.

John son of Thomas and Maria Watkinson (Sheppard) of Sutton, shoemaker, bapt. 25th Aug. by Richard Ward, rector.

Ellen dau. of Samuel and Elizabeth Twelves (Blanksby) of Duckmanton, moulder, bapt. 1st Sept. by Henry Barlow, curate of Dethick.

Mary dau. of John and Elizabeth Unwin (Flint) of Duckmanton, moulder, bapt. 27th Oct. by William Fletcher, curate of Wingerworth.

Reuben posthumous son of George and Mary Revell of Far Duckmanton, labourer, bapt. 15th Dec. by William Fletcher.

Harriett dau. of William and Elizabeth Davison of Duckmanton Moor, coalminer, bapt. [*No date*] by William Fletcher.

Ann Hibbard dau. of John and Ann White (Hibbard) of Sutton, farmer, bapt. 24th Jan. by William Fletcher.

George son of Samuel and Sarah Nixon of Duckmanton, labourer, bapt. 21st Feb. by William Fletcher.

Samuel son of Joseph and Rhoda Richards of Far Duckmanton, labourer, bapt. 27th Feb. by William Fletcher.

[*The following note is appended to the preceding entry and refers back to the baptism of other childen of the same woman registered in Oct. 1824, Feb. 1826, March 1828, April 1830 and Jan. 1832:*] We the undersigned firmly believe that this ought to have been the mode of registering Nos. 243, 267, 302, 335, 361 in this book, since she co-habited illictly with one Abraham Guit. The above-mentioned Rhoda had we believe been married at Sheffield to Joseph Richards previously to Oct. 1824. Witness our hands this sixth day of May 1835. William Fletcher, curate; George Alsop, church warden.

John son of Henry and Ann Bradley of Sutton, labourer, bapt. 2nd March by William Fletcher.

George Herbert son of Joseph and Eliza Anne Plant (Waller) of Far Duckmanton, farmer, bapt. 22nd March by William Fletcher.

Mary dau. of William and Hannah Ordish of Sutton, gamekeeper, bapt. 23rd March by William Fletcher.

Martha dau. of Thomas and Hannah Barlow of Middle Duckmanton, labourer, bapt. 30th March by William Fletcher.

Mary dau. of Hugh and Elizabeth Heath of Duckmanton Moor, farmer, bapt. 12th April by William Fletcher.

Mary dau. of Alsop and Hannah Smith of Sutton Lane, farmer, bapt. 13th April by William Fletcher.

Alfred son of William and Hannah Heath of Sutton, blacksmith, bapt. 20th April by William Fletcher.

Francis son of Joseph and Elizabeth Pearce of Duckmanton, farmer, bapt. 1st May by William Fletcher.

Herbert son of George and Ellen Marsh of Sutton, parish clerk, bapt. 25th May by William Fletcher.

Mary dau. of George and Ann Shaw of Duckmanton Moor, labourer, bapt. 1st June by William Fletcher.

Joseph son of Thomas and Cecilia Sheppard of Shire Lane, Sutton, labourer, bapt. 21st June by William Fletcher.

James son of Joseph and Mary Reddish of Duckmanton, coalminer, bapt. 14th
July by William Fletcher.

Sarah dau. of William and Anne Cooper of Duckmanton, moulder, bapt. 20th
July by William Fletcher.

Elizabeth dau. of James and Hannah Brookes of Calow, labourer, bapt. 17th
Aug. by William Fletcher.

Thomas son of William and Sarah Lievesley (Frith) of Duckmanton, labourer,
bapt. 31st Aug. by William Fletcher.

Job son of George and Elizabeth Marriott of Duckmanton, blacksmith, bapt. 3rd
Sept. by William Fletcher.

John illegitimate son of Charlotte Bennett spinster of Duckmanton bapt. 7th
Sept. by William Fletcher.

Alfred son of John and Sarah Sales of Duckmanton, victualler, bapt. 19th Sept.
by William Fletcher.

Joseph son of William and Mary Chapman of Middle Duckmanton, coalminer,
bapt. 5th Oct. by William Fletcher.

William son of Thomas and Amy Gilstrip of Duckmanton Furnace, labourer,
bapt. 4th Nov. by William Fletcher.

Hannah dau. of John and Ann Unwin of Duckmanton Moor, labourer, bapt. 21st
Dec. by William Fletcher.

John son of Luke and Jane Platts of Duckmanton, labourer, bapt. 25th Dec. by
William Fletcher by certificate from S. Revell dated 17th Nov. 1834.

1835

Henry son of William and Harriette Brookes of Sutton Lane, engine server, bapt.
10th Feb. by William Fletcher.

Herbert son of Joseph and Anne Plant of Shuttlewood, labourer, bapt. 12th Feb.
by Willliam Fletcher.

Jane dau. of Joseph and Jane Hollingworth of Sutton, farmer, bapt. 3rd May by
T.B. Lucas.

Hannah dau. of Solomom and Rebecca Whitcombe of Duckmanton Furnace,
labourer, bapt. 10th May by T.B. Lucas.

Frederick son of Henry and Sarah Revill of Duckmanton, labourer, bapt. 14th
June by T.B. Lucas.

Eliza dau. of John and Elizabeth Unwin of Sheffield, moulder, bapt. 28th June
by T.B. Lucas.

Sarah dau. of Hugh and Elizabeth Heath of Duckmanton Moor, farmer, bapt. 4th
July by Willam Fletcher.

Thomas son of Thomas and Martha Clarke of Duckmanton Moor Top, labourer,
bapt. 19th July by T.B. Lucas.

Elizabeth Lydia dau. of Joseph and Elizabeth Pearce of New Lodge, Sutton, farmer, bapt. 20th July by William Fletcher.

Sarah Anne dau. of Joseph and Elizabeth Bennett of Far Duckmanton, labourer, bapt. 26th July by T.B. Lucas.

Sarah Anne dau. of William and Sarah Pearce of Bolsover, mercer and draper, bapt. 11th Aug. by William Fletcher.

Margaret dau. of William and Sarah Pearce of Bolsover, mercer and draper, bapt. 11th Aug. by William Fletcher.

Elizabeth dau. of Thomas and Maria Watkinson of Sutton, cordwainer, bapt. 16th Aug. by William Fletcher.

Thomas son of Thomas and Alice Bailey of Sutton, gardener, bapt. 13th Sept. by William Fletcher.

Harriett illegitimate dau. of Anne Bennett spinster of Duckmanton bapt. 13th Sept. by William Fletcher.

William son of John and Anne White of Sutton, farmer, bapt. 24th Sept. by William Fletcher.

Elizabeth illegitimate dau. of Sarah Gee spinster of Duckmanton bapt. 28th Sept. by William Fletcher.

William illegitimate son of Ruth Sharman (now Bown) spinster when child was born, bapt. 4th Oct. by William Fletcher.

Sarah Anne dau. of Francis and Mary Windle of Sutton, labourer, bapt. 25th Oct. by William Fletcher.

John Askey illegitimate son of Patience Brocksopp spinster of Sutton bapt. 26th Oct. by William Fletcher.

Thomas son of George and Ann Shaw of Duckmanton Moor, labourer, bapt. 1st Nov. by T.B. Lucas.

Joseph son of William and Amy Wood of Sutton, labourer, bapt. 14th Nov. by William Fletcher.

Ellen dau. of George and Elizabeth Marriott of Duckmanton, blacksmith, bapt. 1st Dec. by William Fletcher.

William son of Caleb and Frances Ellis of Middle Duckmanton, stone cutter, bapt. 1st Dec. by William Fletcher.

William son of Moses and Anne Turner of Duckmanton Furnace, moulder, bapt. 16th Dec. by William Fletcher.

1836

Harriette dau. of William and Elizabeth Davison of Duckmanton Moor, coalminer, bapt. 17th Jan. by William Fletcher.

Jane dau. of Samuel and Elizabeth Twelves of Duckmanton, moulder, bapt. 13th Feb. by William Fletcher.

John son of Thomas and Cecilia Sheppard of Shire Lane, Sutton, labourer, bapt. 20th March by William Fletcher.

Sarah dau. of Thomas and Sarah Wragg of Long Duckmanton, farmer, privately bapt. 3rd April by H. Arkwright.

Eliza Ann dau. of Joseph and Eliza Ann Plant of Far Duckmanton, farmer, bapt. 1st May by F.W. Sharpe.

Henry son of Luke and Jane Platts of Duckmanton, labourer, bapt. 15th May by F.W. Sharpe.

Sarah dau. of James and Hannah Wilson of Duckmanton Furnace, labourer, bapt. 29th May by F.W. Sharpe.

Herbert son of Henry and Ellen Bagaley of Calow, labourer, bapt. 5th June by F.W. Sharpe.

Henry son of Henry and Mary Ann Weeds of Duckmanton, bricklayer, bapt. 10th July by F.W. Sharpe, curate.

Harriet dau. of John and Elizabeth Cooper of Duckmanton, labourer, bapt. 10th July by F.W. Sharpe, curate.

James illegitimate son of Ann Blanksby of Duckmanton bapt. 25th July by F.W. Sharpe, curate.

Joseph son of Joseph and Jane Hollingworth of Sutton, farmer, bapt. 14th Aug. by F.W. Sharpe.

John son of Thomas and Hannah Barlow of Middle Duckmanton, labourer, bapt. 11th Sept. by F.W. Sharpe.

Robert Hewit son of Robert and Charlotte Limb of Sutton, labourer, bapt. 18th Sept. by F.W. Sharpe.

Robert son of William and Sarah Lievesley of Duckmanton, labourer, bapt. 9th Oct. by F.W. Sharpe, curate.

1837

Hannah dau. of Joseph and Mary Reddish of Duckmanton, labourer, bapt. 8th Jan. by F.W. Sharpe.

Hugh son of Hugh and Elizabeth Heath of Duckmanton, farmer, bapt. 15th Jan. by F.W. Sharpe.

Joseph son of Joseph and Elizabeth Pearce of New Lodge, Sutton, farmer, bapt. 26th March by F.W. Sharpe.

John son of Samuel and Elizabeth Twelves of Duckmanton, labourer, bapt. 2nd April by T.B. Lucas.

Alfred son of Thomas and Maria Watkinson of Duckmanton, shoemaker, bapt. 23rd April by T.B. Lucas.

Mary dau. of Richard and Elizabeth Winfield of Sutton, joiner, bapt. 30th April by T.B. Lucas.

Henry son of Solomon and Rebecca Whitcombe of Duckmanton Furnace, labourer, bapt. 7th May by T.B. Lucas.

Mary dau. of George and Ann Holmes of Duckmanton, labourer, bapt. 7th May by T.B. Lucas.

Herbert illegitimate son of Sarah Lievesley spinster of Duckmanton bapt. 18th May by T.B. Lucas.

William son of George and Ellen Marsh of Sutton, clerk, bapt. 20th May by T.B. Lucas.

John son of John and Ann White of Sutton, farmer, bapt. 11th June by F.W. Sharpe.

REGISTER OF BURIALS
1813–37

1813

Ann Hewitt illegitimate dau. of Jane Hewitt spinster bur. 14th March aged 3 days by W.C. Tinsley – convulsions.

William Cantrell of Duckmanton Moor Top bur. 25th April aged 76 by Ralph Heathcote, curate – decay of nature.

Samuel Pattison of Bolsover, late of Sutton, bur. 29th April aged 86 by W.C. Tinsley – decay of nature.

William Cutts of Duckmanton bur. 26th June aged 59 by W.C. Tinsley.

John Wragg, mason of Sutton bur. 1st Aug. aged 28 by Ralph Heathcote – fistula in spine. (Member of Sutton Friendly Society.)

William Barlow senior of Duckmanton bur. 3rd Oct. aged nearly 99 by W.C. Tinsley – natural decay.

John Lowe of Newdale, Duckmanton, bur. 12th Oct. aged 88 by Ralph Heathcote – natural decay.

Mary Unwin of Duckmanton bur. 14th Nov. aged 74 by Joseph Ashbridge, minister of Heath – cancer.

John infant son of Thomas and Mary Bennett of Duckmanton bur. 21st Dec. aged 2 months by Joseph Ashbridge – convulsions.

Mary wife of William Davidson of Tapton bur. 26th Dec. aged 29 by Ralph Heathcote – mortification.

Joseph infant son of William Davidson of Tapton bur. 29th Dec. aged 3 weeks by Joseph Ashbridge – convulsions.

1814

Mary dau. of John Wingfield of Duckmanton bur. 20th Jan. aged 6 by T.B. Lucas, minister – fever.

George Wheeldon of Duckmanton Furnace bur. 17th Feb. aged 13 by J. Ashbridge – fever.

Susannah dau. of James and Mary Plant of Far Duckmanton bur. 10th April aged 8 months by Ralph Heathcote.

John infant son of Hezekiah and Alice Saviere of Duckmanton Furnace bur. 17th July aged 3 days by Ralph Heathcote.

Mary wife of Francis Scales of Sutton bur. 7th Aug. aged 64 by Joseph Ashbridge.

1815

Elizabeth wife of George Dicken of Glapwell bur. 4th Jan. aged 25 by J. Ashbridge – died at Sutton.

Frances infant dau. of Richard Birkett of Duckmanton bur. 24th March aged 3 days by Ralph Heathcote.

Thomas son of Charles and Martha Watts of Brightside Bierlow, Sheffield bur. 9th April aged 7 by Ralph Heathcote.

Joseph Dicken Wilcockson son of Ann Dicken spinster of Sutton bur. 10th April aged 1 year by J. Ashbridge.

Anne Bunting of Duckmanton bur. 10th June aged 75 by J. Ashbridge.

Charles son of John and Mary Cooper of Duckmanton bur. 1st Sept. aged 1 year 7 months by J. Ashbridge.

Ann dau. of Joseph and Amy Sales of Duckmanton bur. 22nd Oct. aged 7 by Ralph Heathcote – burnt to death by clothes taking fire.

William son of Samuel and Elizabeth Bacon of Duckmanton Moor Top bur. 31st Oct. aged 1 day by J. Ashbridge.

Hannah wife of Robert Mallender of Duckmanton Furnace bur. at Chesterfield 19th Nov. aged 57.

Anne wife of Richard Chapman of Duckmanton bur. 22nd Nov. aged 42 by J. Ashbridge.

1816

Elizabeth dau. of Mr Thomas Wragg of Duckmanton bur. 19th Jan. aged 24 by J. Ashbridge.

Mary wife of Samuel Unwin of Duckmanton bur. 24th March aged 79 by Ralph Heathcote.

John Shaw of Sutton bur. 28th March aged 68 by J. Ashbridge.

George Richards of Hasland bur. 5th May aged 19 by J. Ashbridge.

Samuel son of Paul Unwin junior of Duckmanton bur. 11th June aged 3 months by T.B. Lucas.

Thomas Sales of Duckmanton bur. 11th June aged 69 by T.B. Lucas, minister.

Thomas son of Charles and Frances Newbold of Normanton bur. 29th July by T.B. Lucas – an infant.

Ann Bennett widow of Duckmanton bur. 5th Nov. aged 77 by T.B. Lucas, minister.

1817

Samuel Unwin of Duckmanton bur. 5th Aug. aged 76 by T.B. Lucas, minister.
Hannah Hudson widow of Sutton bur. 23rd Oct. aged 64.
Sarah wife of John Marsh, schoolmaster of Sutton bur. 20th Nov. aged 50 by T.B. Lucas, minister.

1818

John son of Humphrey Brookes of Duckmanton bur. 8th Jan. aged 5 weeks by T.B. Lucas.
Robert Atkinson of Duckmanton Furnace bur. 3rd Feb. aged 61 by T.B. Lucas.
Mary wife of Jasper Whitcomb of Duckmanton Furnace bur. 3rd Feb. aged 58 by T.B. Lucas.
William Machin of Duckmanton bur. 15th Feb. aged 18 by T.B. Lucas.
Georgiana dau. of Joseph and Helen Richards of Corbriggs bur. 16th Aug. aged 8 weeks by T.B. Lucas.
Sampson Johnson of Far Duckmanton bur. 23rd Aug. aged 81 by T.B. Lucas.
Esther infant dau. of John Sharman of Sutton bur. 9th Sept. aged 7 months by T.B. Lucas.
Robert son of James and Jane Hewitt of Duckmanton bur. 1st Nov. aged 1 year by T.B. Lucas.
John Pogmore of Duckmanton Moor bur. 11th Dec. aged 82 by T.B. Lucas.

1819

Ann dau. of Paul and Ann Unwin of Duckmanton bur. 16th Feb. aged 1 year by T.B. Lucas.
William Unwin of Sutton bur. 21st Feb. aged 83 by T.B. Lucas.
Harriet Lloyd of Duckmanton bur. 25th Feb. aged 18 by T.B. Lucas.
William Lowe of Sutton, servant to Mrs Dicken bur. 1st March aged 19 by J. Ashbridge.
John son of William Pearce of Duckmanton bur. 28th March aged 13 by T.B. Lucas.
James Newton of Duckmanton bur. 10th May aged 82 by T.B. Lucas.
Ann Godber widow of Duckmanton bur. 17th May aged 78 by T.B. Lucas.

John infant son of Humphrey Brookes of Duckmanton Moor bur. 17th May aged 2 months by T.B. Lucas.

Mary wife of Thomas Lievesley of Duckmanton bur. 11th Nov. aged 73 by T.B. Lucas.

Mary Wood widow of late John Wood of Duckmanton bur. 3rd Dec. aged 80 by T.B. Lucas.

Robert Crofts of Duckmanton bur. 5th Dec. aged 62 by T.B. Lucas.

Elizabeth Hopkinson wife of David Hopkinson, Calow, bur. 7th Dec. aged 68. Received a certificate from Chesterfield minister.

Mary dau. of William Blanksby of Duckmanton bur. 31st Dec. aged 25. Interred at Chesterfield.

1820

Ellen wife of Samuel Wheelhouse of Duckmanton bur. 2nd Jan. Interred at Staveley.

Nicholas Marsh of Sutton bur. 17th Jan. aged 72 by J. Ashbridge.

Paul Unwin of Duckmanton bur. 1st Feb. aged 75 by T.B. Lucas.

Thomas Jarvis of Duckmanton bur. 29th Feb. aged 62 by T.B. Lucas.

Sarah Frost junior of Duckmanton bur. 19th March aged 33 by T.B. Lucas.

Elizabeth dau. of Hezekiah and Alice Saviere of Duckmanton Furnace bur. 9th June aged 10 weeks by T.B. Lucas.

George Britt son of Aaron Britt, Star Inn, New Square, Chesterfield, bur. 13th Aug. aged 16 by Ralph Heathcote.

Sarah wife of Thomas Slack of Duckmanton bur. 17th Aug. aged 23 by J. Ashbridge.

Ann wife of Joseph Oates of Duckmanton bur. 30th Aug. aged 60 by T.B. Lucas.

Caroline infant dau. of Benjamin Marsden of Duckmanton Moor Top bur. 23rd Oct. by T.B. Lucas.

Richard Chapman of Middle Duckmanton bur. 5th Nov. aged 47 by T.B. Lucas.

Mr James Hodgkinson of Middle Duckmanton bur. 7th Nov. aged 80. Interred at Eyam.

Mary Reddish widow of Duckmanton bur. 14th Nov. aged 68 by T.B. Lucas.

Daniel Watkinson of Sutton bur. 18th Nov. aged 48 by T.B. Lucas.

Elizabeth wife of Richard Charlesworth of Duckmanton bur. 18th Dec. aged 28 by T.B. Lucas.

1821

Elizabeth wife of John Machin of Duckmanton bur. 18th Jan. aged 48 by T.B. Lucas.

Elizabeth Lowe spinster of Duckmanton bur. 26th Feb. aged 80 by J. Ashbridge.

Mary dau. of Paul Unwin of Duckmanton bur. 16th May aged 11 months by Rev. Mr Wagstaff.

Sarah infant dau. of Samuel and Elizabeth Bacon of Calow bur. 20th May aged 2 days by Rev. Mr Wagstaff.

Matthew infant son of John and Mary Jepson of Sutton bur. 29th Sept. aged 3 weeks by T. B. Lucas.

Ann Chapman widow of Duckmanton bur. 12th Oct. by J. Ashbridge.

Benjamin son of Benjamin and Elizabeth Marsden of Duckmanton Moor Top bur. 22nd Nov. aged 9 days by T.B. Lucas.

George Britte of Duckmanton bur. 19th Dec. aged 72 by T.B. Lucas.

1822

Elizabeth dau. of Christopher and Elizabeth Britte of Chesterfield bur. 7th May aged 1 year 1 month by J. Ashbridge.

Hugh Heath of Sutton bur. 12th May aged 64 by T.B. Lucas.

Anne dau. of Mr Joseph Woodhead of Duckmanton bur. 15th May aged 37 by T.B. Lucas. (Died at Chesterfield.)

Anne Pogmore wife of John Pogmore of Duckmanton bur. 8th Sept. aged 67 by T.B. Lucas.

Mary infant dau. of Joseph and Elizabeth Horton of Sutton bur. 10th Nov. aged 5 days by T.B. Lucas.

Thomas son of Jane Blanksby widow bur. 19th Dec. aged 3 years by T.B. Lucas.

1823

Thomas son of William Turner of Duckmanton Furnace bur. 7th Feb. aged 5 years by T.B. Lucas.

Elizabeth infant dau. of Richard and Elizabeth Charlesworth of Duckmanton bur. 23rd Feb. aged 9 months by Rev. Thomas Field.

George infant son of Hezekiah Saviere of Duckmanton Furnace bur. 2nd March aged 2 weeks by T.B. Lucas.

Sarah Britt of Duckmanton bur. 7th March aged 70 by J. Ashbridge.

Mr Joseph Woodhead of Duckmanton bur. 2nd April aged 67 by T.B. Lucas.

Hannah Heath widow of Sutton bur. 21st April aged 78 by Joseph Ashbridge.

John Bentley of Sutton bur. 1st May aged 81. Interred at Darley Dale.

Joseph Jarvis of Duckmanton bur. 8th May aged 23. Killed at the Adelphi Colliery by the falling in of an ironstone pit.

Thomas Walker of Duckmanton Furnace bur. 20th June aged 11 by J. Ashbridge.

Thomas Clayton of Chesterfield bur. 21st June aged 56. Died at Duckmanton Moor Top – interred at Wingerworth.

William son of Samuel and Elizabeth Bacon of Calow bur. 2nd Sept. aged 5 days. Parish of Chesterfield.

Mary wife of Mr Peter Smith of Sutton bur. 13th Nov. aged 47.

Joseph infant son of Hugh and Sarah Heath of Calow bur. 18th Dec. aged 8 weeks by J. Ashbridge.

1824

Richard infant son of George and Ellen Marsh of Sutton bur. 23rd March aged 1 week by J. Ashbridge.

John infant son of John and Hannah Nixon of Normanton bur. 25th April aged 14 weeks by A. Auriol Barker – parish of Chesterfield.

Sarah infant dau. of John and Sarah Sales of Duckmanton bur. 6th May aged 2 days by A. Auriol Barker.

William Hewitt of Sutton bur. 21st Oct. aged 44 years by A. Auriol Barker.

Sarah wife of John Charlton of Duckmanton Moor Top bur. 5th Nov. aged 66 by J. Ashbridge.

John Walker of Duckmanton Furnace bur. 21st Nov. aged 47 by G. Alderson. Killed by accidently falling off a cart in the parish of Pleasley.

Francis Scales of Sutton bur. 17th Dec. aged 74 by G. Alderson, curate.

Mr Henry Bramwell of Sutton bur. 24th Dec. aged 72 by G. Alderson. Drowned accidently falling backwards into a water trough in Sutton Hall orchard, whereon he had been accustomed to rest himself.

1825

James Plant Senior of Duckmanton bur. 2nd Feb. aged 84 by J. Ashbridge.

Mary Revill of Duckmanton bur. 11th Feb. aged 80 by G. Alderson, curate.

Anne infant dau. of John Sales of Duckmanton bur. 7th Feb. aged 3 weeks by G. Alderson.

Hannah infant dau. of Rhoda Wheelhouse spinster of Duckmanton Furnace bur. 30th March aged 23 weeks by Rev. Lowe, curate, Wingfield.

Ann wife of William Ferne of Duckmanton bur. 7th May aged 66 by G. Alderson.

Elizabeth Clarke of Whalley bur. 25th May aged 24 by G. Alderson. Died at Sutton.

Sarah infant dau. of James and Ann Booth of Duckmanton bur. 8th July aged 10 days by Rev. W. Carlisle, rector of this parish.

Mrs Ann Bennett of Duckmanton bur. 10th July aged 87 by G. Alderson.

Elizabeth Jervis of Duckmanton bur. 12th July aged 63 by J. Ashbridge.

John Lowe of Duckmanton Common bur. 26th July aged 65 by G. Alderson.

Thomas Reddish of Duckmanton bur. 19th Sept. aged 83. Interred at Bolsover.

John Bowler of Duckmanton bur. 13th Oct. aged 86 by Rev. G. Alderson.

Joseph Parker of Duckmanton bur. 10th Dec. aged 16 by Rev. W. Carlisle.

Mary wife of Samuel Johnson of Duckmanton Moor Top bur. 11th Dec. aged 47 by G. Alderson.

1826

Helen Plant of Duckmanton bur. 25th Jan. aged 78 by G. Alderson, curate.

Harriet Wheelhouse of Duckmanton Furnace bur. 7th Feb. aged 2 by G. Alderson.

Benedicta Parker of Calow bur. 10th Feb. aged 78 by G. Alderson.

Sarah wife of Hugh Heath of Calow bur. 24th March aged 30 by G. Alderson.

Thomas Lievesley of Duckmanton bur. 9th April aged 84 by G. Alderson.

James infant son of Joseph and Ann Plant of Duckmanton bur. 19th April aged 2 days by G. Alderson.

Edward Johnson of Duckmanton bur. 23rd April aged 79 by G. Alderson.

Thomas Booker of Duckmanton bur. 14th May aged 39 years by G. Alderson.

Joseph Bennett of Duckmanton bur. 21st May aged 72 by G. Alderson.

Anne infant dau. of Thomas and Martha Clarke of Duckmanton Moor Top bur. 24th Aug. aged 3 years 6 months by Joseph Ashbridge.

Mary infant dau. of Thomas and Martha Clarke of Duckmanton Moor Top bur. 6th Sept. aged 1 year 3 months by Joseph Ashbridge.

Esther infant dau. of John and Alice Johnson of Middle Duckmanton bur. 8th Oct. aged 9 months by Rev. W. Mountain.

Sarah Moss of Darley, but died at Duckmanton Moor Top, at Thomas Cantrell's, bur. 13th Nov. aged 62 by William Badnall, curate.

Charles infant son of James and Hannah Fidler of Sutton Mill bur. 15th Nov. aged 7 weeks by Joseph Ashbridge.

Joseph Horton, schoolmaster of Sutton bur. 10th Dec. aged 45 by William Badnall.

Francis son of John and Mary Cooper of Duckmanton bur. 24th Dec. aged 14 by William Badnall.

1827

William Sales of Duckmanton bur. 11th Jan. aged 73 by William Badnall.

John Bennett of Duckmanton bur. 20th Feb. aged 69 by William Badnall.

William Cantrell of Duckmanton Moor Top bur. 13th March aged 22 by William Badnall. Killed by Mr Woodhead's cart going over his leg which was amputated and which caused his death within fourteen hours afterwards.

John Machin of Duckmanton bur. 14th March aged 61 by William Badnall.

Samuel Lievesley of Duckmanton bur. 28th March aged 82 by William Badnall.

Charles infant son of John and Jane Wood of Duckmanton bur. 8th April aged 7 months by William Badnall.

John Pogmore of Duckmanton bur. 9th May aged 73 by Andrew Knox.

Abraham Frost of Pleasley bur. 30th May aged 39 by William Badnall.

William Barlow of Middle Duckmanton bur. 6th July aged 73 by William Badnall.

Sarah infant dau. of Thomas and Martha Clarke of Duckmanton Moor Top bur. 12th Sept. aged 1 day by John Clarke.

1828

Emma infant dau. of William and Hannah Taylor of Duckmanton Furnace bur. 4th Feb. aged 6 months by John Clarke.

Richard Marsh of Mosbro' but died at Chesterfield bur. 3rd May aged 45 by Samuel Revell.

Mary Flint of Calow bur. 8th May aged 34 by Rev. Foxlowe.

Elizabeth Blanksby of Duckmanton bur. 4th June aged 67. Interred at Chesterfield.

Hannah wife of Joseph Cantrell of Duckmanton Moor Top bur. 11th June aged 80 by S. Revell.

Joseph Oates of Duckmanton bur. 16th June aged 68 by S. Revell.

Mary dau. of Stephen and Mary Thompston of Duckmanton Furnace bur. 27th June aged 17 by S. Revell.

Tamar Watkinson widow of Sutton bur. 31st July aged 55 by John Clarke.

Mary wife of Thomas Nix of Sutton bur. 4th Aug. aged 25. Interred at Ault Hucknall.

William Booker of Duckmanton bur. 17th Dec. aged 85 by S. Revell.

1829

Judith wife of Richard Marshall of Duckmanton bur. 22nd Feb. aged 68 by S. Revell.

Mary wife of George Shaw of Duckmanton Moor bur. 29th April aged 61 by S. Revell, curate.

Francis Bunting of Ford, parish of North Wingfield, bur. 14th May aged 55 by William Carlisle, rector.

Hannah Wilson of Duckmanton bur. 24th May aged 87 by S. Revell.

Ann Wheelhouse of Far Duckmanton bur. 28th Oct. aged 3 by S. Revell.

Elizabeth wife of Gervase Johnson of Duckmanton bur. 22nd Nov. aged 73 by S. Revell.

Hannah wife of William Taylor of Duckmanton Furnace bur. 10th Dec. aged 45 by S. Revell.

Richard Wood of Duckmanton bur. 12th Dec. aged 64 by S. Revell.

Mary Wood wife of the above bur. 16th Dec. aged 76 by S. Revell.

1830

Elizabeth wife of Thomas Wragg of Duckmanton bur. 2nd Jan. aged 73 by S. Revell.

John son of William and Ann Rodgers of Sutton bur. 9th March aged 16 by S. Revell.

Joshua son of William and Ann Brookes of Calow bur. 23rd March aged 2 months by S. Revell.

John son of William and Ann Brookes of Calow bur. 11th April aged 2 months by S. Revell.

Joseph son of Matthew Joseph and Sarah Oates of Duckmanton bur. 16th April aged 15 months by S. Revell.

Ann wife of William Brookes of Calow bur. 22nd April aged 21 by S. Revell.

Sarah wife of Matthew Joseph Oates of Duckmanton bur. 27th May aged 24.

Matthew Charlton of Duckmanton Moor Top bur. 6th June aged 37 by S. Revell.

Louisa Seviere of Duckmanton Furnace bur. 13th June aged 3 months by S. Revell.

Hannah Belfield of Manchester, late of Sutton, bur. 14th June aged 32 by S. Revell.

Mary Cowley of Calow bur. 1st July aged 19 by S. Revell.

George son of William and Amy Wood of Sutton bur. 17th Aug. aged 1 month by S. Revell.

1831

Hannah wife of Francis Bentley of Sutton bur. 5th Jan. aged 73 by S. Revell.

William Charlesworth of Duckmanton bur. 5th Jan. aged 77 by S. Revell. Interred at Bolsover.

Elizabeth wife of Thomas Stevenson of Fullard, parish of Sutton-in-Ashfield, bur. 13th Jan. aged 61 by S. Revell.

Maria dau. of David Caleb and Ann Britt of Sutton bur. 15th Jan. aged 8 months by S. Revell.

Hannah Bennett widow of Far Duckmanton bur. 20th Jan. aged 77 by J. Ashbridge.

Septimus son of Humphrey and Elizabeth Brookes of Sutton bur. 30th Jan. aged 10 by S. Revell.

Hannah dau. of Thomas and Hannah Barlow of Middle Duckmanton bur. 31st Jan. aged 16 months by S. Revell.

Martha dau. of Thomas and Hannah Barlow of Middle Duckmanton bur. 7th Feb. aged 16 months by S. Revell.

Sarah dau. of Moses and Ann Turner of Duckmanton Furnace bur. 7th Feb. aged 4 by S. Revell.

James Plant of Far Duckmanton bur. 24th April aged 58 by S. Revell.

Mary dau. of James and Sarah Cowley of Calow bur. 10th May aged 5 by S. Revell.

Hannah Lievesley of Duckmanton bur. 29th May aged 26 by S. Revell.

Amy dau. of James and Sarah Cowley of Calow bur. 14th June aged 3 by J. Ashbridge.

Phillis wife of Alexander Steel of Duckmanton bur. 8th July aged 21 by S. Revell.

William Timmis of Keele, Staffs., died at Duckmanton bur. 8th July aged 16 by S. Revell.

James Reddish of Duckmanton bur. 16th July aged 23. Killed at the Adelphi Colliery by lightning which caused his death immediately. Interred at Bolsover.

Joseph Wragg junior of Bolsover, late of Sutton bur. 13th Nov. aged 30 by S. Revell.

1832

Joseph Wragg senior of Sutton bur. 17th March aged 76 by S. Revell.

Henry son of Henry Revell of Duckmanton bur. 25th March aged 4 years 8 months by S. Revell.

George son of Christopher Britt of Chesterfield bur. 8th April aged 5 by S. Revell.

Elizabeth dau. of Luke Platts bur. 17th April aged 9 months by S. Revell.

Mary wife of George Robinson of Duckmanton bur. 4th May aged 31 by S. Revell.

Sarah wife of Luke Platts of Duckmanton bur. 20th May aged 29 by S. Revell.

Martha dau. of George Robinson of Duckmanton bur. 21st May aged 9 weeks by S. Revell.

Robert Dicken of Sutton bur. 9th July aged 77 by S. Revell.

Hannah Wragg of Bolsover bur. 24th July aged 3 by J. Ashbridge.

Hebron son of Daniel and Hannah Piggin of Sutton bur. 26th July aged 5 months by J. Ashbridge.

Hezekiah Saviere of Duckmanton Furnace bur. 26th July aged 47 by J. Ashbridge.

George son of George and Mary Revell of Duckmanton bur. 12th Sept. aged 3 months by S. Revell.

Elizabeth wife of George Beresford of Duckmanton bur. 26th Sept. aged 59 by S. Revell.

Martha Barlow of Duckmanton bur. 17th Nov. aged 74 by S. Revell.

Thomas Bennett of Duckmanton bur. 11th Dec. aged 42 by S. Revell.

1833

Joseph Heath of Sutton bur. 17th Jan. aged 50 by J. Ashbridge.

John Charlton of Duckmanton Moor Top bur. 27th Jan. aged 72 by S. Revell, curate.

Hannah dau. of George and Mary Revell of Far Duckmanton bur. 19th Feb. aged 6 by Rev. John Knight.

Samuel son of Christopher Britt of Chesterfield bur. 3rd March aged 6 months by S. Revell.

John Richards of Corbriggs near Hasland bur. 4th March aged 30 by S. Revell. Killed by accident at William Clarke's colliery at Calow.

Elizabeth wife of Humphrey Brookes of Duckmanton Moor bur. 12th March aged 53 by J. Ashbridge.

George Revell of Far Duckmanton bur. 16th March aged 30 by S. Revell.

George son of Ann Lievesley of Duckmanton bur. 17th May aged 6 months by S. Revell.

William Meakin of Duckmanton bur. 22nd May aged 70 by S. Revell.

Elizabeth wife of William Britt of Duckmanton bur. 10th July aged 45 by S. Revell.

Gervase Johnson of Duckmanton bur. 21st Aug. aged 80 by J. Ashbridge.

Grace wife of John Wingfield of Duckmanton bur. 18th Sept. aged 54 by J. Ashbridge.

William Fearn of Duckmanton bur. 27th Sept. aged 78 by William Fletcher, curate of Wingerworth.

George Shaw of Duckmanton Moor bur. 15th Oct. aged 72 by William Fletcher.

Richard Marshall of Duckmanton bur. 3rd Nov. aged 82 by Richard Ward, rector.

Mary Shaw wife of Thomas Shaw of Duckmanton Moor bur. 18th Dec. aged 72 by William Fletcher.

1834

Elizabeth Turner of Duckmanton Furnace bur. 10th Feb. aged 73 by William Fletcher.

Mary Middleton of Middle Duckmanton bur. 11th Feb. aged 61 by William Fletcher.

Thomas son of Thomas and Sarah Wragg of Duckmanton bur. 14th April aged 9 months by C.J. Callow.

Alfred son of William and Hannah Heath of Sutton bur. 1st May aged 2 weeks by William Fletcher.

Elizabeth Lievesley of Duckmanton bur. 20th July aged 46 by William Fletcher.

Herbert son of George and Ellen Marsh of Sutton bur. 24th July aged 2 months by William Fletcher.

Job son of George and Elizabeth Marriott of Duckmanton bur. 9th Sept. aged 10 days by William Fletcher.

Amy Hewitt widow of Sutton Lane bur. 14th Sept. aged 50 by William Fletcher.

Henry son of Solomon and Rebecca Whitcomb of Duckmanton Furnace bur. 16th Sept. aged 3 by William Fletcher.

Harriette dau. of William and Elizabeth Davison of Duckmanton Moor bur. 16th Nov. aged 10 months by William Fletcher.

1835

Joseph Renshaw of Duckmanton Moor bur. 23rd March aged 18 by William Fletcher.

June Birkett of Long Course bur. 1st May aged 55 by T.B. Lucas.

Richard Birkett of Long Course bur. 27th May aged 56 by T.B. Lucas.

Sarah Cowley of Calow bur. 17th July aged 32 by William Fletcher.

Sarah Horton of Sutton Lane bur. 25th July aged 15 by William Fletcher.

James Booth of Duckmanton Furnace bur. 24th Aug. aged 32 by William Fletcher.

Lydia Bunting of The Ford, North Wingfield bur. 27th Sept. aged 54 by William Fletcher.

Robert Frith of Duckmanton bur. 29th Sept. aged 67 by William Fletcher.

John Hodgekinson of Duckmanton bur. 29th Sept. aged 71 by William Fletcher.

Elizabeth Cowley of Top of Ox Pasture bur. 13th Oct. aged 59 by William Fletcher.

James Brookes of Calow bur. 27th Oct. aged 22 by William Fletcher.

Hannah Meakin of Duckmanton bur. 31st Oct. aged 76 by T.B. Lucas.

William Woodhead of Calow Green bur. 5th Dec. aged 84 by William Fletcher.

1836

Hannah Whitcomb of Duckmanton Furnace bur. 8th Jan. aged 9 months by William Fletcher.

William Pearce of Duckmanton bur. 1st March aged 60 by William Fletcher.

Thomas Stevenson of Sutton-in-Ashfield bur. 5th March aged 72 by William Fletcher.

Herbert Cooper of Sheffield bur. 10th May aged 5 by F.W. Sharpe.

Rhoda Johnson of Calow bur. 17th May aged 26 by F.W. Sharpe.

Mary Ann Unwin of Sheffield bur. 8th June aged 2 years 8 months by F.W. Sharpe.

Thomas Wragg of Duckmanton bur. 23rd Sept. aged 73 by F.W. Sharpe.

Robert Hewit Limb of Sutton bur. 9th Oct. aged 3 weeks by F.W. Sharpe, curate.

John Cantrell of Duckmanton Moor bur. 23rd Nov. aged 14 by F.W. Sharpe, curate.

Sarah Sales of Duckmanton bur. 14th Dec. aged 80 by F.W. Sharpe.

1837

George Thompson of Duckmanton Furnace bur. 21st Jan. aged 16 by Francis Hodgson.

Elizabeth Birkett of Long Course Farm bur. 2nd Feb. aged 23 by F.W. Sharpe.

Paul Unwin of Duckmanton bur. 19th Feb. aged 24 by F.W. Sharpe.

Elizabeth Bennett of Duckmanton Moor bur. 28th Feb. aged 5 by F.W. Sharpe.

John Poolsmith of Duckmanton Moor bur. 8th March aged 71 by F.W. Sharpe.

John Poolsmith of Duckmanton Moor bur. 8th March aged 71 by F.W. Sharpe.
John Barlow of Middle Duckmanton bur. 8th March aged 7 months by F.W. Sharpe.
Martha Barlow of Middle Duckmanton bur. 10th March aged 3 by F.W. Sharpe.
Moses Britt of Temple Normanton bur. 10th March aged 71 by F.W. Sharpe.
Matthew Charlton of Duckmanton Moor bur. 15th March aged 10 by C. Currey, vicar of Heath.
Catherine Renshaw of Duckmanton Moor bur. 1st May aged 63 by T.B. Lucas.
Sarah Cooper of Duckmanton bur. 14th May aged 20 by T.B. Lucas.
William Lloyd of Duckmanton bur. 2nd June aged 78 by C. Currey.

REGISTER OF MARRIAGES
1813–37

1813

John Richardson bachelor of Bolsover and Ann Reddish spinster of this parish, mar. 6th May by Ralph Heathcote.

Thomas Bennett bachelor and Mary Hawkins widow, both of this parish, mar. 12th July by R. Heathcote.

William Needham bachelor and Else Whitcombe spinster, both of this parish, mar. 25th Nov. by Edward Heathcote.

Thomas Barlow bachelor of this parish and Hannah Frith of Staveley mar. 13th Dec. by R. Heathcote.

1814

George Bennett bachelor of this parish and Martha Wells spinster of Whitwell mar. 3rd Jan. by J. Ashbridge.

Francis Whitworth bachelor of Heath and Dorothy Watkinson spinster of this parish mar. 6th June by J. Ashbridge.

John Wingfield bachelor of this parish and Esther Harrison spinster of Bolsover mar. 18th July by J. Ashbridge.

John Bunting bachelor of this parish, age 40 years and upwards, and Susannah Smith spinster of this parish, aged 40 years and upwards, mar. by licence 7th Nov. by J. Ashbridge.

1815

Thomas Hudson bachelor and Anne Chapman spinster, both of this parish, mar. 16th Jan. by J. Ashbridge.

Richard Charlesworth bachelor and Elizabeth Kenyon spinster, both of this parish, mar. 16th Jan. by J. Ashbridge.

Joseph Brown of Bolsover and Elizabeth Sharman of this parish mar. 20th Feb. by J. Ashbridge.

Cornelius Amos of Mansfield and Elizabeth Cutts of this parish mar. 10th April by J. Ashbridge.

Thomas Huntingdon of Bolsover and Jane Hewitt of this parish mar. 29th May by J. Ashbridge.

John Wragge bachelor of this parish and Mary Smith widow of Calow mar. by licence 20th Sept. by J. Ashbridge.

Robert Barber bachelor of Whittington and Ann Nelson spinster of this parish mar. by licence 13th Nov. by J. Ashbridge, curate *pro tempore*.

Thomas Cooke bachelor and Ellen Bamford spinster, both of this parish, mar. 27th Nov. by J. Ashbridge.

1816

Richard Chapman widower and Ann Reddish spinster, both of this parish, mar. 19th Feb. by J. Ashbridge.

Francis Reddish bachelor of this parish, aged over 21, and Mary Yates spinster of Bolsover, age 18 years and upwards, mar. by licence with consent of William Yates, father, 18th Sept. by T.B. Lucas.

Hugh Heath bachelor and Sarah Lowe spinster, both of this parish, mar. 1st Oct. by T.B. Lucas.

Henry Revill bachelor and Sarah Lievesley spinster, both of this parish, mar. 31st Dec. by T.B. Lucas.

1817

Joseph Woodhead bachelor of Mansfield and Elizabeth Hudson spinster of this parish, both aged 21 and upwards, mar. by licence 3rd May by T.B. Lucas.

Joseph Staniforth bachelor and Dorothy Brailsford spinster, both of this parish, mar. 5th May by T.B. Lucas.

William Britt bachelor of this parish, aged over 21, and Elizabeth Britt spinster of Brimington, over 21, mar. by licence 27th May by T.B. Lucas.

William Lievesley bachelor of this parish and Sarah Frith spinster of Staveley mar. 23rd June by T.B. Lucas.

John Meakin bachelor of this parish and Charlotte Saxelby spinster of Bolsover mar. 11th Aug. by T.B. Lucas.

Thomas Berry bachelor of Alt Hucknall and Sarah Meakin spinster of this parish, mar. 24th Sept. by T.B. Lucas.

Joseph Nixon bachelor of this parish and Ann Smith spinster of Whittington mar. 26th Nov. by T.B. Lucas.

1818

William Wilson bachelor of Stretton (N. Wingfield) and Ellen Smith spinster of this parish, mar. by licence 25th Aug. by T.B. Lucas.

William Wragg bachelor and Jane Saxelby spinster both of this parish, mar. 13th Nov. by T.B. Lucas.

John Flint bachelor and Elizabeth Shepherd spinster, both of this parish, mar. 1st Dec. by T.B. Lucas.

George White bachelor and Elizabeth Smith spinster, both of this parish, mar. 24th Dec. by T.B. Lucas.

1819

William Mettam bachelor of Brimington and Elizabeth Pearce spinster of this parish, mar. 13th Dec. by T.B. Lucas.

1820

Joseph Plant bachelor and Anne Walker spinster, both of this parish mar. 24th Jan. by T.B. Lucas.

Richard Alsop bachelor of Chesterfield and Ellen Charlton spinster of this parish, mar. by licence 19th July by T.B. Lucas.

John Johnson bachelor and Alice Varley spinster, both of this parish mar. 13th Oct. by T.B. Lucas.

William Davison widower and Elizabeth Cantrell spinster, both of this parish, mar. 11th Dec. by T.B. Lucas.

1821

Charles Eastwood bachelor and Martha Wheelhouse spinster, both of this parish, mar. 5th June by T.B. Lucas.

Richard Charlesworth widower of this parish and Elizabeth Middleton widow of Bolsover mar. 14th June by T.B. Lucas.

John Brocksopp widower of Hault Hucknall and Hannah Shaw widow of this parish, mar. by licence 16th July by T.B. Lucas.

John Chapman bachelor and Mary Reddish spinster, both of this parish, mar. 20th Aug. by J. Ashbridge.

George Conway bachelor of Leeds (a minor) and Elizabeth Berrisford spinster of this parish, mar. by licence with father's consent 28th Aug. by J. Ashbridge.

Godfrey Flint junior bachelor of Chesterfield and Sarah Limb spinster of this parish, mar. 23rd Oct. by J. Ashbridge.

William Hibbert bachelor of Dronfield and Ann Lievesley spinster of this parish, mar. 3rd Dec. by T.B. Lucas.

William Berry bachelor of Alt Hucknall and Mary Meakin spinster of this parish, mar. 18th Dec. by T.B. Lucas.

1822

George Clarke bachelor of Chesterfield and Hannah Booth spinster of this parish, mar. 17th June by J. Ashbridge.

William Chapman bachelor of Chesterfield and Sarah Charlton spinster of this parish, both over 21, mar. by licence 23rd July by T.B. Lucas.

Job Smedley bachelor of Sutton-in-Ashfield and Ann Lievesley of this parish, mar. 12th Aug. by T.B. Lucas.

John Goodwin bachelor of Chesterfield and Elizabeth Shaw spinster of this parish, both over 21, mar. 7th Oct. by J. Ashbridge.

John Maxfield bachelor of Bolsover and Lydia Allwood spinster of this parish, mar. 28th Oct. by T.B. Lucas.

Edmund Armstrong bachelor of Scarcliffe and Elizabeth Fidler (a minor) of this parish, mar. by licence with father's consent 13th Dec. by J. Ashbridge.

1823

Samuel Lievesley bachelor and Elizabeth Meakin spinster, both of this parish, mar. 22nd April by J. Ashbridge.

George Marsh bachelor and Helen Frith spinster, both of this parish mar. 20th May by J. Ashbridge.

John Sales bachelor and Sarah Hewitt spinster, both of this parish mar. 5th Aug. by J. Ashbridge.

Solomon Wickdom bachelor and Rebecca Harvey spinster, both of this parish, mar. 24th Aug. by A.A. Barker, curate.

William Bennett bachelor and Elizabeth Machin spinster, both of this parish, mar. 3rd Nov. by A.A. Barker.

John Revill bachelor and Ann Pogmore spinster, both of this parish, mar. 12th Nov. by A.A. Barker.

1824

Thomas Hopkinson bachelor and Ann Watkinson spinster, both of this parish, mar. 1st Jan. by A.A. Barker.

Christopher Haywood bachelor and Ann Taylor spinster, both of this parish, mar. 11th Jan. by A.A. Barker.

William Ward of Warsop and Mary Greaves spinster of this parish mar. 2nd Feb. by A.A. Barker.

James Booth bachelor and Ann Barber widow, both of this parish, mar. 28th June by J. Ashbridge.

George Alsop bachelor of Chesterfield and Mary Charlton spinster of this parish mar. by licence 29th June by J. Ashbridge.

George Robinson bachelor and Mary Waller spinster, both of this parish, mar. 25th Dec. by George Alderson, curate.

1825

John Wood bachelor of Sheffield and Jane Johnson spinster of this parish, mar. by licence 25th Feb. by G. Alderson.

George Frith bachelor of this parish and Elizabeth Wood spinster of Bolsover mar. 26th May by G. Alderson.

John Platts bachelor and Rebecca Watkinson spinster, both of this parish, mar. 30th May by E.W. Lowe.

Thomas Harvey bachelor and Hannah Webster spinster, both of this parish, mar. 22nd Aug. by G. Alderson.

Thomas Limb widower and Mary Chapman spinster, both of this parish mar. 5th Dec. by G. Alderson.

1826

Thomas Reddish bachelor of this parish and Ann Taylor spinster of Heath mar. 13th Feb. by G. Alderson.

Moses Turner bachelor and Ann Wicksall spinster, both of this parish, mar. 26th March by G. Alderson, now rector of Harthill.

Thomas Nix bachelor of N. Wingfield and Mary Turner spinster of this parish, mar. by licence 9th July by Stephen Cragg.

1827

Thomas Watkinson bachelor and Maria Sheppard spinster, both of this parish, mar. 2nd Jan. by Wm Badnall, curate.

Robert Littler bachelor of Liverpool and Ann Parker spinster of this parish mar. by licence 2nd March by J. Ashbridge.

Joseph Wragg bachelor of this parish and Mary Hardwick spinster mar. 5th June by Wm Badnall.

William Purslove bachelor and Ann Lievesley spinster, both of this parish, mar. 3rd July by Wm Badnall.

Charles Fowler bachelor and Hariett Hewitt spinster, both of this parish, mar. by licence 14th Oct. by Samuel Revell, curate.

1828

Matthew Joseph Oates bachelor and Sarah Barlow spinster, both of this parish, mar. by licence 12th Aug. by S. Revell.

John Frith bachelor and Mary Fearne spinster, both of this parish, mar. by licence 27th Sept. by Francis Foxlowe, vicar of Elmton.

John Booth bachelor of this parish and Hannah Gladwin spinster of Chesterfield mar. by licence 28th Oct. by S. Revell.

Samuel Marriot bachelor of Bolsover and Jane Cantrell spinster of this parish, mar. 8th Dec. by S. Revell.

1829

John Bennett bachelor and Ann Bacon spinster, both of this parish, mar. 20th April by S. Revell.

George Shaw bachelor and Ann Harvey spinster, both of this parish, mar. 29th June by S. Revell.

John Levick bachelor of Eckington and Sarah Sales spinster of this parish mar. by licence 29th June by S. Revell.

Edward Adderson bachelor of Chesterfield and Anne Evans spinster of this parish mar. by licence 26th July by S. Revell.

William Brookes bachelor and Ann Cowley spinster, both of this parish, mar. 12th Oct. by S. Revell.

Jasper Fidler bachelor and Sarah Walker spinster, both of this parish, mar. 29th Nov. by S. Revell.

John Jepson the younger bachelor and Mary Oakley spinster, both of this parish, mar. 6th Dec. by S. Revell.

1830

William Wood bachelor and Amy Sharman spinster, both of this parish, mar. 1st Feb. by S. Revell.

William Meakin widower and Sarah Thorpe spinster, both of this parish, mar. 2nd Aug. by S. Revell.

1831

William Cantrell bachelor and Mary Parker spinster, both of this parish, mar. by licence 10th Jan. by S. Revell.

Alexander Steel bachelor and Phyllis Lloyd spinster, both of this parish, mar. 10th Jan. by S. Revell.

Thomas Heath bachelor and Hannah Watkinson spinster, both of this parish, mar. 21st Jan. by S. Revell.

John Lievesley bachelor and Mary Fogg spinster, both of this parish, mar. 24th Jan. by S. Revell.

Richard Marsh bachelor and Elizabeth Brailsford spinster, both of this parish, mar. by licence 4th May by S. Revell.

Job Pether bachelor and Hannah Shaw spinster, both of this parish, mar. 19th June by S. Revell.

Joseph Tansley bachelor and Mary Unwin spinster, both of this parish, mar. 5th Sept. by S. Revell.

William Unwin bachelor of this parish and Mary Windle spinster of Chesterfield mar. 21st Oct. by S. Revell.

William Hill of Clowne and Susannah Woodhead of this parish mar. by licence 10th Nov. by Thomas Hill.

1832

Thomas Sheppard bachelor of this parish and Cecilia Hopkinson spinster of Heath mar. 6th Feb. by S. Revell.

Samuel Trickett of Mansfield Woodhouse and Catherine Thompson spinster of this parish, mar. 21st May by S. Revell.

John White bachelor and Ann Hibbard spinster, both of this parish, mar. by licence 6th Aug. by S. Revell.

Luke Platts widower of this parish and Jane Coulson spinster of Chesterfield mar. 27th Aug. by S. Revell.

Samuel Nixon bachelor and Sarah Unwin spinster, both of this parish, mar. 26th Nov. by S. Revell.

1833

William Turner bachelor of Ashover and Elizabeth Nixon spinster of this parish, mar. 17th June by J. Ashbridge.

Henry Bradley bachelor and Ann Bowler spinster, both of this parish, mar. 22nd July by S. Revell.

William Pogmore bachelor and Mary Bowns widow, both of this parish, mar. 26th Aug. by J. Ashbridge.

William Lievesley bachelor and Mary Crooks spinster, both of this parish, mar. 3rd Nov. by Richard Ward, rector.

George Marriott bachelor of Heath and Elizabeth Clay spinster of this parish, mar. by licence 22nd Dec. by W. Fletcher, curate.

1834

George Smith bachelor and Ann Booker spinster, both of this parish mar. 10th June by John Wright, curate, Bolsover.

John Bacon bachelor of Bolsover and Julia Johnson spinster of this parish, mar. 13th June by Charles Smith, curate, Barlow.

Caleb Ellis and Frances Hallam, both of this parish, mar. 3rd Aug. by Wm Fletcher, curate.

Henry Millward and Mary Cook, both of this parish, mar. 17th Aug. by Wm Fletcher.

1835

Francis Windle bachelor of Dronfield and Mary Hewitt spinster of this parish, mar. 26th Feb. by Wm Fletcher.

Henry Winchester Harley and Charlotte Cook, both of this parish, mar. 23rd Aug. by Wm Fletcher.

Thomas Bowns of Bolsover and Ruth Sharman of this parish mar. 1st Oct. by Wm Fletcher.

Robert Lovett bachelor and Eliza Smith spinster, both of this parish, mar. by licence 28th Oct. by Wm Fletcher.

John Swain bachelor of Chesterfield and Eliza Heath spinster of this parish, mar. 7th Dec. by Wm Fletcher.

1836

Peter Bradley bachelor of this parish and Mary Elliott spinster of Chesterfield mar. 24th Jan. by Wm Fletcher.

William Woodhead Smith bachelor and Jane Kirk spinster, both of this parish, mar. by licence 8th March by Wm Fletcher.

William Britt widower and Grace Middleton spinster, both of this parish, mar. by licence 8th March by Wm Fletcher.

Robert Limb bachelor and Charlotte Horton spinster, both of this parish, mar. 29th Aug. by F.W. Sharpe, curate.

Richard Winfield bachelor and Elizabeth Atkin spinster, both of this parish, mar. 6th Sept. by F.W. Sharpe.

1837

Alfred Bennett bachelor and Ann Wingfield spinster, both of this parish, mar. by licence 17th Jan. by F.W. Sharpe.

Luke Parker bachelor and Ida Matilda Hilliard, both of this parish mar. 17th Feb. by F.W. Sharpe.

Joseph Hewitt bachelor and Hannah Wright spinster, both of this parish, mar. 27th March by Charles Currey, vicar of Heath.

John Longdil bachelor and Martha Thompson spinster, both of this parish, mar. 14th May by T.B. Lucas.

Joseph Calow bachelor and Mary Bennett spinster, both of this parish mar. 26th June by F.W. Sharpe.

INDEX OF PLACES

Plain references to Duckmanton and Sutton have not been indexed; for places within the parish see under Duckmanton and Sutton. County suffixes are only given for parishes outside Derbyshire.

Duckmanton New Colliery in 49, 50, 51, 53, 55, 99, 100, 102
Duckmanton School in 103
Duckmanton Works, *see* Duckmanton Furnace
Far Duckmanton in 46, 97, 106, 140, 143, 148, 149, 150, 152, 153, 154, 156, 157, 159, 161, 167, 168, 169
Long Duckmanton in 157
Longcourse (Long Course) in 44, 45, 47, 48, 52, 56, 84, 86, 95, 140, 144, 170, 171
Middle Duckmanton in 43, 45, 134, 148, 150, 152, 154, 155, 156, 157, 162, 165, 166, 168, 170, 172
Newdale in 98, 159
Ox Pasture in 171
Sutton Lane End in 55
Duxford, Cambs. 105

Eastwood, Notts. 130
Ecclesfield, Yorks. 128
Eckington 123, 130, 178
Mosborough (Mosbro') in 166
Elmton, vicar of 178
Ely, Cambs. 105
Exeter, Devon 103

Far Duckmanton, *see* Duckmanton, Far Duckmanton in
Ford, *see* North Wingfield, Ford in
Fullard, *see* Sutton-in-Ashfield, Fullard in

Glapwell 160

Hagg, *see* Sutton, Hagg in
Handsworth, Yorks. 132
Harewood (Harwood) Grange, *see* Beeley, Harewood Grange in
Harthill with Woodall, Yorks. 124
rector of 177
Harwood Grange, *see* Beeley, Harewood Grange in
Hasland 95, 96, 160
Corbriggs in 161, 169
Hault Hucknall, *see* Ault Hucknall
Heath 26, 69, 70, 71, 73, 118, 119, 173, 177, 180
curate of 119
minister of 159
Owlcotes (Old-Coates) in 71
vicar of 181
Hexham, Northumberland 104

Inkersall, Inkersell, *see* Staveley, Inkersall in

Keele, Staffs. 168
Kent, *see* Ulcombe

Lancashire, *see* Liverpool, Manchester
Leeds, Yorks. 97, 176
Leicester, St Martin's parish in 122
Lilleshall, Shropshire 105
Lincoln 112
Lincolnshire, *see* ?Careby, Lincoln, Market Deeping, Syston
Liverpool, Lancs. 178
London 103
see also Westminster
Long Course, *see* Duckmanton, Longcourse in
Long Duckmanton, *see* Duckmanton, Long Duckmanton in

Manchester, Lancs. 167
Mansfield, Notts. 128, 173, 174
Mansfield Woodhouse, Notts. 179
Mapleton (Mappleton) 97
Market Deeping, Lincs. 105
Middle Duckmanton, *see* Duckmanton, Middle Duckmanton in
Middleton & Smerrill (Middleton, Youlgreave) 119
Moor Top, *see* Duckmanton Moor Top
Morton 128
Mosbro', *see* Eckington, Mosborough in

New Colliery, *see* Duckmanton New Colliery
New Furnace, *see* Duckmanton Furnace 57
New Lodge, *see* Sutton, New Lodge in
New Works, *see* Duckmanton Furnace
Newdale, *see* Duckmanton
Norfolk, *see* Cawston
Normanton, *see* South Normanton, Temple Normanton
Normanton Lodge, *see* Temple Normanton, Normanton Lodge in
North Wingfield 94, 121, 122, 124, 125, 128, 129, 130, 131, 177
curate of 164
Ford in 167, 171
Northumberland, *see* Hexham
Norton 124
Nottingham 47, 51, 54, 94, 113
Nottinghamshire, *see* Cuckney, Eastwood, Mansfield, Mansfield Woodhouse, Nottingham, Sutton-in-Ashfield, Teversal, Warsop

Old-Coates, Owlcotes, *see* Heath, Owlcotes in
Ox Pasture, Top of, *see* Duckmanton, Ox Pasture in

INDEX OF PERSONS

This index includes the names of all those entered in the register as baptised, married or buried; it does not include the parents or spouses of such people. Christian names have been silently modernised, except in cases of doubt; variant spellings of surnames are given in brackets at the head of each entry.

186

187

192

194